Guide to the Healthcare Industry

This book is for all those who work in the healthcare industry not just as a career but as a calling, especially those who took such good care of me in Hilo and Honolulu during the medical emergency I experienced amidst writing this book and Chris Frueh, my husband and fellow clinical psychologist since graduate school.

Guide to the Healthcare Industry

Karen L. Pellegrin
University of Hawai'i at Hilo

S Sage Reference

FOR INFORMATION:

2455 Teller Road
Thousand Oaks, California 91320
E-mail: order@sagepub.com

1 Oliver's Yard
55 City Road
London, EC1Y 1SP
United Kingdom

Unit No 323-333, Third Floor, F-Block
International Trade Tower Nehru Place
New Delhi – 110 019
India

18 Cross Street #10-10/11/12
China Square Central
Singapore 048423

Printed in the UK

Library of Congress Cataloging-in-Publication Data:

ISBN: 9781071909973

Acquisitions Editor: Kaitlin Ciarmiello
Development Editor: Olivia Sigmund
Associate Editor: Elizabeth Hernandez
Production Editor: Syeda Aina Rahat Ali
Copy Editor: Tammy Giesmann
Typesetter: Hurix Digital
Proofreader: Ellen Brink
Indexer: Integra
Cover Designer: Dally Verghese
Marketing Manager: Gabrielle Perretta

24 25 26 27 28 10 9 8 7 6 5 4 3 2 1

Brief Contents

Detailed Contents

Preface

This book is designed to guide students, healthcare professionals, leaders, and innovators through the structure of the healthcare industry from a business perspective and to demonstrate the dynamics that shape it. Michael E. Porter's evidence-based framework for industry analysis is used as a disciplined and rigorous approach to support understanding of this highly complex industry. This guide covers each of the competitive forces in healthcare, describes the social and environmental factors shaping the future of the industry, applies these forces in real world business cases, and provides insights to support innovation. While the book focuses on the healthcare industry within the United States, given its size and uniqueness, international and global issues are included throughout.

Chapter 1 describes Porter's framework and demonstrates its application to the healthcare industry. The immense challenges disrupting the industry are highlighted by the failure of a joint venture between three of the most successful businesspersons in the United States—Warren Buffett, Jeff Bezos, and Jamie Dimon. The size of the global healthcare industry is included with comparisons in per capita health expenditures by country. Chapters 2 through 6 cover each of Porter's competitive forces as applied to the healthcare industry. In Chapter 2, key barriers to entry into the healthcare industry are described with a focus on the complexities of federal and state regulations that make it so difficult for industry outsiders to break in. Amazon's long but ultimately successful push into healthcare is featured. Chapter 3 examines the suppliers of healthcare, including the hospitals, clinics, pharmaceutical companies, and workforce that provide patient care, along with suppliers of public health and research. The factors that increase the power of suppliers to drive up costs of healthcare are featured. Chapter 4 examines the factors that increase the power of buyers to negotiate price and types of buyers of healthcare, including health insurance companies, employers, governments, taxpayers, and patients. Chapter 5 addresses the potential substitutes that threaten to replace conventional healthcare, including online care, alternative and complementary providers, self-treatment with over-the-counter supplements, and wearable devices and apps that help consumers adopt healthier lifestyles to reduce the need for so much healthcare. In Chapter 6, the intensity and basis of competition in the healthcare industry are explored, with a focus on the impacts of decelerating industry growth and improvements in price transparency.

After covering the competitive forces within the industry, the next two chapters address key issues that are influencing the future of healthcare and how value is defined. Chapter 7 examines health disparities, social determinants of health, and potential opportunities to improve health by focusing efforts outside of the healthcare system. Chapter 8 addresses the environmental impact of the healthcare industry and describes the promising One Health approach to resolving both human and environmental health issues. Chapter 9 presents six real-world case studies that illustrate the dynamics of the competitive forces covering organizations including Amazon's One Medical, the hospital chain HCA, the nonprofit Civica, the biopharmaceutical company Pfizer, the health insurance company Elevance, and the small business ZetrOZ. Finally, Chapter 10 considers opportunities for innovators to improve healthcare value not only through new technologies but also through new care models and payment methods and concludes with the importance of better healthcare value to the broader economy.

Acknowledgments

I am deeply grateful to the Sage Publishing team for their focus on the healthcare industry, including Rebecca Frankel for many years of collaboration on the Healthcare Management series in Sage Business Cases and the editorial team for this book—Kaitlin Ciarmiello for the invitation, Carole Maurer for the encouragement, and Olivia Sigmund for obsessing over details with me and (more or less) keeping me on schedule. Many thanks to all the Sage team members who have worked to launch this book. I would also like to acknowledge the scholarly work of Michael E. Porter, which spans a half-century, has improved the performance of organizations across industries and around the globe, and provides the framework for this book. May his work guide those who are dedicated to improving the healthcare industry.

Acknowledgments

I am deeply grateful to the Sage Publishing team for their focus on the healthcare industry, including Rebecca Plenkel for many years of collaboration on the Healthcare Management series in Sage Business Cases and the editorial team for this book—Katlin Giarmillo for the invitation, Carole Maurer for the encouragement, and Olivia Sigmund for absorbing over details with me and (more or less) keeping me on schedule. Many thanks to all the Sage team members who have worked to launch this book.

I would also like to acknowledge the scholarly work of Michael E. Porter, which spans a half-century, has inspired the performance of organizations across industries and around the globe, and provides the framework for this book. May his work guide those who are dedicated to improving the healthcare industry.

Introduction

Porter's Framework in the Healthcare Industry

W arren Buffett, one of the most well-known and successful business-persons and investors, described the healthcare industry as a "hungry tapeworm," detrimental to the U.S. economy as it consumes significant income without significant return on those investments. In 2018, Buffett announced that he was joining forces with two other business luminaries, Amazon's Jeff Bezos and JPMorgan Chase's Jamie Dimon, in the launch of a new company, Haven, that would focus on improving healthcare value. At the launch of the venture, Bezos stated that reducing the burden of healthcare on the economy is a worthwhile endeavor that requires "talented experts, a beginner's mind, and a long-term orientation." Three years later, these business leaders dissolved the new company, with Buffett acknowledging how difficult it was to make progress on improving healthcare value. The failure of Haven, despite the resources and business acumen of its founders, reflects the challenges of the healthcare industry that are analyzed in this guide.

Though medical advances continue to inspire awe and save lives, healthcare often fails to deliver good value to those who pay for it. While costs have continued to increase, quality improvements arguably have not kept pace. Some assert that business, and specifically profit, should be driven out of healthcare, a sentiment reflected in the Buffett-Bezos-Dimon team decision to launch Haven as not-for-profit. This guide invites business and healthcare students and professionals to consider that sound evidence-based business practices may be able to counteract the negative effects of the healthcare industry on the economy.

Development of Porter's Framework

The organization of this guide is based on one of the soundest evidence-based business frameworks: Michael E. Porter's approach to analyzing industries to support effective competitive strategy by delivering value. Porter's framework has been tested and applied for nearly a half-century across many industries. That it has not been routinely applied or adopted in the healthcare industry suggests there is great untapped opportunity to improve value in this industry through Porter's more disciplined approach. Porter is a distinguished emeritus professor at Harvard Business School, where he earned an MBA and a PhD in business economics. At a time when the field of strategy was in its infancy and the simplistic strengths-weaknesses-opportunities-threats (SWOT) analysis was the primary strategy tool taught in business schools and used in industry, Porter set out to create a more robust, disciplined, and useful framework. His 1980 book *Competitive Strategy: Techniques for Analyzing Industries and Competitors* marked the beginning of the modern era of business strategy and has been translated into 19 languages.

Porter's core tenet is that organizations should choose a generic strategy, low-cost leadership or differentiation and choose whether to compete within a focused niche or the total industry-wide market. Empirical evidence supports this approach. Organizations that align with a generic strategy tend to outperform those that do not across industries and types of organizations.

Five Competitive Forces of Porter's Framework

In 2008, Porter identified five competitive forces that are essential to understanding an industry's structure and the strategic positioning of a company to perform better. These five forces are the threat of entry, the power of suppliers, the power of buyers, the threat of substitutes, and rivalry among existing competitors.

The Threat of Entry

New entrants in an industry can intensify competition as they seek market share by offering lower prices and differentiated products and services, pressuring incumbents to respond by making investments to protect their market share. Porter identified that new entrants already established in other markets or industries can be particularly disruptive if they can leverage existing resources to rapidly gain a competitive advantage in the new market. One of Porter's examples of this is Microsoft leveraging its dominant position in the market for operating system software for personal computers to enter the market for internet browser software.

From the perspective of existing businesses in an industry, the competitive landscape is not limited to current competitors but includes the potential for new competitors to enter the market. The threat of entry to incumbents is a strong force if it is easy for new competitors to enter the market and a weak force if there are significant barriers to entry. After many years and attempts, big tech companies are accelerating their push into the healthcare market. With the size of the market, the surprise is not their interest in healthcare but rather why they haven't been more successful breaking in. Key barriers to entry have made the threat of entry a relatively weak force for existing healthcare organizations. These barriers include the complexity of federal and state policies and regulations, including Medicare and Medicaid rules; the Affordable Care Act; privacy and security requirements; health information sharing requirements; Physician Self-Referral law; licensing laws; pricing requirements; telehealth laws; drug and device marketing laws; and laws governing federally qualified health clinics, rural health clinics and other federally designated entities. Amazon's moves into healthcare demonstrate that acquisition (i.e., buy rather than build) may be the most viable approach for new entrants—even those with the vast scale and resources Amazon has—given the industry's complexity. Other barriers to entry in some segments of the healthcare industry include the need for economies of scale (e.g., healthcare insurance) or capital investments (e.g., hospitals and other specialized facilities), as well as other incumbent advantages (e.g., clinical expertise) and potential responses that discourage new entrants.

The Power of Suppliers

Suppliers provide goods and labor to a business, and they affect the profitability of the business. Every business has suppliers—the people and organizations the business pays in the process of running the business. The company's key business expenses reflect its key suppliers, such as employees or contractors, sources of raw materials and finished products used in production or service delivery, computers and other technology used by the business, and building owners from whom office or retail space is leased. When key suppliers are very powerful, the business has little leverage to negotiate how much they pay. Powerful suppliers can charge higher prices, which reduce the profitability of the business that uses the supplies if it cannot pass the cost on to its customers.

The healthcare industry includes vast and diverse suppliers that are used to deliver healthcare. The COVID supply chain disruptions affected most industries worldwide; in healthcare, these disruptions made it difficult to maintain adequate clinical staffing levels, adequate inventory of high-grade masks and other safety gear, and adequate medications and life-saving equipment. The suppliers in the healthcare industry are highly specialized, which adds to their power. This includes suppliers of information technology, for example suppliers of electronic medical record software, suppliers of equipment and facilities, and suppliers of labor—doctors, nurses, pharmacists, and other healthcare workers who need a specialized license that determines scope of practice. Health profession associations can increase the power of these clinical suppliers by advancing or protecting their respective scopes of practice and otherwise lobbying for regulations that increase their power.

The Power of Buyers

Every business has buyers—the people or organizations that pay the business for the products and services they offer. The company's key business revenues reflect its key buyers. When key buyers are very powerful, the business has little leverage to negotiate how much the buyers pay them. Powerful buyers can reduce the profitability of the business by driving prices and revenue down and by demanding higher quality products or services, which increases business expenses. Typically, buyers are considered the customers or users, but not in all industries. For example, in the social media industry, the users typically do not pay for use of the media. Rather, the key buyers are the advertisers who buy ads with the media companies to reach their users. While patients are typically considered the key customers of healthcare, they frequently are not the key buyers of healthcare. In some cases, patients are partial or indirect buyers and in other cases, patients are not buyers at all. Patients may have employer-based insurance wherein their employer buys insurance while the insurer buys most of the healthcare, and patients make copayments. In addition, taxpayers pay for healthcare of others via government insurance programs, which are key buyers of healthcare for program beneficiaries.

The healthcare industry is highly unique in the extent to which suppliers are paid by insurance (private or public) as the primary direct buyers. This is in stark contrast to other industries, such as the auto industry and real estate industry, where auto and homeowners pay for most maintenance and repairs and rely on insurance to pay only in rare exceptions. Thus, insurers play a dominant role as direct buyers in the healthcare industry. However, the primary buyers of that insurance are employees and employers. While individual employees are not powerful as buyers of insurance, employers—especially large ones—are.

To the extent that employers are unhappy with insurance companies serving as the healthcare buyers for their employees, they can self-insure and buy healthcare directly. In some cases, large buyers that are unhappy with available suppliers will themselves enter the market to provide their own supply, including in the healthcare industry. Increasingly, large employers, unhappy with the value of healthcare they buy for their employees, are entering the healthcare industry themselves. These are classic examples of buyers becoming suppliers and disrupting the competitive environment in the quest for better value.

The Threat of Substitutes

The extent to which a product or service could be replaced by another that offers the same or similar function but in a different way that delivers value to the buyer is the threat of substitutes. When Amazon was launched, it offered a different way to buy books, a substitute for shopping at local bookstores. Similarly, e-books and e-readers offer a different way to read, a substitute for physical books. Substitutes may be downstream. For example, e-readers are also a substitute for bookshelves, and software that allows e-books to be downloaded directly from the internet rather than shipped to the customer on a disc is a substitute for book warehouses and book wholesalers.

There are potential substitutes for every business's product or service. The extent to which those substitutes offer a compelling relative value— quality for the cost—to buyers determines how big a threat it is to the business. While regulations and the nature of some health conditions limit potential substitutes for some hospital and emergency care, other aspects of healthcare face the threat of being substituted. Urgent care clinics and concierge medicine are potential substitutes for traditional primary care, while telehealth and mail-order pharmacies are alternatives to in-person care. During the pandemic, many healthcare providers began offering healthcare visits virtually. In particular, the availability and use of virtual mental healthcare services grew dramatically as technology startups modified the delivery of mental health services. The increasing availability of innovative consumer products threatens to replace traditional healthcare. Examples include Kardia (home EKGs for heart monitoring), wearables to promote health and prevention (e.g., Whoop, Apple), and online help (e.g., WebMD resources for consumers, Roman's direct-to-consumer online care targeting men's health issues). Many consumers globally also turn to over-the-counter supplements, herbal medicine, and traditional healers as substitutes for conventional medicine.

Rivalry Among Existing Competitors

Existing competitors can vie for market share by reducing their prices, offering new versions of their products, enhancing service, and launching advertising campaigns. The greater the rivalry, the greater the limitations are on industry profitability as competitors must sacrifice revenue via lower prices or spend more on product enhancements or advertising to maintain or grow their market share. The extent to which profitability is limited depends on both the intensity of the rivalry and whether the rivalry is based on price competition or differentiation among products and services.

Competitors within an industry or segment compete for existing buyers within a market and to grow the market by finding new buyers.

Price sensitive buyers seek acceptable quality for the lowest cost, inspiring price competition, while other buyers shop for various levels of quality at an acceptable cost, inspiring competition around differentiated quality (e.g., customer service, speed, convenience, durability, luxury, status, experience). In the healthcare industry, buyers have had great difficulty shopping for value because of lack of transparency to allow comparisons of price and quality. In addition, the complexity of healthcare makes evaluation of the quality of care challenging for most buyers. Competitors in the healthcare industry often use nonmarket approaches to protect their turf from competition. This includes competing over legislation regarding price controls and transparency, marketing of drugs and other health products, and scopes of practice—for example, who can diagnose conditions and prescribe medications. Fraud and corruption as nonmarket strategies are unfortunately not uncommon in healthcare in the competition for buyers. These unethical organizations often prey on price-sensitive buyers who do not have the capacity to meaningfully compare healthcare options based on quality.

Porter's Framework in Action in the Healthcare Industry

Governments play a major role in shaping the competitive forces of healthcare within nations, and differences in this role provide opportunities for comparative analyses. Nations vary in the extent to which public funding is provided for healthcare, whether all citizens have health insurance coverage, the benefits and services that are covered, to what extent prices are set and how they are set, whether providers are public or private and for profit or nonprofit, and the extent to which new treatments are developed and available. In their 2020 review of 20 countries, the Commonwealth Fund provided a detailed comparison of healthcare systems and insurance coverage and financing. The report indicated that only two nations studied, India and the United States, do not have universal coverage and provided detailed comparisons of the user fees and safety nets by country. The report provided type of ownership—public or private—of the primary care providers and hospitals, along with comparisons of how they are paid and the extent of gatekeepers in using the facilities. Medical education models—whether medical schools are public or private and whether tuition is charged to the student or subsidized—are also compared by nation in the report.

There is broad recognition that the healthcare system in the United States is the most unique across the diversity of national systems. Healthcare in the United States can be described as lacking in system-ness, as a fragmented collection of partial systems and independent organizations. The United States is consistently an outlier in terms of its high costs per capita, inspiring efforts to identify the root causes, reduce costs, and improve quality. In 2022, the Organisation for Economic Co-operation and Development (OECD) conducted an analysis to explain the high cost of healthcare in the United States relative to the OECD average and the other Group of Seven (G7) nations of advanced economies. The analysis found that per capita spending in the United States cannot be explained solely by higher income levels, as it remains an outlier after accounting for income. Relative aging across nations partially masks the extent to which the United States is a high-cost outlier, as age adjustments reported by the OECD reveal even greater cost differences between the United States and other nations. The OECD report indicates no simple explanations can be found in differences in lifestyle. While the United States has a higher portion of the population that is overweight or obese, it is among the lowest in portion of the population that smokes daily. The quality of care also does not provide easy explanations, with the United States performing relatively better on effective cancer care and survival and relatively worse on effective primary care in the management of diabetes.

The OECD analysis identifies significant differences between the United States and the other G7 nations in terms of the funding sources of healthcare. In the other nations, approximately three-fourths of healthcare expenditures are funded by government compared with only about half in the United States. In other G7 nations, private health insurance is supplementary, funding less than 15% of healthcare expenditures, compared with funding approximately one-third in the United States, where private insurance is the primary or only health insurance for many. In terms of proportion of per capita spending, administrative costs are particularly high in the United States relative to the other G7 nations, accounting for 8% of expenditures, though completely eliminating this expense would do little to close the total per capita healthcare spending gap. The OECD report documents that the higher per capita healthcare spending in the United States relative to other G7 nations is due to both greater consumption of healthcare and higher prices for that care.

Put into Porter's framework, in other nations, the government buyers are much more powerful relative to the United States. When there is only one buyer—that is, a buyer's monopoly such as single-payer healthcare systems—that buyer has tremendous power over the healthcare suppliers to drive down supply prices to whatever it wants and to limit consumption by restricting what it will buy. The only options for suppliers in response are to accept the reduced income, cut expenses, or exit the market. In the United States, where physician income is significantly higher than in other countries, the cost of medical school tuition has soared, so accepting reduced income makes it more difficult for the physician to achieve return on that educational investment. With lower income, cutting expenses is another option, though doing so without jeopardizing quality of care may be challenging.

Barriers to exiting the healthcare market, specifically the specialized nature of healthcare resources that cannot be easily repurposed in other industries, would likely keep some incumbents in the market accepting lower income, while other incumbents would likely dissolve, and new entrants would be discouraged from entering the market. In response to the suppliers' actions, the single buyer might choose to increase the price they will pay to prevent a decline in quality or availability of healthcare suppliers. The buyer might also seek substitutes for traditional healthcare (e.g., substitute lower cost practitioners who have less training for more highly trained and expensive physicians). Finally, the monopoly buyer might enter the market itself as a healthcare supplier (e.g., establish and operate public hospitals, clinics, pharmacies, and pharmaceutical manufacturers). The only other check on the power of a single government buyer of healthcare is the voting power of the public in nations that hold free and fair elections.

In the United States, the federal government is a powerful buyer, but it is not the only buyer of healthcare. However, as it continues to struggle to sustain its insurance programs in the face of an aging population and federal deficits, it is increasingly exercising its buying power. In response, healthcare suppliers have increasingly consolidated into large healthcare systems (e.g., growing into larger hospital, clinic, and pharmacy chains) and other large companies (e.g., pharmaceutical companies and healthcare technology companies) to increase their power in negotiating prices with the government and other large buyers. These larger suppliers are demanding even higher prices from private insurance buyers to make up for cuts by government buyers. Some providers are refusing to accept patients with certain federal insurance, both Medicaid and Medicare, due to the low prices they pay. Private insurance companies then, which are also consolidating to increase their buying power, are passing along the higher prices they are paying healthcare suppliers to the employees and employers in the form of higher health insurance premiums. These higher health insurance premiums translate to higher business expenses for employers across all industries and lower discretionary income among their employees, which harms the U.S. economy.

Sizing Up the Healthcare Industry

In 2022, the World Health Organization stated that healthcare spending hit $9 trillion in 2020, representing 11% of the global gross domestic product. The United States accounted for nearly half of those expenditures at $4 trillion, and high-income countries combined accounted for more than 80% of global healthcare expenditures. High income countries spend significantly more than other countries as a percentage of gross domestic product and as a percentage of government spending. On a per capita basis, healthcare

Figure 1   Current Health Expenditure Per Capita in USD in 2020

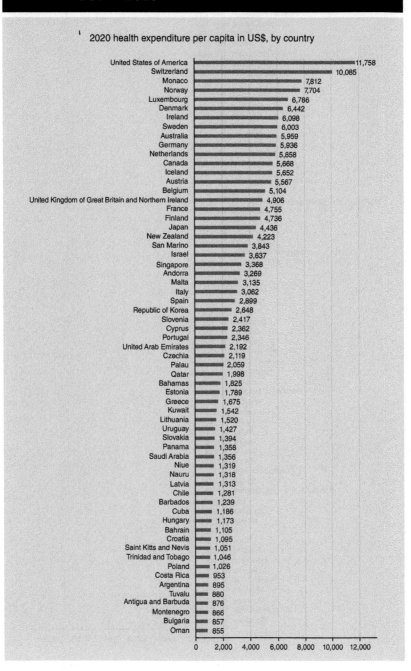

2020 health expenditure per capita in US$, by country

United States of America	11,758
Switzerland	10,085
Monaco	7,812
Norway	7,704
Luxembourg	6,786
Denmark	6,442
Ireland	6,098
Sweden	6,003
Australia	5,959
Germany	5,936
Netherlands	5,858
Canada	5,668
Iceland	5,652
Austria	5,567
Belgium	5,104
United Kingdom of Great Britain and Northern Ireland	4,906
France	4,755
Finland	4,736
Japan	4,436
New Zealand	4,223
San Marino	3,843
Israel	3,637
Singapore	3,368
Andorra	3,269
Malta	3,135
Italy	3,062
Spain	2,899
Republic of Korea	2,648
Slovenia	2,417
Cyprus	2,362
Portugal	2,346
United Arab Emirates	2,192
Czechia	2,119
Palau	2,059
Qatar	1,998
Bahamas	1,825
Estonia	1,789
Greece	1,675
Kuwait	1,542
Lithuania	1,520
Uruguay	1,427
Slovakia	1,394
Panama	1,358
Saudi Arabia	1,356
Niue	1,319
Nauru	1,318
Latvia	1,313
Chile	1,281
Barbados	1,239
Cuba	1,186
Hungary	1,173
Bahrain	1,105
Croatia	1,095
Saint Kitts and Nevis	1,051
Trinidad and Tobago	1,046
Poland	1,026
Costa Rica	953
Argentina	895
Tuvalu	880
Antigua and Barbuda	876
Montenegro	866
Bulgaria	857
Oman	855

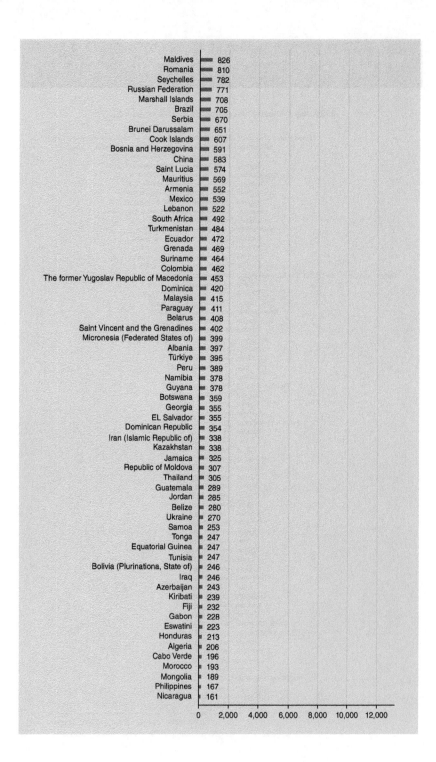

Maldives	826
Romania	810
Seychelles	782
Russian Federation	771
Marshall Islands	708
Brazil	705
Serbia	670
Brunei Darussalam	651
Cook Islands	607
Bosnia and Herzegovina	591
China	583
Saint Lucia	574
Mauritius	569
Armenia	552
Mexico	539
Lebanon	522
South Africa	492
Turkmenistan	484
Ecuador	472
Grenada	469
Suriname	464
Colombia	462
The former Yugoslav Republic of Macedonia	453
Dominica	420
Malaysia	415
Paraguay	411
Belarus	408
Saint Vincent and the Grenadines	402
Micronesia (Federated States of)	399
Albania	397
Türkiye	395
Peru	389
Namibia	378
Guyana	378
Botswana	359
Georgia	355
EL Salvador	355
Dominican Republic	354
Iran (Islamic Republic of)	338
Kazakhstan	338
Jamaica	325
Republic of Moldova	307
Thailand	305
Guatemala	289
Jordan	285
Belize	280
Ukraine	270
Samoa	253
Tonga	247
Equatorial Guinea	247
Tunisia	247
Bolivia (Plurinationa, State of)	246
Iraq	246
Azerbaijan	243
Kiribati	239
Fiji	232
Gabon	228
Eswatini	223
Honduras	213
Algeria	206
Cabo Verde	196
Morocco	193
Mongolia	189
Philippines	167
Nicaragua	161

0   2,000   4,000   6,000   8,000   10,000   12,000

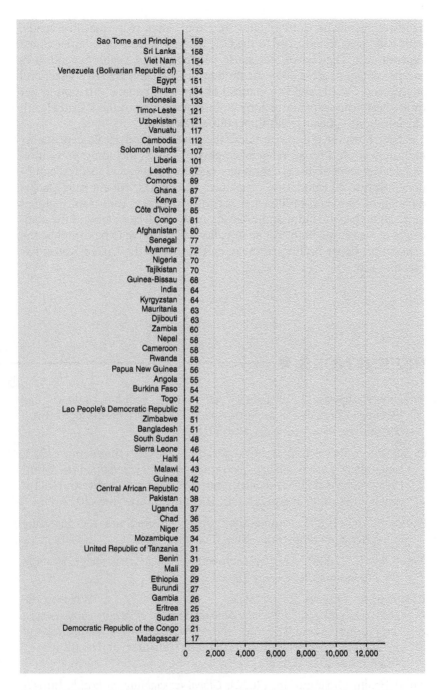

Sao Tome and Principe	159
Sri Lanka	158
Viet Nam	154
Venezuela (Bolivarian Republic of)	153
Egypt	151
Bhutan	134
Indonesia	133
Timor-Leste	121
Uzbekistan	121
Vanuatu	117
Cambodia	112
Solomon Islands	107
Liberia	101
Lesotho	97
Comoros	89
Ghana	87
Kenya	87
Côte d'Ivoire	85
Congo	81
Afghanistan	80
Senegal	77
Myanmar	72
Nigeria	70
Tajikistan	70
Guinea-Bissau	68
India	64
Kyrgyzstan	64
Mauritania	63
Djibouti	63
Zambia	60
Nepal	58
Cameroon	58
Rwanda	58
Papua New Guinea	56
Angola	55
Burkina Faso	54
Togo	54
Lao People's Democratic Republic	52
Zimbabwe	51
Bangladesh	51
South Sudan	48
Sierra Leone	46
Haiti	44
Malawi	43
Guinea	42
Central African Republic	40
Pakistan	38
Uganda	37
Chad	36
Niger	35
Mozambique	34
United Republic of Tanzania	31
Benin	31
Mali	29
Ethiopia	29
Burundi	27
Gambia	26
Eritrea	25
Sudan	23
Democratic Republic of the Congo	21
Madagascar	17

Source: WHO, the Global Health Observatory Indicators: Current Health Expenditure per capita in 2020 (https://www.who.int/data/gho/data/indicators/indicators-index)

expenditures in the United States were more than twice that in Canada, with only Switzerland close to the U.S. amount at 86% of U.S. per capita expenditures. The United States also has the highest health expenditures as a percentage of gross domestic product at 19% compared to Switzerland at 12% and Canada at 13%. Figure 1 shows the dramatic variation in per capita healthcare expenditures by country according to the World Health Organization's Global Health Expenditure Database.

Cost, however, is only one side of the value equation. Healthcare quality indicators cover a broad range of important topics, including prevention and management of disease, mortality rates for surgery and medical conditions, overuse and underuse of medical procedures, patient safety, coordination of care, end-of-life care, patient experience, care team member satisfaction, health equity, and innovation. While debates around the challenges of measuring both cost and quality will continue to be complex, the demand for better healthcare value, particularly in the United States, has become clear.

REFERENCES

Berkshire Hathaway. (2018, January 30). *Amazon, Berkshire Hathaway and JPMorgan Chase & Co. to partner on U.S. employee healthcare.* https://berkshirehathaway.com/news/jan3018.pdf

Organisation for Economic Co-operation and Development. (2022, September). *Understanding differences in health expenditure between the United States and OECD countries.* https://www.oecd.org/health/Health-expenditure-differences-USA-OECD-countries-Brief-July-2022.pdf

Porter, M. E. (1980). Competitive strategy: Techniques for analyzing industries and competitors. New York: Free Press.

Porter, M. E. (2008). The five competitive forces that shape strategy. *Harvard Business Review, 86*(1), 78.

Tikkanen, R., Osborn, R., Mossialos, E., Djordjevic, A., & Wharton, G. (2020 December). *2020 international profiles of health care systems.* The Commonwealth Fund. https://www.commonwealthfund.org/sites/default/files/2020-12/International_Profiles_of_Health_Care_Systems_Dec2020.pdf

World Health Organization. (2022). *Global expenditure on health.* https://apps.who.int/iris/bitstream/handle/10665/365133/9789240064911-eng.pdf

World Health Organization. *Global health expenditure database.* https://apps
.who.int/nha/database/Select/Indicators/en

World Health Organization. *Indicators.* https://www.who.int/data/gho/data/
indicators/indicators-index

FURTHER READINGS _____

Bradburd, R. M., & Ross, D. R. (1989). Can small firms find and defend
strategic niches? A test of the Porter hypothesis. *The Review of Economics
and Statistics*, 258–262. https://doi.org/10.2307/1926971

Dess, G. G., & Davis, P. S. (1984). Porter's (1980) generic strategies as
determinants of strategic group membership and organizational
performance. *Academy of Management Journal*, 27(3), 467–488. https://
doi.org/10.2307/256040

Kling, J. A., & Smith, K. A. (1995). Identifying strategic groups in the
US airline industry: An application of the Porter model. *Transportation
Journal*, 26–34.

Mazzarol, T. W., & Soutar, G. N. (2008) Strategy matters: Strategic positioning and performance in the education services sector. *International
Journal of Nonprofit and Voluntary Sector Marketing*, 13(2), 141–151.
https://doi.org/10.1002/nvsm.313

Pellegrin, K. L., & Pezzuto, J. M. (2011). Strategic direction for high
demand degrees: an analysis of the US pharmacy degree competitive
market. *International Journal of Management in Education*, 5(2–3),
285–300. https://doi.org/10.1504/IJMIE.2011.039490

White, R. E. (1986). Generic business strategies, organizational context
and performance: An empirical investigation. *Strategic Management
Journal*, 7(3), 217–231. https://doi.org/10.1002/smj.4250070304

CHAPTER

2

The Healthcare Market

Barriers to Entrants

If a company like Amazon—with vast access to capital, technology capabilities, and business acumen—cannot easily enter the healthcare market, the barriers to entry are significant, making the threat of entry a relatively weak force for healthcare incumbents. In 1999, just two years after its initial public offering, Amazon first attempted to enter the healthcare market by purchasing a 46% stake in drugstore.com and selling its over-the-counter products via Amazon's online store. However, as a step toward entering the prescription drug market, Amazon's first effort failed due to challenges dealing with the myriad of complicated regulations, logistics, and existing business partnerships that became stronger in the face of an outsider like Amazon. In 2011, prescription drug retailer incumbent Walgreens acquired drugstore.com, paying a 102% premium for the company, and then shut it down just a few years later to focus on making improvements to its own website Walgreens.com. While the premium purchase and shutdown marked a financial loss for Walgreens, the strategic gain was the elimination of its online competitor drugstore.com and of Amazon's ability to leverage the company to enter Walgreen's prescription drug market turf.

From the perspective of healthcare incumbents, the threat of entry is both from large corporations like Amazon wanting to move in and from new startup companies like drugstore.com. Just two years before Walgreens shut down its drugstore.com threat, PillPack launched as a new, independent pharmacy aiming to take market share from Walgreens and other big retail pharmacy chains. PillPack is known for its online ordering and home delivery of medications in presorted pill packets, each of which is marked for a specific day and time with support from a medication reminder app. By the time drugstore.com was closed, PillPack was operating in 48 U.S. states. According to PillPack cofounder and then-CEO TJ Parker, they launched the online pharmacy to transform the process of managing medications for those who take them regularly. Their goal was to streamline not only the daily process of sorting and remembering which pills to take when but also the process of getting the prescriptions filled by seamlessly connecting with prescribers and health insurance companies to ensure the patient always has a supply of the medications they need with the convenience of home delivery.

In 2018, Amazon outbid Walmart—a major existing competitor and pharmacy incumbent—to purchase PillPack for nearly $1 billion, causing major declines in shares of Walgreens, other chain retail pharmacies, and pharmacy middlemen (e.g., pharmacy benefit managers and wholesalers) due to concerns about the potential for Amazon to disrupt the pharmacy market and its supply chain. Nearly 20 years after Amazon first attempted to enter the prescription drug market via drugstore.com, Amazon was in with PillPack. Their acquisition of the company allowed Amazon to enter the market much faster relative to building their own in-house online pharmacy. While this purchase made entering the market quick, Amazon still faced complex healthcare regulations and a network of complicated relationships between established incumbents that threatened the success of its new pharmacy business.

However, Amazon's goal was not the success of its pharmacy business; its goal was the success of its business more broadly, and PillPack was just a first step into healthcare toward that goal. A year later, Amazon launched Amazon Care, a healthcare service for its employees that was built in-house as part of Amazon's Haven venture with Berkshire Hathaway and JP Morgan. Amazon Care outlasted Haven, but not for long. It was launched for employees in the Seattle area, offering virtual urgent care and consultations as well as in-person visits and delivery of prescription medications to the employee's home or office.

Amazon Care expanded rapidly to offer in-person care in multiple cities and telehealth services in all 50 states landing contracts with Hilton and other corporations to offer the Amazon Care benefit to their employees. However, three years after the launch of the Amazon Care pilot, Amazon shut it down and announced the acquisition of primary care provider One Medical for nearly $4 billion. Specifically, Amazon indicated that its Amazon Care service was not comprehensive enough for its employer customers. Amazon's abandonment of its internally built outpatient service in favor of buying one underscores the benefits of the acquisition approach as the most viable way to deal with barriers to entry for healthcare industry outsiders.

Amazon's aggressive push into healthcare with the purchase of One Medical—a topic further addressed in the first business case in Chapter 9— has raised many questions about where it might be headed next. Amazon's pharmacy and primary care investments do not include suppliers of the sector that consumes the largest share of the U.S. healthcare expenditure— hospital care—which accounts for about one-third of the annual $4 trillion total spending. Yet Amazon's moves have sent a strong reminder to healthcare incumbents that the barriers to entry are not impenetrable. This section dissects these barriers that protect incumbents and daunt any organization aiming to enter the healthcare industry. Identified by Porter, these entry barriers give incumbents a competitive advantage by making it difficult for potential new competitors to enter the market.

Economies of Scale in Production

In any industry, larger businesses have a competitive advantage because they can produce at a lower per-unit cost than smaller businesses—this is also known as supply-side economies of scale. Production costs can be divided into fixed costs and variable costs. Fixed costs are those that don't change with the volume produced (e.g., buildings, equipment, management salaries). Variable costs change with volume and include the cost of the raw materials and the product/service workforce (i.e., the workers who turn raw materials into finished products or provide services). Organizations that produce larger volume have lower costs per unit because they are spreading out their fixed costs over more units. Greater volume also means better negotiating power in the purchase of supplies needed for production as well as more opportunities to use more efficient technologies in the production process. This barrier requires new competitors to either enter the market with economies of scale in order to be cost competitive or to compete on differentiation.

In the healthcare industry, the economies of scale are a barrier to entry across major segments. In 2023, the Drug Channels Institute reported that in the retail pharmacy market, CVS and Walgreens continue to dominate with a combined total of about 41% of the total U.S. prescription dispensing revenue in 2022. The top 15 companies claim 76% of the market share. Amazon is not among the top 15, the smallest of which has less than a half-percent of the market share. Amazon does not have local community pharmacies unlike its major retail competitor Walmart, which was among the top 15 pharmacies with 4% of the market share of prescription revenue in 2022. With mail order as the only option, some customers might be reluctant to switch to Amazon's pharmacy if they prefer the simplicity and flexibility of using one pharmacy with both virtual and in-person options.

The economies of scale are so essential in the retail pharmacy market that Target's nearly 2,000 stores were not enough to stay viable in this market. Despite $4 billion in annual sales, Target's pharmacy business was losing money, so in 2015, Target announced it was selling its pharmacy business to CVS, which had nearly 8,000 stores at the time. CVS thus leveraged and expanded its vast economies of scale in its drug supply chain with the purchase of Target's pharmacies while also eliminating Target as a competitor in the pharmacy market.

Although the massive retail chains CVS and Walgreens have put many pharmacies out of business, particularly small independent pharmacies, by leveraging economies of scale, some small community pharmacies continue to thrive on a differentiation strategy. They offer specialized niche products and services not offered by the chains, and often have customers referred to them from the chains. PillPack demonstrated that a small independent pharmacy not only can enter the market but also can grow into a national competitor through a differentiation strategy, such as PillPack's unique customer-friendly packaging and mobile app.

With PillPack, Amazon's move into primary care services reflects a widespread acceleration of national pharmacies growing their economies of scale from prescriptions to prescribers. To address stagnant growth, Walgreens acquired a majority stake in VillageMD, a primary care clinic chain, with the plan to attach clinics to hundreds of Walgreens pharmacies. Meanwhile, CVS announced a deal to purchase Oak Street Health, a company specializing in primary care for older adults with over 100 locations across the US, for $10.6 billion.

The moves by these major pharmacy players have been part of a larger trend in the consolidation of outpatient medical care, which used to be delivered largely by solo and small local group practices. In 2021, The American Medical Association reported that the percent of physicians working in private practice—defined as a practice that is wholly owned by physicians—dropped below 50% for the first time in 2020. The percent working in a practice partially or wholly owned by a hospital increased to more than 30%, and the percent working in a practice owned by a private equity firm—an emerging trend—has increased to more than 4%. Regardless of ownership, the increasing importance of economies of scale as a barrier to entry continues to be seen in physician practices. The percent of physicians working in a practice with fewer than five physicians dropped to one-third in 2020 (from 49% in 2012), and those working in a practice with 50 or more physicians grew to 17%—up from 12% in 2012.

The increase in hospital ownership of physician practices is part of the trend in hospital consolidation aiming for economies of scale. Hospitals, like physician practices and pharmacies, used to be mostly single independent entities serving their local communities. Definitive Healthcare reported that, as of 2022, only 20% of hospitals are independent—that is, not part of a healthcare system or network—while the existing healthcare systems continue to grow through mergers with and acquisitions of more hospitals and physician practices. Mergers and acquisitions in other segments of the healthcare industry—from health insurance to drug development and manufacturing to home health, hospice, and other health services—also reflect the drive toward achieving greater economies of scale in production that protect incumbents.

Network Effects

The other side of the economies of scale in production (which increase an organization's capacity to compete on cost by reducing per unit production cost) are network effects, otherwise known as demand-side economies of scale. Network effects are the increases in the value of a product or service to users or buyers that are due to increases in the number of users or buyers. This can occur, for example, when a large company becomes recognized as a trusted brand, which drives more users. In 2022, Newsweek reported that among retail pharmacy chains, CVS has both the largest market share and is voted by consumers as being the most trusted brand in the United States. Walgreens comes in second place, both in market share and consumer trust.

Examples of network effects in e-commerce include Amazon and eBay, both of which rely on platforms that connect buyers and sellers and become more valuable to users with the increased number of users. Increases in users can add value in e-commerce by increasing the number and sources of products available for purchase as well as by adding more information to guide purchases via customer ratings and comments about products. Social media companies rely heavily on network effects. Increases in the number of Facebook and LinkedIn users, for example, enrich the user experience. Network effects can be very powerful barriers to entry once incumbents have captured sufficient market share in segments where market share itself, as with social media and e-commerce companies, is a key part of the value proposition to customers.

These network effects that have helped to create big technology *platform companies* and protect their market share from new entrants can be leveraged as they move into other sectors. As Amazon begins to penetrate the barriers that have thwarted its efforts to enter the healthcare industry, it will aim to use its platform to capture sufficient market share such that the network effects become a key barrier that will reduce the threat of other entrants. This approach is evident in its purchase of PillPack, whose cofounder and then-Chief Technology Officer Elliot Cohen described PillPack's PharmacyOS software on which the company operates: "PharmacyOS is more than a rethinking of a pharmacy system. It truly represents the early stages of a platform that over time will create a radical shift in chronic care management."

Investments in platform companies in healthcare are expected to continue to grow because they offer solutions to many key problems in the industry. In particular, these companies are expected to erect new barriers to entry due to the network effects from eliminating inefficient middlemen in the healthcare supply chain, improving access to healthcare knowledge and expertise, and improving transparency to enhance consumer decision making around pricing and quality. While critical mass to realize these benefits is difficult to achieve, particularly in the healthcare industry, the platform companies that get there first will make it very difficult for others to enter.

The healthcare industry is in the early stages of being radically transformed by e-platforms that connect healthcare providers, health insurance companies, and consumers in a way that adds value to all those who use it. Companies that create and operate these healthcare platforms and successfully grow the number of users to a critical mass will benefit from the network effects that increase barriers to entry. This will allow them to grow their healthcare business through use of the platform by diverse healthcare participants rather than through mergers and acquisitions. Incumbents that invest in the creation of healthcare platforms will not need to control more of the supply chain through vertical integration.

Amazon has grown into a retail giant, not by acquiring all the suppliers that use its platform, but through the creation and operation of a user-friendly retail platform that is beneficial to buyers and suppliers. When the strength and competitive advantage of network effects as a barrier to entry are understood, it becomes quite easy to imagine that Amazon's PillPack Pharmacy OS acquisition, Haven venture, Amazon Care program, and One Medical acquisition have been key efforts to find and develop the right platform to reach that critical mass in the healthcare ecosystem. Network effects are not currently a significant entry barrier, but as big technology companies move in, they will be.

Customer Switching Costs

Switching costs are the fixed costs—in money, time, effort, and/or psychological cost—when a customer switches from one supplier to a competitor. These can serve as barriers that help lock in customers when a company offers a unique enough product or service and that help lock out new entrants. However, companies that offer equivalent products to their competitors will typically have low switching costs (and low barriers to entry), particularly as the internet makes the cost of comparing and switching even lower. Exit fees, such as an administrative fee for closing an account or an early termination fee, are used by some companies to reduce switching. Companies can also increase switching costs by making it a hassle to switch, such as needing to wait in line or complete paperwork. Costs of switching also may include additional investment of time to learn how to use a new product after switching. Companies with equivalent products can increase switching costs by offering convenience (e.g., number of locations or ease of buying products) that customers would lose by switching to an otherwise equivalent competitor. Finally, companies that build strong relationships and trust with customers make it more difficult for customers to switch due to the emotional and other psychological costs (e.g., sense of risk) from switching.

In the prescription drug market, patents and market exclusivity provide a period of legal restrictions against competition, allowing the pharmaceutical company that developed the drug to maintain higher pricing. This period of market exclusivity provides incentives for drug companies to invest in research and development. At the end of this period, generic drug companies can legally enter and begin competing, offering much lower prices for an equivalent drug. Sometimes the brand name drug company will offer incentives—such as copay assistance programs—to entice patients not to switch to the generic drug after market exclusivity ends. Some patients might also experience psychological costs of switching to a generic to the extent that they have a sense of trust in the brand name company.

However, organizations that bear at least some of the risk for managing drug costs have Pharmacy and Therapeutics (P&T) committees that facilitate switching from brand to generic when available. These committees continuously review and evaluate new drugs approved by the FDA as well as available generics and maintain a preferred drug list (i.e., *formulary*) based on cost-effectiveness. This results in higher out-of-pocket expenses for patients who want to continue taking the brand name drug rather than switching to the generic. Thus, switching costs implemented by brand name companies are generally not a significant barrier to generic companies entering the market. As Amazon Pharmacy grows as a healthcare platform, its tools that allow customers to more easily compare prescription drug prices will likely further lower the switching costs as a barrier for new entrants.

In the healthcare industry, a more significant switching cost that serves as a barrier to entry pertains to consumer choices in selecting a health plan and healthcare providers. This has been studied in countries where there is competition in health insurance markets, such as the United States and Switzerland. In the United States, there are generally low rates of customers switching health plans (both within or between insurance companies) and even lower rates of switching to a different insurance company. Medicare Advantage plans for older adults in the United States are offered by private companies under Medicare rules that limit the amount of annual out-of-pocket costs for patients, though typically require patients to use healthcare providers who are part of the plan's network. For patients with Medicare Advantage plans, there are higher switching costs when a patient chooses a different insurance company due to the structure of the Medicare program. Specifically, the high number of choices of plans (even with limited number of insurance companies) means significant complexities in comparing plans across companies, making the decision to switch to a different company particularly time-consuming and potentially risky. In 2020, Adam Atherly and colleagues sampled beneficiaries with a Medicare Advantage plan and found that the beneficiary needed to be compensated $233 per month on average to switch to a different plan with the same insurance company and $1,107 per month to switch to a different plan with a different company.

In Switzerland, the government requires that all residents purchase health insurance from private nonprofit companies. In addition, residents may purchase supplemental private insurance for services that are not covered by the mandatory health insurance. This supplementary insurance gives residents access to a greater choice of physicians and the ability to obtain better accommodations in hospital settings. According to a 2020 report by Karine Lamiraud and Stadelmann, analysis of consumer behavior in Switzerland indicated that low-priced supplemental insurance products are important in the health insurance market both in attracting customers and in keeping them from switching to other companies. Again, the complexities of the health plans and lack of access to user-friendly comparisons across insurance options and companies is considered a significant cost of switching in the Swiss health insurance market.

The importance of comparative information in overcoming switching costs is also apparent in a study of consumer choice of a primary care provider. Enrollment in Sweden's universal health system is automatic, and provider fees and patient copayments are set regionally. In 2021, Anders Anell and colleagues published research on two large field experiments, in which participants were randomly selected to receive information sent out via mail by the regional healthcare authority, which contained comparative information on the accessibility, quality, and available services of the individual's primary care provider as well as the provider's three geographically closest competitors. In addition, a subset of those participants received a prepaid choice form to make it easy to choose a new provider if desired. The results indicate that those who received this intervention were significantly more likely to switch providers.

The cost for consumers to switch providers is a significant barrier to entry for new competitors, largely because there is a lack of user-friendly information about the choices available. Switching providers also costs the consumer time in transferring their medical history from one provider to the next. These barriers of complex choices, limited consumer access to information to support informed decision making, and medical record management are just the types of problems platform companies like Amazon may solve by creating more consumer-friendly healthcare ecosystems.

In the United States, the Affordable Care Act launched a health insurance exchange system that gives consumers easier access to individual health insurance, including the ability to compare plans within and across health insurance companies via a national website. New entrants have increased with this exchange system, likely due at least in part to the reduced uncertainties of switching. Research by the AMA in 2023 further supports the effect of the health insurance exchange on reducing barriers to entry for new health insurance plans to enter new markets. Their analyses indicate that larger health insurance companies have generally gotten smaller, while smaller companies have grown.

Healthcare incumbents that have previously benefited from the switching costs incurred by consumers—in time, effort, and risk—will continue to face a stronger threat of entry as more user-friendly information becomes available to help consumers compare options.

Capital Requirements

Large capital investments needed to compete can be a significant barrier to entry; however, to the extent that investments are likely to provide an adequate return, the capital requirement barrier is not as significant. The healthcare industry, though very labor intensive, has major capital requirements to compete in certain areas, including fixed facilities and equipment (e.g., hospitals, drug manufacturing plants, research and development laboratories). Pharmacies and the pipeline that supplies them need to maintain adequate drug inventory to meet the demand for prescription medications, and pharmaceutical research companies need major capital investments to develop new drugs. In 2020, Olivier Wouters and colleagues reported that, based on an analysis of new drugs and biologic agents approved by the U.S. Food and Drug Administration, the median capitalized cost to bring one new medicine to market is $1.1 billion, including the cost of failed products. In the insurance industry, regulators set the minimum amount of capital required to support operations and write coverage. In the U.S. healthcare industry, insurance companies must maintain a minimum surplus (i.e., assets minus liabilities) level per regulations. Most health insurance companies maintain a surplus level well above this minimum required.

In 2019, Deloitte reported findings from their analyses of return on capital in the healthcare industry by segment as a measure of efficiency in turning capital investments into profit. They measured return on capital as the ratio of earnings before interests and taxes to capital employed, with capital employed measured as total assets minus current liabilities. They found that hospitals have the lowest return on capital (about 6%). In the medtech sector—composed of companies that create tools to diagnose or treat patients, such as magnetic resonance imaging, microscopy, implantable medical devices such as pacemakers, and dialysis machines—the return on capital was approximately 10% in 2017, down from 14% in 2011. Health insurance companies and pharmacy benefit management (PBM) companies—which manage prescription drug benefits on behalf of insurance companies by negotiating contracts with drug manufacturers, wholesalers, and retail pharmacies or their agents—have a 12% return on capital. Return on capital among pharmaceutical companies dropped from over 16% in 2011 to 12% in 2017, among drug wholesalers from 18% to under 15%, and among pharmacies from under 20% to almost 18%.

The Deloitte authors note that pharmacies and wholesalers tend to have lower profitability and slim margins relative to other healthcare industry segments, particularly compared to the pharmaceutical and medtech life sciences companies that advance medical innovations. Yet because they have lower capital requirements, pharmacies and wholesalers demonstrate higher relative return on capital. Life sciences companies, which have very high capital requirements to innovate and develop new products, experienced the greatest decline in return on capital between 2011 and 2017.

Companies with a focus strategy tend to have higher return on capital performance; for example, return on capital was 17% among pharmaceutical companies specializing in a therapeutic area compared to 9% for diversified companies. Generics-focused and primary care–focused pharmaceutical companies were similar to diversified companies in return on capital performance. Medtech companies with a specialty focus also outperformed those with a diversified portfolio, with 11% return on capital versus 9%. Similarly, specialty hospitals tended to outperform general hospitals.

Although return on capital has declined across most healthcare segments, the healthcare industry continues to be attractive for investors. In 2022, Sharon Fry and colleagues reported that the internal rate of return on private equity deals in healthcare has increased over the past two decades, and the median rate in the healthcare industry is 27% compared to 21% across all industries. This robust performance indicates that, even where capital requirements in the healthcare industry are significant, they are not likely to be a major barrier to entry.

Incumbency Advantages Independent of Size

Porter described several ways incumbents can have cost or quality advantages that are not available to new entrants and not dependent on company size. These include proprietary technology, special access to raw materials, special geographic location, established brand identity, and production experience. A key advantage CVS and Walgreens had over aspiring entrant Amazon, despite its scale, was deep pharmacy industry experience. Successful entrant PillPack had no scale at startup but did have two generations of pharmacy experience on its core team. PillPack's CEO and pharmacist TJ Parker not only learned the traditional pharmacy business working in his father's pharmacy, but he also recruited him to serve as vice president of pharmacy for PillPack. Father and pharmacist Lenny Parker started Northeast Pharmacy, which delivered medications to nursing homes and assisted living facilities. Lenny joined his son after TJ and PillPack cofounder Elliot Cohen won a Boston hackathon pitching their concept for a new pharmacy model. The PillPack team then leveraged this experience and invested heavily to develop proprietary software (PharmacyOS) to streamline and automate the complexities of managing prescription renewals, billing insurance, obtaining authorizations from providers, and sending notifications to customers. This customer-friendly proprietary software created by experienced industry insiders was a barrier to others entering the market, making it the right acquisition target for Amazon to enter the market with a differentiation strategy it could further protect through scaling.

Brand identity can also be a powerful barrier to entry in the healthcare industry. When Walgreens registered to do business in Hawai'i in 2004, the state's leading pharmacy chain was California-based Longs Drug Stores, which had more than 500 stores across several states. Walgreens' first Hawai'i store opened in 2007 as part of its aggressive national expansion, putting additional market share pressure on Longs, which was already experiencing competition from Walmart and Safeway. In addition, there were rumors that Target—which had been registered to do business in Hawai'i since 1999—was looking for store locations to enter the Hawai'i market across the islands.

Longs had nearly 40 stores in Hawai'i and a 50-year history of doing business in the state when CVS acquired the regional chain less than two years after Walgreens opened its first Hawai'i store. CVS converted the hundreds of stores in Longs' home state of California and in other states to the CVS brand but kept the Longs brand for its Hawai'i stores. This was because of the strong Longs brand identity and loyalty among customers in Hawai'i, where Longs was considered local despite its headquarters being located in California.

While Target entered the Hawai'i market in 2009, adding to the pharmacy competition in the state, CVS continued to grow its Hawai'i market share by leveraging the Longs brand. The 50th Longs store to open in Hawai'i was the first to pilot the CVS layout with wider aisles arranged in a different configuration. Yet, CVS maintained the local traditions of the Longs brand in Hawai'i, including opening the store with a traditional Hawaiian blessing and stocking inventory of popular island footwear, local foods, and lei. While there have been some complaints that Longs has lost some of its local appeal under CVS management, the Longs brand has endured. When CVS acquired Target's pharmacy business in 2015, the CVS pharmacy brand became a key feature in Target stores across the United States, except in Hawai'i where the Longs brand was used. Today, CVS owns 61 stores across four counties in Hawai'i, including its Target stores, while Walgreens owns only 13 across two counties.

The power of an established brand identity as a barrier to new entrants is also seen in other segments of the healthcare industry. Many academic medical centers—those owned by or affiliated with a medical school—have brands associated with prestige and innovation. For example, Massachusetts General Hospital promotes its status as Harvard medical school's first and largest teaching hospital where most of the physicians are Harvard faculty. Academic medical centers do not just deliver care; they advance it through cutting edge research and help sustain it through the clinical training they provide to future generations of healthcare professionals. This tripartite mission, however, has been challenging to manage, particularly when reimbursement models began changing under managed care, leaving academic medical centers at a disadvantage because of their relatively higher cost structure and production inefficiencies.

Challenges of managed care in the 1990s led the MD Anderson Cancer Center at the University of Texas to financial decline, despite its history and national reputation as a top hospital. They were losing business to lower cost community hospitals. After reading Porter's book *Competitive Advantage*, Mendelsohn, a cancer researcher and the hospital's new president, told the *Wall Street Journal* in 2000 that Porter "taught me that you can be Kmart or Saks Fifth Avenue, but you can't be both . . . I decided I wanted to compete on quality." MD Anderson's success demonstrates the applicability of Porter's core concepts to academic medical centers.

MD Anderson doubled down on its quality differentiation strategy by leveraging its brand, investing in national advertising, staff, and customer service, and being an early adopter in the use of the internet to recruit patients willing to travel to get the best care. It also applied its scientific expertise to study ways to improve efficiencies in the clinical processes without adverse impacts on patient outcomes. It found that better quality can also reduce costs by reducing complications and the need for subsequent treatments. Meanwhile, it defended its practices that focused on the best patient care even when it added cost.

Over the years, instead of focusing on patients coming to MD Anderson, it began partnering with hospitals across the nation to bring MD Anderson's clinical care to patients where they live. The MD Anderson Cancer Network partners deliver the same treatment protocols and are held to the same standards of care as those in place at MD Anderson. The benefits to the network partners include rapid implementation of best practice high quality specialty care for their local cancer patients, access to the MD Anderson cancer experts, participation in cutting edge cancer research, and cobranding their facilities with MD Anderson's highly regarded and recognized name and reputation.

This network has expanded the reach of MD Anderson's clinical and research operations, strengthening its brand as a barrier to entry for new entrants in cancer care. This brand also serves to differentiate the quality of care among its partner hospitals as they compete for cancer care business in their respective local communities. Thus, an established brand identity, along with other incumbent advantages independent of size—such as proprietary technology and production experience—are significant barriers to entry that can be leveraged by healthcare industry incumbents.

Unequal Access to Distribution Channels

As described above, the MD Anderson Cancer Network is more than just a branding barrier for new entrants. This network provides MD Anderson with special access to its network partners, which serve as distribution channels through which MD Anderson delivers its clinical care and research opportunities to patients globally. Distribution channels are the steps involved in getting a product or service from its producer to the end customer, which typically occurs through intermediaries, such as wholesalers, distributors, retailers, and the internet.

In the healthcare industry, the service of patient care is typically delivered to the end customer in a hospital or clinic facility by the producer—that is, the clinician. Thus, unequal clinician access to these facilities as distribution channels is a barrier to new clinician entrants. For example, hospitals often contract with physician groups to deliver medical care services in key areas, such as the emergency department (delivered by *emergency physicians*) or inpatient care (delivered by *hospitalists*). Traditionally, these physician group companies were focused on one specialty area—hospitalist companies competed with each other for the inpatient care business, while emergency medicine companies competed with each other for emergency department business. However, some emergency medicine companies began offering these services as an integrated package with hospitalist care. These integrated service companies solve a key hospital problem—the coordination of resources for patients who transition from the emergency department to an inpatient unit. Thus, companies that have developed this more seamless coordination between physician groups can gain better access to hospital facilities, which serves as a barrier to new physician group companies entering the market offering standalone emergence medicine or hospitalist services.

While much of healthcare must still be delivered in person at hospital or clinic distribution channels, the internet now serves as an important new channel for delivering patient care services. The use of telehealth and investments in digital health companies increased dramatically with the COVID-19 pandemic—accounting for nearly one-third of all outpatient visits—as did physicians' comfort level delivering care virtually, according to a 2022 McKinsey report. The internet has reduced barriers to new entrants that have taken market share from traditional channels and have expanded markets by reaching consumers in areas where there are clinician shortages via traditional channels and in rural and remote areas that lack easy access to traditional in-person patient care distribution channels.

The product side of healthcare is dominated by prescription medications, most of which follow the path from the manufacturer through a wholesale distribution company to a pharmacy then to the patient.

According to a 2022 HDA report, approximately 94% (nearly $600 billion) of all pharmaceutical sales were channeled through distributors in 2021. More than 1,300 manufacturers use distributors to deliver their pharmaceutical products to more than 180,000 locations where they are dispensed. As of 2018, AmerisourceBergen, Cardinal Health, and McKesson, the *Big Three* pharmaceutical companies, claimed 95% of the market share. The use of wholesale distributors to supply pharmacies has increased over time as these wholesalers have developed highly efficient methods that consolidate payments to manufacturers (rather than receiving payments from each pharmacy), consolidate deliveries to each pharmacy (rather than having deliveries from each manufacturer), eliminate the need for retailers to have their own warehouses, and perform numerous compliance functions such as verifying licenses, inspecting pharmacies, and monitoring for suspicious orders per federal *know your customer* policy.

As the value distributors provide and the market share they hold have increased, so has their control over access to the primary drug distribution channel. In particular, generic medication manufacturers that do not have a contract with one of the three major wholesale distributors are largely blocked from the market. Thus, incumbents with established contracts have preferential access to pharmacies, an advantage that serves as a barrier to entry for new generic drug companies. Because by regulation generic medications are equivalent to the brand drug in safety and effectiveness, generic drug manufacturers compete on price in their efforts to obtain and retain contracts for market access via wholesalers. With Amazon's purchase of PillPack, access to distribution channels might become more equal if it offers generic manufacturers an alternative to the current three wholesalers as it uses its supply chain management expertise to gain prescription medication market share.

Restrictive Government Policy

Federal and state regulations are a key reason why the U.S. healthcare industry is considered so complicated and why industry outsiders face significant barriers to entry. PillPack's cofounder and founding CEO TJ Parker's ability to navigate this barrier as a new startup entrant was, in part, because he was a second-generation pharmacist. As a teen, Parker worked in his father's pharmacy and delivered medications to customers' homes, which inspired his career choice and his passion to find a better way to help customers who take multiple medications. Parker's experience and credentials guided him in the arduous tasks of getting PillPack licensed to operate in all 50 states in the United States and to earn national accreditation. Amazon gained this regulatory experience when it acquired PillPack and retained Dr. Parker as CEO.

Government restrictions are a significant barrier to entering nearly every part of the healthcare system in the United States. State licensing laws restrict scope of practice among each type of clinician (e.g., physicians, pharmacists, nurses, psychologists). State *certificate of need* laws restrict the creation or expansion of healthcare facilities while federal regulation now prohibits the establishment of new physician-owned hospitals and prohibits the expansion of existing physician-owned hospitals. Likewise, state and federal regulations establish requirements for health insurance companies. Federal *conditions of participation* and *conditions for coverage* determine standards hospitals, clinics, and other healthcare organizations must meet to participate in Medicare and Medicaid programs—the largest healthcare payers in the United States. Federal regulations govern every step of bringing a new drug to market, from preclinical testing in animals, to testing in humans, to what must be included in advertisements, and federal regulations require health information technology to meet industry-specific privacy and security standards.

Local restrictions are a barrier to entry across intranational markets, and national restrictions are a barrier to entry across international markets. Internationally, healthcare systems differ in key structural ways that restrict new entrants, including policies that determine who has health insurance and who owns the care providers. Some governments require all residents to have health insurance or pay a fine. In countries or regions where health insurance is universal and provided by a single payer, private insurers face a solid barrier to entry and can only enter the supplemental plan market. In countries or regions where the government provides insurance, owns the facilities, and employs the clinicians, there are solid barriers that deter new healthcare providers from entering the market.

The United States has a mixture of all these models with both government-funded and private insurance options. The Patient Protection and Affordable Care Act (also known as "Obamacare") mandated that all residents have insurance or pay a fine for the first time in U.S. history. However, in 2017, the fine was removed. Michelle Doty and colleagues' 2020 international survey of physicians in 11 high-income countries demonstrated that there is fragmentation in the U.S. healthcare industry in primary care settings. U.S. physicians reported the lowest levels of receiving timely information from other providers that is needed for managing care, conducting home visits themselves or through a member of their team, and having an after-hours care system for their patients to avoid use of the emergency department when nonemergency care is needed.

While this lack of a coordinated healthcare system has created many problems, the lack of federally mandated single system means that government restrictions as a barrier to entry into the healthcare market are significantly weaker in the United States relative to other countries. In fact, there are examples where the U.S. government has advocated for reducing state-level barriers to entry or implemented policy changes at the federal level to reduce barriers.

Certificate of Need (CON) laws are a major barrier to entry. Over half of all U.S. states and Washington D.C. continue to have CON laws, which require state approval before establishing new major healthcare facilities or expanding existing facilities, a significant deterrent to new hospitals and other healthcare facilities entering the market in those states. While the original intent of these laws, which vary by state, was to control costs, there is little evidence that CON laws have served this purpose.

In 2008, the Antitrust Division of the U.S. Department of Justice and the Federal Trade Commission issued a joint statement on "Competition in Health Care and Certificates of Need" before the Illinois Task Force on Health Planning Reform that was convened to evaluate Illinois' CON program and identify recommended changes to improve the healthcare system in the state. The federal joint statement included several arguments against CON laws. They stated that CON laws harm consumers by protecting healthcare incumbents from potential new competitors offering better value—that is, higher quality, lower prices, or both. The statement said these laws "impede the efficient performance of health care markets" because they "undercut consumer choice, stifle innovation, and weaken markets' ability to contain health care costs." Another argument against CON laws relates to payment model changes. As described further in Chapter 3, the payment model for hospitals changed dramatically in 1983 from paying hospitals based on their cost of care to paying them a fixed amount per hospital admission. The federal joint statement explains the historical link between healthcare payment models and CON laws, which were designed to prevent further increases in healthcare costs. In their joint statement, the federal agencies posited that these laws are no longer justified under current payment models because healthcare payors no longer reimburse on a cost-plus basis. Furthermore, the claim that CON laws help control healthcare costs is not substantiated. The joint statement noted that "the best empirical evidence shows that 'on balance . . . CON has no effect or actually increases both hospital spending per capita and total spending per capita,'" concluding that these laws have not fulfilled their intended purpose.

The joint statement reported that CON laws facilitate the use of harmful nonmarket approaches to securing market share, including tactics focused on protecting turf rather than increasing value to customers, unethical soft corruption reflecting abuse of power afforded under CON laws, and even illegal forms of corruption. Several organizations were found to have exploited the CON process to prevent new competition from entering the market and to protect their own revenues. In one example, the agencies noted in their joint statement that a member of the Illinois board that approved a hospital CON was convicted for accepting a kickback from the construction company that benefited from the approval.

The two federal agencies that authored the compelling arguments against CON laws support repealing them to remove this barrier to entry that deprives consumers from the benefits of competition. They concluded their statement by urging the state of Illinois to consider the net harms of their CON laws relative to their purported benefits. In 2008, the Illinois Task Force on Health Planning Reform recommended that the CON state laws be continued, with a goal to ensure "a predictable, transparent and efficient CON process."

Today, facilities regulated under Illinois' CON laws continue to include, hospitals, long-term care facilities, dialysis centers, ambulatory surgery centers, alternative health care delivery models, free-standing emergency centers, and birthing centers. Illinois state legislation enacted in 2019 added the requirement of CON approval for *closing* a healthcare facility, creating a new barrier to *exit*. Exit barriers keep struggling organizations in a market longer than they would otherwise stay, which, as Porter noted, causes harm to the healthy organizations in the market.

While CON laws remain as state-level barriers to new and expanded healthcare facilities, some federal government policies reduce these barriers. In rural areas where there is less access to care due to insufficient population size to sustain a hospital, federal laws support critical access hospitals entering these markets through cost-based reimbursement subsidies. In addition, federal laws allow cost-based reimbursement subsidies for designated Rural Health Clinics and Federally Qualified Health Clinics. Federal laws and funding also subsidize the development of new drugs and other treatments by funding biomedical research via the National Institutes of Health (NIH). This funding helps reduce barriers to new companies entering the market by reducing the capital investments required to develop treatments. In 2022, Berna Uygur and colleagues observed that early-stage companies that receive funding from or collaborate with the NIH National Cancer Institute are more likely to have a successful exit (e.g., be acquired, merge, or issue an Initial Public Offering) and less likely to file for bankruptcy or be dissolved compared to other companies.

In another example, U.S. legislation has been proposed to address the physician shortage by reducing a significant barrier to new physicians entering the market—completion of clinical training. While the number of medical students in the United States has increased, the residency slots available to provide the required clinical training for medical school graduates to practice medicine independently has not kept up. The federal government pays teaching hospitals for providing graduate medical education to physician *residents* (i.e., those who have completed medical school and are in clinical training) but caps the number of federally funded resident slots at each hospital. These caps, along with challenges finding other funding sources for these residency slots, have created a bottleneck in new physicians available to enter the market. Bipartisan legislation proposes to increase these caps, particularly in areas with significant physician shortages. Thus, government policies can and do increase and decrease the barriers to new entrants across all segments of the healthcare industry.

Expected Retaliation

Porter (2008) notes that potential entrants' expectations of retaliation by incumbents—which can be based on observation of responses to previous entrants—can be a barrier to entry if these expectations dissuade entry. If there is little growth in the industry, potential entrants might expect greater retaliation by incumbents who stand to lose more market share. Incumbents threatened by a new entrant might cut their prices to make it difficult for the newcomer to compete on price. Incumbents with special relationships with suppliers and customers might leverage those ties to try to squeeze out the new entrant.

Large incumbents tend to be slower and less aggressive in retaliating against new entrants. The CEOs of both Walgreens and CVS reported not being worried about Amazon's purchase of PillPack, yet after Amazon became their new competitor, the two big retail chain pharmacies began showing signs of retaliation by rejecting customers' requests to transfer their prescriptions to PillPack, claiming PillPack did not obtain proper consent. In 2019, CNBC reported that PillPack's spokesperson, Jacquelyn Miller, responded: "While incumbent pharmacies may be disappointed in the loss of business, it is unacceptable to make unsubstantiated allegations about PillPack's practices while simultaneously creating systemic barriers that make it harder for a customer to switch pharmacies."

While PillPack was on a mission to compete with the big retail pharmacies, smaller entrants can reverse retaliatory tendencies of larger incumbents by entering with complementary products and services that benefit the incumbent. Small independent pharmacies often complement retail chains by offering products and services not offered by the chains. Then, these pharmacies can share rather than fight over customers in ways that benefit them both.

Barriers to entry impact organizations in the healthcare industry globally. Despite the number and complexity of government policies in the United States, the U.S. healthcare industry has fewer impenetrable barriers relative to other countries. Thus, potential new for-profit and nonprofit entrants, both large and small, will continue to take aim at this large market.

REFERENCES

American Medical Association. (2023). *Bipartisan graduate medical education and physician workforce legislation.* https://www.ama-assn.org/system/files/2023-nac-action-kit-gme-physician-workforce.pdf

Anell, A., Dietrichson, J., Ellegård, L. M., & Kjellsson, G. (2021). Information, switching costs, and consumer choice: Evidence from two randomised field experiments in Swedish primary health care. *Journal of Public Economics, 196.* 104390. https://doi.org/10.1016/j.jpubeco.2021.104390

Atherly, A., Feldman, R. D., Dowd, B., & van den Broek-Altenburg, E. (2020). Switching Costs in Medicare Advantage. *Forum for Health Economics & Policy, 23*(1), 20190023. https://doi.org/10.1515/fhep-2019-0023

Cohen, E. (n.d.). *PharmacyOS.* PillPack by Amazon Pharmacy. https://www.pharmacyos.com/

Cordina, J., Fowkes, J., Malani, R., & Medford-Davis, L. (2022, February 22). *Patients love telehealth—physicians are not so sure.* McKinsey & Company. https://www.mckinsey.com/industries/healthcare/our-insights/patients-love-telehealth-physicians-are-not-so-sure

Definitive Healthcare. (2022). *Top 10 largest independent hospitals.* https://www.definitivehc.com/blog/top-10-largest-independent-hospitals

Deloitte. (2019). *The role of distributors in the US health care industry.* https://www2.deloitte.com/us/en/pages/life-sciences-and-health-care/articles/the-role-of-distributors-in-the-us-health-care-industry.html

Doty, M. M., Tikkanen, R., Shah, A., & Schneider, E. C. (2020). Primary care physicians' role in coordinating medical and health-related social needs in eleven countries. *Health Affairs (Project Hope), 39*(1), 115–123. https://doi.org/10.1377/hlthaff.2019.01088

Drug Channels Institute. (2023, March 8). The top 15 U.S. pharmacies of 2022: Market shares and revenues at the biggest companies. https://www.drugchannels.net/2023/03/the-top-15-us-pharmacies-of-2022-market.html

Fry, S., Kapur, V., Jain, N., Klingan, F., Podpolny, D., & Murphy, K. (2022, March 15). *Healthcare private equity deal returns: Look to revenues and multiples.* Bain & Company. https://www.bain.com/insights/deal-returns-global-healthcare-private-equity-and-ma-report-2022/

Healthcare Distribution Alliance. (2022). *HDA Factbook.* https://www.hda.org/publications/93rd-edition-hda-factbook-the-facts-figures-and-trends-in-healthcare/

Illinois Department of Public Health. (2008, December 31). *Final report of the Task Force on Health Planning Reform.* http://www.idph.state.il.us/tfhpr/reports/TFHPR%20Final%20Report.pdf

Johannes, L. (2000, August 29). M.D. Anderson works to build ties with the HMOs it once combated. *The Wall Street Journal.* https://www.wsj.com/articles/SB967500656782012753

Kane, C. K. (2021). *Recent changes in physician practice arrangements: Private practice dropped to less than 50 percent of physicians in 2020.* American Medical Association. https://www.ama-assn.org/system/files/2021-05/2020-prp-physician-practice-arrangements.pdf

Lamiraud, K., & Stadelmann, P. (2020). Switching costs in competitive health insurance markets: The role of insurers' pricing strategies. *Health Economics, 29*(9), 992–1012. https://doi.org/10.1002%2Fhec.4111

Leste, T., Siegal, Y., & Shukla, M. (2019, April 30). *Return on capital performance in life sciences and health care.* Deloitte. https://www.deloitte.com/global/en/our-thinking/insights/industry/health-care/return-on-capital-health-care.html

Newsweek. (2022). *America's Most Trusted Brands 2022.* https://www.newsweek.com/americas-most-trusted-brands-2022

U.S. Department of Justice. (2008, September 15). *Competition in health care and certificates of need.* https://www.justice.gov/archive/atr/public/press_releases/2008/237153a.htm

Uygur, B., Ferguson, S., & Pollack, M. (2022). Hiding in plain sight: surprising pharma and biotech connections to NIH's national cancer institute. *Journal of Commercial Biotechnology, 27*(2), 5. https://doi.org/10.5912/jcb1020

Wouters, O. J., McKee, M., & Luyten, J. (2020). Estimated research and development investment needed to bring a new medicine to market, 2009–2018. *JAMA, 323*(9), 844–853. https://doi.org/10.1001/jama.2020.1166

FURTHER READINGS

Academy of Managed Care Pharmacy. (2019) *Formulary management.* https://www.amcp.org/about/managed-care-pharmacy-101/concepts-managed-care-pharmacy/formulary-management

Carlton, S., Lee, M., & Prakash, A. (2022, August 3). *Insights into the 2022 individual health insurance market.* McKinsey & Company. https://www.mckinsey.com/industries/healthcare/our-insights/insights-into-the-2022-individual-health-insurance-market

Fein, A. J. (2022, March). *The 2022 economic report on U.S. pharmacies and pharmacy benefit managers*. Drug Channels Institute. https://drugchan nelsinstitute.com/files/2022-PharmacyPBM-DCI-Overview.pdf

Hayes, D., Killian, R., & Kolli, S. (2020, February). *Capital requirements for health insurers*. Milliman. https://www.milliman.com/-/media/ milliman/pdfs/articles/capital_requirements_for_health_insurers.ashx

Mulcahy, A. W., & Kareddy, V. (2021). *Prescription drug supply chains: An overview of stakeholders and relationships*. RAND Corporation. https://www.rand.org/pubs/research_reports/RRA328-1.html

National Conference of State Legislatures. (2021, December 20). *Certificate of need state laws*. https://www.ncsl.org/health/certificate-of-need-state-laws

Seeley, E. (2022, July 20). *The impact of pharmaceutical wholesalers on U.S. drug spending*. The Commonwealth Fund. https://www .commonwealthfund.org/publications/issue-briefs/2022/jul/impact-pharmaceutical-wholesalers-drug-spending

Stobierski, T. (2020, November 12). *What are network effects?* Business Insights Blog. Harvard Business School Online. https://online.hbs.edu/ blog/post/what-are-network-effects

United States Government Accountability Office. (2021, May). *Caps on Medicare-funded graduate medical education at teaching hospitals*. https:// www.gao.gov/assets/gao-21-391.pdf

Healthcare Suppliers
Driving Healthcare Costs

The people, products, raw materials, facilities, equipment, science, and technology that encompass the healthcare supply chain account for 93% of total national health expenditures in the United States. The remaining 7% is composed of the cost of government administration and the net cost of health insurance, which are discussed in Chapter 4. Collectively, these national health expenditures have accounted for an increasing percentage of the gross domestic product (GDP), with total expenditures in the United States rising from 5% in 1960 to 18.3% in 2021 according to the U.S. Department of Health and Human Services (HHS). HHS projects these national expenditures will be 19.6% of the GDP by 2030.

The more than $4 trillion spent on healthcare per year in the United States is a comprehensive total based on HHS accounting methods that reflect the major categories of suppliers of healthcare goods and services across the industry. Figure 1 shows that the majority is spent on personal healthcare suppliers. As a percentage of the total national health expenditures, this personal healthcare portion has remained consistent over the decades, with an average of 84% since 1960.

Federal, state, and local governments are suppliers of public health services like disease prevention and surveillance. Since 1990, public health expenditures remained consistently around 3% of total health expenditures until 2020 when that percentage doubled in the midst of the COVID-19 pandemic. Investments in research, medical structures, and equipment also reflect important suppliers in the healthcare industry, representing 5–6% of total annual health expenditures. Labor is a primary component of all categories of healthcare suppliers. In 2020, Ryan Nunn and colleagues estimated that the healthcare industry employs 11% of workers in the United States. Given this large pool of labor suppliers, workforce dynamics are included throughout this chapter.

Porter identified several key factors that increase the power suppliers have to drive up costs of a product or service. These include high supplier concentration, low dependence on revenue from a single industry, high buyer switching cost, differentiated offerings, lack of substitutes, and feasibility of forward integration.

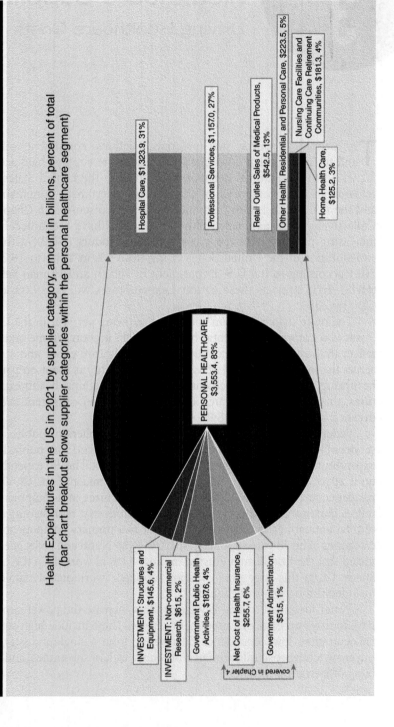

Figure 1 Health Expenditures in the United States in 2021 by Supplier Category

Health Expenditures in the US in 2021 by supplier category, amount in billions, percent of total (bar chart breakout shows supplier categories within the personal healthcare segment)

Hospital Care, $1,323.9, 31%

Professional Services, $1,157.0, 27%

Retail Outlet Sales of Medical Products, $542.5, 13%

Other Health, Residential, and Personal Care, $223.5, 5%

Nursing Care Facilities and Continuing Care Retirement Communities, $181.3, 4%

Home Health Care, $125.2, 3%

PERSONAL HEALTHCARE, $3,553.4, 83%

INVESTMENT: Structures and Equipment, $145.6, 4%

INVESTMENT: Non-commercial Research, $61.5, 2%

Government Public Health Activities, $187.6, 4%

Net Cost of Health Insurance, $255.7, 6%

Government Administration, $51.5, 1%

covered in Chapter 4

High Supplier Concentration

When there are many buyers and few suppliers, the buyers concentrate their purchases on those suppliers, which gives the suppliers more power in negotiating what the buyer will pay. In the healthcare industry, consolidation of hospitals and physicians has been driven by economic challenges that make it difficult for these providers to operate independently and by efforts to improve negotiating power through reducing the number of suppliers in a market.

Low Dependence on a Single Industry for Revenue

In the healthcare industry, most of the labor, facilities, equipment, and technology is highly specialized to and dependent on the industry, thus, making these suppliers less powerful. To the extent that Amazon and other large corporations enter the healthcare industry, their low dependence on revenue from healthcare gives them greater power than those operating exclusively within the industry.

High Switching Cost to Buyers

Healthcare buyers can often switch suppliers without significant costs, thus reducing supplier power. For example, patients can switch primary care providers without paying fees, though they will pay a small price in time and effort to transmit their medical history to a new provider. However, the increasing concentration of providers reduces availability of options to switch to. In addition, these providers may experience switching costs as buyers of the supply chain they rely upon to deliver care. For example, suppliers of electronic medical records and other healthcare technology often have increased power because of the switching costs for the hospitals and physicians that buy them. Switching to a new technology supplier can involve significant expenses including vendor fees, the cost of training the workforce on the new technology, the potential loss of productivity as the workforce adapts to new workflows, and operating downtime that translates to lost revenue.

Differentiated Offerings

In healthcare, science-based standards of care guidelines limit clinical differentiation across providers. Thus, providers have sought other ways to differentiate themselves, such as hotel-like amenities within hospitals and concierge physician practices. However, the suppliers of the science that set new standards of care can wield substantial power. For example, pharmaceutical companies have market exclusivity when a new drug they develop is legally protected from generic competition for a period of time after market approval by the Food and Drug Administration (FDA), giving them significant negotiating power with their buyers. Similarly, medical centers that offer participation in research protocols to test new treatments are differentiated from those providers offering only standard care. These medical centers have more power in negotiating payments from the buyers of the research, such as the National Institutes of Health.

Lack of Substitute for Supplier Offering

The availability of substitutes for some healthcare suppliers weakens their negotiating power. Telehealth technology and remote monitoring have become common substitutes for traditional, in-person visits for some personal healthcare, and artificial intelligence continues to advance in ways that may weaken the power of the healthcare workforce as suppliers of clinical judgments (e.g., diagnoses and treatment decisions) and scientific discoveries. However, other suppliers are not so easily replaced, like emergency and acute care providers, life-saving medications and devices, and the supply chains of people and materials through which these types of care are delivered. The lack of substitutes for these suppliers gives them greater negotiating power with buyers.

Feasibility of Forward Integration of a Supplier Into Buyers' Markets

In the healthcare industry product segment, technology—such as Amazon's existing business platform and PillPack's advanced pharmacy platform—may increase the power of pharmaceutical companies and other manufacturers by allowing them to bypass wholesale distributors to sell their products directly to consumers. On the service side, more hospitals and healthcare providers are taking steps to forward integrate into the health insurance market to increase power.

Personal Healthcare Suppliers

Personal healthcare, which HHS measures as all the revenue, grants, subsidies, and philanthropic funds received by healthcare providers, makes up a majority of healthcare expenditures in the United States. The two biggest categories of personal healthcare, hospital care and professional services (e.g., physician and other services), account for over half of total national health expenditures.

Hospital Care

Accounting for nearly one-third of total national health expenditures, hospital care suppliers include general medical and surgical hospitals, psychiatric and substance abuse hospitals, and other specialty hospitals. In their publication *Fast Facts on U.S. Hospitals, 2024*, the American Hospital Association (AHA) reported there were more than 6,000 hospitals and more than 34 million annual hospital admissions in the United States as of 2022. To deliver this care, hospitals must receive sufficient revenue to cover the cost of the patient rooms and facilities, clinical and support staff, and equipment and supplies for the care, including inpatient pharmacy and ancillary services such as operating room and other hospital-based services. The continued trend of hospital consolidation into large national or regional chains is due to revenue constraints while the costs of delivering care continues to increase. These financial pressures also have resulted in a trend of hospital closures, particularly in rural areas across the United States. The AHA reported in April of 2023 that more than 140 rural hospitals closed between 2010 and 2022. The trend in hospital closures accelerated during the pandemic.

The AHA described the hospital payment system in the United States as *broken* as there are too many buyers that do not pay enough to cover the cost of providing the care, with nearly one-fourth of hospitals losing money. By 2019, more than one-third of hospitals had an annual loss, and more than half were in the red in 2022. Hospital expenses then increased by 17.5% from 2019 to 2022, while reimbursements did not keep pace.

Prior to 1983, hospitals in the United States were retrospectively reimbursed by major payers based on their costs, which provided no incentives for efficiency and led to large increases in annual national expenditures on hospital care. Since the passage of the Social Security Amendments of 1983, hospital reimbursement shifted to a prospective payment system in which hospitals are reimbursed at a fixed payment per hospitalization based on the patient's diagnosis-related group (DRG). This system groups patients based on similar demographic data (e.g., age), diagnoses (i.e., principal diagnosis and secondary diagnoses), and treatment (e.g., surgical or other procedures), which drive the level of resources needed to care for the patient during the hospitalization. Resource intensity includes length of stay in the hospital and use of specialized units and services such as the operating room and radiology. This complex classification system requires documentation by the clinical team and expert coders to support reimbursement of the correct DRG for each patient. This includes accurate documentation and coding of what conditions are present on admission, which may result in a patient DRG with a higher payment versus those conditions that are hospital acquired, harmful preventable events like infections, and errors that reflect poor quality of care, which are not eligible for higher-paying DRGs. This DRG system was originally developed by the Yale University School of Organization and Management in the 1970s. Since it was implemented for hospital payments in 1983, there have been more than 30 versions of the DRG classification system, all of which have been updated by 3M Health Information Systems under contract with the federal Centers for Medicare and Medicaid Services (CMS) based on changes in medical technology and practices as well as reviews of the classification system performance to support hospital payments.

Just three years after the Social Security Amendments of 1983 began limiting hospital payments through the prospective DRG system, the Emergency Medical Treatment & Labor Act (EMTALA) was passed by Congress. EMTALA prohibits hospitals from denying emergency services to patients based on their ability to pay. Also known as the Patient Anti-Dumping Law, EMTALA imposes significant penalties on hospitals for violations of this law. Specifically, EMTALA requires hospital emergency services to provide any patient presenting to the hospital a medical screening examination for emergency medical conditions, including individuals in active labor. Hospitals are required to stabilize these emergency patients or, if the hospital is not capable of doing so, make an appropriate transfer to another hospital, which is similarly prohibited from denying emergency stabilization services if capable. In 2017, Sophie Terp and colleagues reported that 9% of all hospitals in the United States were investigated and 4.3% were cited for EMTALA violations annually, with a rate of 3.9 EMTALA investigations and 1.7 citations per million emergency department visits over a decade.

Despite these major legislative changes that limit hospital revenue and increase cost burden of unfunded hospital care since the 1980s, the number of for-profit hospitals has increased rather than decreased, reversing the trend from the previous half-century. Research by economics professor Carson W. Bays documented that for-profit hospitals were on the decline prior to the implementation of the DRG payment system in 1983. He reported that more than half of all hospitals in the United States were for profit in 1910 and were established primarily in areas of rapid population growth where government and philanthropic funds were not available to support growth of nonprofit hospitals to meet the new demand. As populations stabilized, some for-profit hospitals struggled to compete with the nonprofits and either closed or converted to nonprofits. Others were bought by or merged with other for-profit hospitals such that 90% of all for-profit hospitals were part of a hospital chain by 1977, by which time the percentage of hospitals that were for profit had declined to only 10% of all hospitals in the United States.

Hospitals are often classified by type of ownership (i.e., nonprofit, government run, or for profit). Figure 2 showcases the change in percentage of hospitals that are for profit in the United States from 1910 to 2022. The percentage of for-profit hospitals decreased from 1910 until the implementation of the DRG payment system in 1983 when the percentage began to

Figure 2   Percentage of U.S. Hospitals That Are for Profit From 1910 to 2022

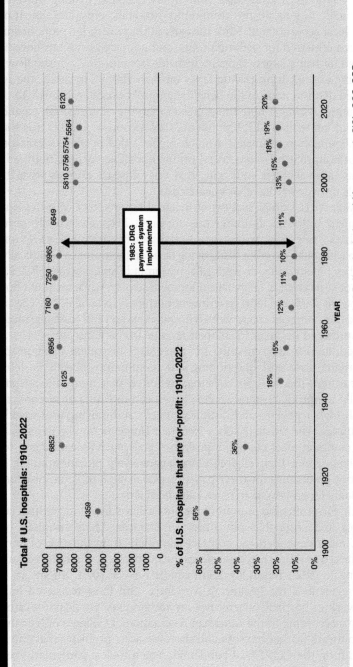

Total # U.S. hospitals: 1910–2022

% of U.S. hospitals that are for-profit: 1910–2022

1983: DRG payment system implemented

YEAR

Source: Bays, C. W. (1983). Why most private hospitals are nonprofit. *Journal of Policy Analysis and Management, 2*(3), 366–385. Centers for Disease Control and Prevention. *Table 89. Hospitals, beds, and occupancy rates, by type of ownership and size of hospital: United States, selected years 1975–2015.* (2017). https://www.cdc.gov/nchs/data/hus/2017/089.pdf

slowly increase again. Figure 3 breaks down all the hospitals in the United States by type as of 2022 with community hospitals making up 84% of all hospitals. Among all the community hospitals, only 15% are run by state or local governments. Since the early 20th century, for-profit hospitals have been criticized for seeking profits, and nonprofit hospitals have been criticized for being largely indistinguishable from for-profit hospitals while also being exempt from paying taxes on their profits. In 2022, the AHA estimated that the value of the benefits nonprofit hospitals provide to their communities is almost nine times greater than the estimated tax payments they avoid, more than $12.4 billion in 2019. However, in 2023, the Kaiser Family Foundation estimated a much higher value of the tax exemption status of nonprofit hospitals based on methods that include both federal and state taxes avoided, indicating that this value far exceeds what these hospitals provide in total charity care costs.

A *Wall Street Journal* analysis of financial reports filed with the federal government by hospitals found that for-profit hospitals actually provide more charity care as a percentage of total patient revenue than nonprofit charitable hospitals do while also paying taxes on their profits. Specifically, in 2022, they reported that, in aggregate, nonprofit hospitals wrote off 2.3% of their patient revenue as financial aid for medical bills, while for-profit hospitals wrote off 3.4% and local government hospitals wrote off 4.7%. They also reported one nonprofit chain with 18 hospitals and several academic medical centers provided less than 1% of their revenue in charitable aid.

In addition to documenting the percentage of patient revenue spent on charitable care and questioning how community benefit is defined and measured, the *Wall Street Journal* reported that nonprofit hospitals, especially nonprofit hospital chains, have been moving out of communities with higher poverty and healthcare needs and moving into wealthier communities. The *Journal's* series *Nonprofit Hospitals Are Big Business* also reports common practices of nonprofit hospitals, such as avoiding informing patients about their eligibility and aggressively pursuing billing and collections procedures for these patients, that make it difficult for patients who qualify for assistance to receive financial aid.

Both for-profit and nonprofit hospitals have faced increasing labor shortages and costs that put stress on finances. Many hospitals have become more dependent on contract labor, which, in the case of nurses, has increased to more than three times the median cost of employed nurses according to 2022 report by KaufmanHall. As of 2023, nurses are the largest segment of the healthcare workforce, and most registered nurses (RNs) work in hospitals where they are the primary providers of care for inpatients according to the American Association of Colleges of Nursing.

Healthcare worker burnout and shortages were problems that only got worse during the COVID-19 pandemic, which took a particularly heavy toll on nurses and other hospital workers who care for the sickest patients.

Figure 3 U.S. Hospitals by Type, 2022

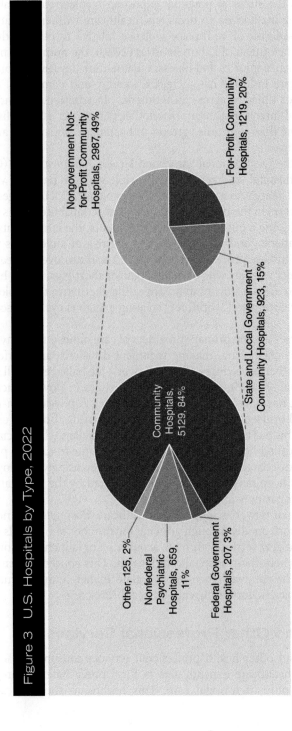

Source: American Hospital Association. (2023). *Fast facts on U.S. hospitals.* https://www.aha.org/statistics/fast-facts-us-hospitals

In addition to the stress of potential exposure to infectious diseases and routinely facing life-and-death decisions, healthcare workers are at significantly increased risk of workplace violence relative to other industries. According to the Bureau of Labor Statistics (2020), the number of nonfatal workplace violence injuries and illnesses that require days away from work in the healthcare industry has increased steadily and comprises 73% of such injuries or illnesses across all industries. In addition, the incidence rate of nonfatal intentional injury by another person per 10,000 full-time workers is more than four times greater in hospitals compared to ambulatory care settings.

In 2015, the Occupational Safety and Health Administration (OSHA) reported that hospital workers experience violence from patients, visitors, and others and likely underreport workplace violence. OSHA suggests several unique factors in the healthcare industry may contribute to this underreporting, including a culture of service to patients, the ethical duty to do no harm to patients, and an acceptance of the risk of violence as part of some patients' disease process. Burnout-related staff turnover increases the need for contract workers who earn high pay for short gigs, giving hospital employees who are not burnt out an appealing alternative to employment via joining the contracted workforce, creating a vicious cycle of escalating labor costs.

While nurses are the primary providers of care in hospitals, physicians are essential to diagnosing, making treatment decisions, and performing surgeries and other procedures. Physician work-life balance as well as efficiency and quality factors have led to major shifts in how medical care is provided in hospitals. In the traditional model, a physician in private practice would oversee their patients' care across settings from the clinic to the hospital. This has been largely replaced by physicians who specialize in hospital care, called hospitalists, who do not continue to care for patients after they are discharged. These physicians are increasingly employees of the hospital or hospitalist group practice contracted by the hospital rather than owners or partners in a private practice.

To build their power as suppliers of healthcare, hospitals have not only consolidated horizontally through growing the number of hospitals within their chains but also vertically through acquisition or launch of ambulatory care services where their hospitals are located. This concentration within local markets has allowed them to negotiate higher reimbursement for services from payers, further driving up healthcare costs.

Medical and Other Professional Services

Medical and other health professional services consume 27% of the total national healthcare expenditures in the United States according to HHS, second only to hospital care. This healthcare supplier category includes services rendered in establishments of physicians, dentists, and other medical professionals, including chiropractors, optometrists, podiatrists, mental health practitioners, audiologists, and physical, occupational, and speech therapists. This also includes services in other outpatient establishments such as centers for family planning, substance abuse, and outpatient surgery, along with medical laboratories and diagnostic imaging centers.

Broadly, these outpatient care establishments can be divided into primary care and specialty care. Primary care providers are generalists who are often the first point of contact for care outside of hospital settings, including health screenings, diagnosis, and prevention services such as vaccinations. In some cases, specialists only see patients who have been referred to them by another provider, typically a primary care physician who then serves as the gatekeeper to the specialists.

The consolidation of these outpatient providers from individual or small group practices into large practices or, in the case of consolidation with hospitals, into healthcare systems, has increased their power to negotiate higher prices. Healthcare workforce shortages that existed before and continue beyond the pandemic have been due at least in part to an aging population. The greater number of older adults in need of healthcare has coincided with more healthcare workers retiring while there is insufficient capacity for training new healthcare professionals. The COVID-19 pandemic affected hospital workers and clinic-based care workers differentially. HHS reported that, while hospital-trained nurses and other clinicians were in short supply during the pandemic, many outpatient healthcare workers were furloughed or had reduced hours as many ambulatory services closed or limited available services. In fact, HHS reported that from May of 2020 until February of 2022, nonhospital healthcare workers were about as likely as workers outside of the healthcare industry to report that they were unable to work because their employer closed or lost business during the pandemic.

While the nursing shortage is most severe in hospital settings, the physician shortage is most severe in primary care, where physicians earn substantially less than specialists. Less adequate primary care, including screening and prevention services, then increases the need for hospital care that might otherwise have been prevented. In 2021, the Association of American Medical Colleges (AAMC) projected that by 2034, the United States will have a shortage of at least 17,800 primary care physicians, 15,800 surgeons, 3,800 medical specialist physicians (e.g., internal medicine and pediatric subspecialties), and 10,300 other specialist physicians, along with an oversupply of at least 2,700 hospitalists.

The supply of physicians and other healthcare workers has been significantly affected by professional associations that have formed to represent them. The American Medical Association (AMA) has effectively influenced legislation to limit physician supply in response to projections there would be too many and now lobbies to help address projected shortages. Meanwhile the field of nursing has made significant advances from functioning to care for the sick and help prevent disease without the ability to diagnose and prescribe treatments to the creation of doctoral level nursing degrees and licensing procedures that allow them to function independently of physicians and with the authority to diagnose and prescribe treatments.

The path to becoming a physician is rigorous and expensive in terms of time, tuition, and opportunity cost. After completing an undergraduate degree that includes pre-medicine requirements for medical school, aspiring physicians who are accepted complete four years of medical school to earn the Doctor of Medicine (MD) degree or the Doctor of Osteopathic Medicine (DO) degree. They must then pass a licensing exam—and possibly other requirements based on state law—and successfully compete for a resident physician position where they will spend three to seven years in clinical training in their chosen field of medicine. In addition to this training, most employers will expect physicians to obtain board certification in their field. The AMA has vigorously defended its profession against encroachment by nonphysician healthcare professionals through state and federal lobbying. For example, their #StopScopeCreep campaign has helped defeat legislation that would have expanded the respective scopes of practice of nurses, physician assistants (PAs), pharmacists, and chiropractors, and they have provided funding to other organizations to advocate for the protection of physician-led, team-based care.

From a resource perspective, particularly given the shortage of physicians, all members of the healthcare team should be authorized to work at their respective *top of license*. This would mean, for example, that it is wasteful for a physician to diagnose and prescribe appropriate treatment for an infection when a nurse practitioner (NP) can do so at a lower cost, for an NP to administer the treatment when a registered nurse can do so at a lower cost, and for a registered nurse to check the patient's vital signs when a nursing assistant can do so at a lower cost. This approach allows physicians to oversee the care of more patients because they are leading a team of nonphysicians who can competently perform tasks the physician would otherwise have to do. While this *top of license* concept is simple in theory, it can be difficult to implement given the complexities of federal and local laws, billing policies, and standards for scopes of practice across a myriad of types of healthcare workers and the dynamics of available supplies of each type within each local market.

Another challenge to the optimal implementation of the physician-led team is that, despite physicians undergoing the lengthiest training among the healthcare professions, there are many aspects of evidence-based healthcare in which physicians receive little or no training. Physicians, therefore, may tend to recommend the therapies they know best first (e.g., medications, medical procedures, or surgery) rather than refer patients to specialists such as a nutritionist for a dietary prescription, a physical therapist for exercise therapy, or a psychologist for cognitive behavioral therapy in addition to or as a first line of treatment when scientific evidence indicates these therapies are at least as effective as medications with a lower risk of adverse side effects.

Physician organizations have increasingly recognized the limitations of their profession's scientific scope of expertise and lobbying efforts. For example, for nearly a century the AMA fought for the demise of the chiropractic profession. A 1976 lawsuit against the AMA, which lasted more than a decade, revealed the extent of the physician organization's efforts and plans to undermine the chiropractic profession, and in 1987, the AMA was found guilty of violating the Sherman Antitrust Act for their organized attempts to eliminate chiropractors as competitors. The American College of Physicians and other physicians have since adopted evidence-based treatment guidelines for low back pain, a very common ailment among the adult population, which recommend non-drug therapies first, including spinal manipulation, a procedure that is typically performed by a chiropractor.

Healthcare professionals continue to fight over prescriptive authority, the ability to write a prescription for medications not available over the counter. Physicians have the broadest prescriptive authority, including the authority to prescribe controlled substances, which have higher risk of dependence and harm if misused. Over decades, with physician shortages, PAs and NPs have been given limited prescriptive authority across states while pharmacists and psychologists have limited prescriptive authority in some states under certain circumstances. In some cases, these healthcare professionals are only allowed to practice this prescriptive authority under the supervision of a physician. The core debate centers on the risks and benefits of limiting prescriptive authority to physicians when there are shortages versus expanding access to medications by granting this authority to some nonphysician healthcare professionals.

Retail Sellers of Medical Products

The category of medical products includes spending on products purchased or leased through retail stores and mail-order companies such as pharmacies but excludes spending on these supplies in other settings (e.g., hospitals buy medications and other supplies from distributors, not retail stores, so these are included in the cost of hospital care). The largest expenditure within this medical products category is prescription medications, which has accounted for approximately 9–10% of total annual healthcare expenditures since 2000 according to HHS. This category also includes durable medical equipment (e.g., prescription eyeglasses, wheelchairs, and blood sugar meters) and other nondurable medical products (e.g., over-the-counter medications, wound care dressings), each at approximately 2% of total national healthcare expenditures.

The cost of prescription medications has been a bipartisan concern, with partisan proposals to resolve the issue. This concern may be considered disproportionate given that these drug costs are approximately 13% of total health expenditures when including prescription drug expenditures in nonretail settings as estimated by HHS in 2022. In comparison, hospital care and healthcare professional services, after subtracting the estimated cost of prescription drug expenses in these nonretail settings, are still more than 50% of total national health expenditures. The 2022 Inflation Reduction Act allowed the U.S. federal government to negotiate prescription drug prices for the first time in its history. Most other developed countries have already implemented regulations that allow this or other drug price control mechanisms. Pharmaceutical companies and the U.S. Chamber of Commerce have filed federal lawsuits claiming this new drug price negotiation power is unconstitutional. They also claim that price controls harm their ability to develop future drugs as revenue from new drugs is used to support drug development.

In 2020, Olivier J. Wouters and colleagues reported that the median cost to bring a new drug to market is estimated to be more than one billion dollars, with the cost of a new cancer drug being the highest at approximately $2.8 billion. The drug development process and cost include many drugs that fail to make it to approval. New molecular entities must undergo lab and animal testing (i.e., preclinical research) before they are tested in humans (i.e., clinical research). This also includes getting regulatory approvals from the FDA at each phase and then marketing the drug before the patent protections allowing market exclusivity expire, permitting generic drug manufacturers to compete. In 2021, the Congressional Budget Office reported that most new entities never make it into clinical trials, and only 12% of those that do are eventually approved by the FDA.

Once a drug is approved, the FDA regulates how it is manufactured. Quality issues in the manufacturing process are the primary cause of drug shortages, which can also occur because of delays in receiving essential raw materials or one or more manufacturers discontinuing drug production. Pharmaceutical companies with market exclusivity on a differentiated product have significant, though time-limited, power as the sole source of a drug. However, sometimes manufacturers of older drugs, such as insulin, have significant power to increase prices because the generic suppliers are few and demand is high.

Once manufactured, most prescription drugs are distributed through wholesalers to the point of dispensing where the prescription is filled and delivered to the patient. While pharmaceutical companies traditionally targeted their marketing dollars on physicians and other prescribers as key gatekeepers, direct to consumer advertisement spending has increased substantially since the FDA eased regulations to allow it in 1997. The United States and New Zealand are the only countries that allow this type of advertising. These marketing efforts increase patient awareness about the medical condition and the drug available to treat it, resulting in patients going to their doctors seeking a prescription.

Pharmaceutical companies are increasingly exploring and expanding direct to patient sales, which bypass the traditional physicians as prescribers, traditional retail pharmacies as dispensers, and traditional health plans as payers. In direct-to-patient sales, a pharmaceutical company's direct-to-consumer advertisement points potential customers to a website where they can create an account and enter a credit card for payment, interact with a licensed prescriber who gathers health information and prescribes the medication if appropriate indication is confirmed. This medication is then shipped to the patient from a mail-order pharmacy or warehouse. As Amazon has entered the prescription drug business with the purchase of PillPack and the prescriber business with the purchase of One Medical, this e-commerce giant is well positioned to serve as the preferred, user-friendly platform for pharmaceutical companies to use for direct-to-patient sales. While the Deloitte consultants indicate that direct-to-patient sales is meant to complement rather than replace consumer relationships with their traditional primary care physicians and retail pharmacies, Amazon is likely aiming to be more than complementary.

Nursing and Continuing Care Facilities

At 4% of national health expenditures according to HHS, nursing and continuing care facilities include freestanding facilities that primarily provide inpatient nursing care and rehabilitation care, including retirement facilities with on-site nursing care. Hospital-based nursing home care is excluded from this category as it is included in hospital care. Nursing and rehabilitation care facilities are essential to the efficient use of acute care hospitals for patients who no longer need high intensity medical monitoring but are unable to be discharged home due to a continued need for nursing support or other therapy to regain ability to function independently. Shortages of these nursing facilities result in delays in patient discharges from acute care facilities, driving up costs, creating bottlenecks in the process of admitting new patients to the hospital, and ultimately straining emergency department resources as patients wait to be admitted.

In their 2023 report, Katherine Miller and colleagues found that the number of nursing care facility beds per 10,000 population aged 65 and older has decreased by more than 20% from 2011 to 2019, due in part to a decrease in the absolute number of nursing care beds and in part because of an increase in the aging population. These researchers also reported a small increase in the proportion of nursing care beds that were for profit and a small decrease in the proportion of nursing care beds that received four-star or five-star quality ratings as measured by CMS. The continued trend of nursing homes closing is caused by the same challenges faced by hospitals, staffing shortage and financial strain. According to an HHS 2022 report, nursing homes have changed ownership much more frequently than hospitals, potentially indicating consolidation to increase power for this supplier segment.

Home Health Care

Home health care includes expenditures for freestanding home health agencies to provide healthcare services delivered in patients' homes, including nursing care, personal care, physical therapy, occupational therapy, medications and medical equipment, counseling, nutrition services, speech therapy, and audiology services. In 1980, home health care expenditures were less than 1% of total expenditures while inpatient nursing care was 6%. Since then, home health care expenditures have grown to 3% while inpatient nursing care has decreased to 4%, reflecting the shift in preference for home-based care over nursing homes. Several national home healthcare companies have been acquired by retail pharmacy chains and health plans, signaling the expectation that home healthcare revenues will continue to grow and that these home-based services offer strategic synergies.

Other Care

Other care makes up 5% of total health expenditures and includes personal healthcare, such as school-based care, worksite care, home and community-based care provided under a state Medicaid waiver program, ambulance services, and residential mental health, substance abuse, and developmental disability facilities.

Medical Structure and Equipment Suppliers

The medical structure segment of the national health expenditures includes investments in new construction for medical facilities, such as new buildings, additions, alterations, major replacements, mechanical and electric installations, architectural and engineering work, and site preparation. This category excludes maintenance and repair as well as the new construction of retail establishments. The medical equipment segment of the national health expenditures includes investments in new capital equipment in medical establishments, including nonstructural equipment like X-ray machines, beds, and software. According to HHS data, combined medical structures and equipment investments have decreased as a percentage of total national health expenditures from 6.9% in 1960 to 3.4% in 2021.

The AHA has brought attention to the aging physical condition of America's hospitals and urged investments of federal funds to ensure these critical facilities are appropriately upgraded to meet the required standards of care. Because of the specialized nature of healthcare facilities—for example, the importance of engineering and design features to control the spread of infections—the AHA offers certifications for healthcare facilities managers. There are also construction companies that specialize in healthcare facilities. Total bed capacity has decreased in the United States due to hospital and service closures such that expansion of hospital facility infrastructure is needed to ensure sufficient capacity to meet an aging population and future emergencies.

According to a 2017 report by Andrea Park Chung and colleagues, the AHA's call for federal funding to increase hospital capacity has precedent based on research from previous investments. These researchers documented that the public subsidies from the 1946 Hospital Survey and Construction Act resulted in significant and lasting improvements in the healthcare system capacity. Specifically, from 1948 to 1975, this funding resulted in a net increase of more than 70,000 hospital beds nationwide, which represents 17% of the total growth during that period. Moreover, this capacity was sustained for more than two decades and had a particularly strong effect in geographic regions that were lacking adequate facilities. The net increase in beds included increases in nonprofit and public hospital beds but a decrease in for-profit hospital beds, a finding that raises discussions about to what extent the hospital infrastructure investments should be from public or private sources.

In the 21st century, the federal government has made massive investments to accelerate the digitization and better use of health information. The 2009 Health Information Technology for Economic and Clinical Health (HITECH) Act provided approximately $35 billion to help hospitals and physicians adopt health information technology. This funding was specifically focused on the adoption of electronic medical records that can be exchanged across providers through interoperable standards, allowing providers to have efficient access to information they need to make the best treatment decisions. A 2020 publication from Samual Lite and colleagues indicated that this federal investment might have also triggered a rapid increase in venture capital (VC) investments in this segment. Specifically, they found that federal HITECH investments were associated with a rate of increased VC investments in healthcare information technology and electronic health record companies that was higher than the rate of increase in VC investments overall across segments. They also found that the proportion of investments in seed companies increased more than 5%. Consolidation of these health information technology suppliers continues, with big tech companies like Amazon and Microsoft acquiring, rather than building, the expertise needed to compete in the specialized healthcare market, which requires compliance with industry-specific privacy and security regulations and understanding of diverse user needs and preferences.

Public Health Service Suppliers

Governments are key suppliers of public health services, which focus on population-level health services for the general public rather than individual patient care. According to HHS, this segment accounts for 4% of national health expenditures and includes health surveillance, vaccination services, disease prevention programs, and operation of public health laboratories. Excluded are functions such as public works, water supplies, sanitation and sewage treatment, and emergency planning. At the federal level, the majority of expenditures for the public health activities are for operation of the Centers for Disease Control and Prevention (CDC) and the Food and Drug Administration (FDA). Since the September 11, 2001, terrorist attacks, public health activities are also funded through the Public Health and Social Services Emergency Fund and the Department of Homeland Security. State and local governments also fund public health activities which are also included in these expenditures.

The COVID-19 pandemic challenged the global public health infrastructure and revealed significant weaknesses in the public health supply chain. This resulted in lack of available testing and personal protection equipment, particularly for healthcare workers on the frontlines. Assessment of vulnerabilities in the United States demonstrated that the public health infrastructure was compromised by several key factors. The widespread adoption of just-in-time inventory management systems and lean operations that prioritize efficiency over robustness reduced slack resources while high dependency on foreign sources of supplies and raw materials needed for the production of supplies meant the United States had limited capacity to produce its own supplies when shortages occurred. Likewise, inadequate monitoring of critical supplies in the Strategic National Stockpile led to a lack of identification, correction, and prevention of shortages prior to an emergency.

In addition, HHS failures to comply with regulatory requirements enacted to better prepare for a pandemic exacerbated the crisis. In 2006, the Pandemic and All-Hazards Preparedness Act was passed, requiring that HHS develop and implement an electronic network of interoperable systems to enable the simultaneous sharing of public health information needed to enhance situational awareness at the federal, state, and local levels by the end of 2008. Failure to comply resulted in the reauthorization of this act in 2013, which included additional requirements to improve federal biosurveillance activities. In 2019, after continued noncompliance by HHS and just a few months before the first human was infected with COVID-19, another Pandemic and All-Hazards Preparedness Act was passed reiterating the mandate to improve public health situational awareness and surveillance through an interoperable network. In their 2022 report on their study of the impact of HHS noncompliance with these acts, the Government Accountability Office (GAO) surveyed state-level public health officials about the challenges they faced in the management of public health information during the pandemic. The most significant challenge was manual processing of data and data collection. Most of these officials also reported the following to be *very challenging*: interoperability among systems, human-capital-related IT resources, and clarity in roles and responsibilities. The GAO documented that these major gaps in compliance remain as a key vulnerability in the United States public health infrastructure.

Despite these weaknesses, the pandemic also revealed key strengths in the public health system. Prior to the pandemic, the FDA had been working with the pharmaceutical industry to monitor and resolve drug shortages. The number of new drug shortages peaked at 250 in 2011, which led to regulatory changes that directed the FDA to expedite reviews of new drug applications, require drug manufacturers to report temporary interruptions of production as well as planned discontinuations, and improve planning and communications to support the prevention and mitigation of effects from drug shortages, including identifying the root causes of shortages and potential solutions to address them.

These changes have helped reduce annual new drug shortages to approximately 50 or less per year since 2013. In the wake of the pandemic, the FDA was granted additional authority to prioritize the inspection and review of drug applications, where appropriate, to prevent or address a drug shortage, to require manufacturers to develop redundancy plans to mitigate the risk of shortages in the production of drugs and the active pharmaceutical ingredients used to make drugs, and to require manufacturers to provide annual reports on the amount of each drug they have produced for commercial distribution.

During the pandemic, the FDA also issued guidance regarding how the companies developing vaccines could accelerate the process while meeting FDA requirements, which helped expedite the process leading to the Emergency Use Authorization (EUA) by the FDA for the Moderna and Pfizer/BioNTech vaccines. In addition, HHS facilitated identification of manufacturing partners to address capacity issues and procurement of scarce but essential reagents, chemicals, and equipment needed to produce the vaccines and deployment of staff to mitigate workforce shortages at vaccine manufacturers.

Noncommercial Health Research Suppliers

Noncommercial health research supplier spending includes investments in noncommercial research by nonprofit organizations and governments. This excludes research and development expenditures by commercial entities because these expenses are assumed to be incorporated into product prices and accounted for through sales. A large portion of this category is research funded by the National Institutes of Health (NIH), but it also includes research funding from other federal agencies as well as state, local, and private funding for health research. As a percentage of total national health expenditures, these investments have decreased from 2.6% in 1960 to 1.4% in 2021.

The NIH is the world's largest supplier of noncommercial (i.e., public or philanthropic) health research, with research expenditures that are more than seven times the second largest supplier, the European Commission. According to NIH, they spend most of their annual budget, $48 billion in fiscal year 2023, on medical research, including research conducted by more than 6,000 scientists located at NIH laboratories in Maryland, North Carolina, Montana, and Arizona and research funding awarded to more than 300,000 scientists at universities and other research institutes across the United States. NIH-funded researchers have conducted basic, animal, and human studies that have contributed to significant advancements in understandings of human health and diagnosis and treatment of diseases across the life span.

Despite the many successes of NIH, including its important role in supporting the rapid development of COVID-19 vaccines, there have been calls for reform of the NIH mission, culture, funding award processes, and transparency practices to produce more tangible results that justify investments. A key criticism has been that NIH is too conservative with its funding decisions, largely resulting in support for low-risk, low-reward science rather than groundbreaking innovations that translate to specific improvements in patient outcomes. Adding to the concerns are reports of inadequate quality control by NIH, including reports of NIH-funded research being published in predatory journals (i.e., online journals that do not adhere to accepted scientific standards of peer review). In a 2017 report of a random sampling of nearly 2,000 articles published in more than 200 of these predatory journals, David Moher and colleagues found that NIH was the most frequently cited funding source, while most of the articles did not report a funding source. At best, NIH-funded research reported in these journals is legitimate but unusable for advancing science given a naïve researcher chose to publish the work in an untrustworthy journal. At worst, the researcher cut corners in the research, so it was not suitable for publication in a legitimate scientific journal. Either way, these federal resources were wasted and the public's trust in the NIH and, more generally, in science was eroded.

Perhaps because of concerns about the feasibility of reforming or reinventing a giant federal agency, the NIH now has a new startup competitor. In 2022, federal law authorized the establishment of the Advanced Research Projects Agency for Health (ARPA-H) within HHS. The mission of ARPA-H is to fund research that leads to major medical breakthroughs targeting sustainable solutions for specific health problems and results in substantial improvements in health outcomes and equity. They use a model that keeps the agency independent from NIH and empowers program managers to collaborate broadly with partners using different approaches and incorporating programmatic evaluation. The inaugural director of ARPA-H has indicated the agency's initial focus will be on meeting the objectives of President Biden's Cancer Moonshot, kicking off the competition with NIH's prestigious National Cancer Institute, which had a head start since the president's ambitions were announced in 2016. While ARPA-H's budget is just a fraction of the National Cancer Institute budget, to the extent that ARPA-H can truly differentiate itself from NIH, it has the potential to become NIH's most powerful competitor.

REFERENCES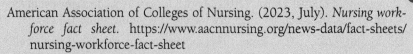

American Association of Colleges of Nursing. (2023, July). *Nursing workforce fact sheet.* https://www.aacnnursing.org/news-data/fact-sheets/nursing-workforce-fact-sheet

American Hospital Association. (2017, September). *Fact sheet: Hospital billing explained.* https://www.aha.org/system/files/2018-01/factsheet-hospital-billing-explained-9-2017.pdf

American Hospital Association. (2023). *Fast facts on U.S. hospitals.* https://www.aha.org/statistics/fast-facts-us-hospitals

American Hospital Association. (2023, April). *The financial stability of America's hospitals and health systems is at risk as the costs of caring continue to rise.* https://www.aha.org/system/files/media/file/2023/04/Cost-of-Caring-2023-The-Financial-Stability-of-Americas-Hospitals-and-Health-Systems-Is-at-Risk.pdf

Assistant Secretary for Planning and Evaluation. (2022). *Trends in prescription drug spending, 2016–2021*. Office of Science and Data Policy, US Department of Health and Human Services. https://aspe.hhs.gov/sites/default/files/documents/88c547c976e915fc31fe2c6903ac0bc9/sdp-trends-prescription-drug-spending.pdf

Assistant Secretary for Planning and Evaluation, Office of Health Policy. (2022, April 20). *Changes of ownership of hospital and skilled nursing facilities*. U.S. Department of Health and Human Services. https://aspe.hhs.gov/sites/default/files/documents/be6f3366294b-d30a08a8ae90c84f3894/aspe-datapoint-change-ownership-pecos.pdf

Assistant Secretary for Planning and Evaluation, Office of Health Policy. (2022, May 3). *Impact of the COVID-19 pandemic on the hospital and outpatient clinician workforce*. U.S. Department of Health and Human Services. https://aspe.hhs.gov/sites/default/files/documents/9cc72124a bd9ea25d58a22c7692dccb6/aspe-covid-workforce-report.pdf

Bays, C. W. (1983). Why most private hospitals are nonprofit. *Journal of Policy Analysis and Management, 2*(3), 366–385. https://doi.org/10.2307/3324447

Centers for Medicare & Medicaid Services. (2023, September 6). *National health expenditure data*. U.S. Department of Health and Human Services. https://www.cms.gov/research-statistics-data-and-systems/statistics-trends-and-reports/nationalhealthexpenddata

Chung, A. P., Gaynor, M., & Richards-Shubik, S. (2017). Subsidies and structure: The lasting impact of the Hill-Burton program on the hospital industry. *The Review of Economics and Statistics, 99*(5), 926–943. https://www.jstor.org/stable/26616170

Congressional Budget Office. (2021, April). *Research and development in the pharmaceutical industry*. https://www.cbo.gov/publication/57126

IHS Markit Ltd. (2021, June). *The complexities of physician supply and demand: Projections from 2019 to 2034*. Association of American Medical Colleges. https://www.aamc.org/media/54681/download

KaufmanHall. (2022, May 11). *A special workforce edition of the national hospital flash report*. https://www.kaufmanhall.com/insights/research-report/special-workforce-edition-national-hospital-flash-report

Lite, S., Gordon, W. J., & Stern, A. D. (2020). Association of the meaningful use electronic health record incentive program with health information technology venture capital funding. *JAMA Network Open, 3*(3), e201402. https://doi.org/10.1001/jamanetworkopen.2020.1402

Miller, K. E. M., Chatterjee, P., & Werner, R. M. (2023). Trends in supply of nursing home beds, 2011–2019. *JAMA Network Open, 6*(3), e230640. https://doi.org/10.1001/jamanetworkopen.2023.0640

Moher, D., Shamseer, L., Cobey, K. D., Lalu, M. M., Galipeau, J., Avey, M. T., Ahmadzai, N., Alabousi, M., Barbeau, P., Beck, A., Daniel, R., Frank, R., Ghannad, M., Hamel, C., Hersi, M., Hutton, B., Isupov, I., McGrath, T. A., McInnes, M. D. F., Page, M. J., . . . & Ziai, H. (2017). Stop this waste of people, animals and money. *Nature, 549*(7670), 23–25. https://doi.org/10.1038/549023a

Nunn, R., Parsons, J., Shambaugh, J., & Contreras, A. (2020, March 10). *A dozen facts about the economics of the US healthcare system.* Brookings. https://www.brookings.edu/research/a-dozen-facts-about-the-economics-of-the-u-s-health-care-system/

Occupational Safety and Health Administration. (2015, December). *Workplace violence in healthcare.* https://www.osha.gov/sites/default/files/OSHA3826.pdf

Office of Inspector General. (2023, January 25). *The National Institutes of Health and EcoHealth Alliance did not effectively monitor awards and subawards, resulting in missed opportunities to oversee research and other deficiencies.* U.S. Department of Health and Human Services Office of Inspector General. https://oig.hhs.gov/oas/reports/region5/52100025.pdf

Terp, S., Seabury, S. A., Arora, S., Eads, A., Lam, C. N., & Menchine, M. (2017). Enforcement of the Emergency Medical Treatment and Labor Act, 2005 to 2014. *Annals of Emergency Medicine, 69*(2), 155–162.e1. https://doi.org/10.1016/j.annemergmed.2016.05.021

U.S. Bureau of Labor Statistics. (2020, April). *Workplace violence in healthcare, 2018.* https://www.bls.gov/iif/factsheets/workplace-violence-healthcare-2018.htm

U.S. Government Accountability Office. (2022, June). *Report to congressional addressees: COVID-19 pandemic lessons highlight need for public health situational awareness network.* https://www.gao.gov/assets/gao-22-104600.pdf

Wall Street Journal. (2022). *Nonprofit hospitals are big business.* https://www.wsj.com/news/collection/nonprofit-hospitals-679fab59

Wouters, O. J., McKee, M., & Luyten, J. (2020). Estimated research and development investment needed to bring a new medicine to market, 2009–2018. *JAMA, 323*(9), 844–853. https://doi.org/10.1001/jama.2020.1166

FURTHER READINGS

Agocs, S. (2011). Chiropractic's Fight for Survival. *AMA Journal of Ethics, 13*(6), 384–388. https://doi.org/10.1001/virtualmentor.2011.13.6.mhst1-1106

American Medical Association. (2023, May 15). *AMA successfully fights scope of practice expansions that threaten patient safety.* https://www.ama-assn.org/practice-management/scope-practice/ama-successfully-fights-scope-practice-expansions-threaten

Flaherty, M., & Lou, R. (2020, October 1). *Direct-to-patient (DTP) sales channels might be the next frontier for pharmaceutical companies.* Deloitte Consulting LLP. https://www2.deloitte.com/us/en/blog/health-care-blog/2020/direct-to-patient-sales-channels-might-be-the-next-frontier-for-pharmaceutical-companies.html

Godwin, J., Levinson, Z., & Hulver, S. (2023, March 14). *The estimated value of tax exemption for nonprofit hospitals was about $28 billion in 2020.* Kaiser Family Foundation https://www.kff.org/health-costs/issue-brief/the-estimated-value-of-tax-exemption-for-nonprofit-hospitals-was-about-28-billion-in-2020/

Keeling, A. W. (2016, May 31). Historical perspectives on an expanded role for nursing. *OJIN The Online Journal of Issues in Nursing, 20*(2). https://doi.org/10.3912/OJIN.Vol20No02Man02

Pierson, L. (2022, March 15). *The AMA can help fix the health care shortages it helped create.* Bill of Health. https://blog.petrieflom.law.harvard.edu/2022/03/15/ama-scope-of-practice-lobbying/

Public Health Emergency. *National strategy for a resilient public health supply chain.* (2021, July). U.S. Department of Health & Human Services. https://www.phe.gov/Preparedness/legal/Documents/National-Strategy-for-Resilient-Public-Health-Supply-Chain.pdf

Sood, N. (2023, March 23). *Should the government restrict direct-to-consumer prescription drug advertising? Six takeaways on their effects.* University of Southern California. https://healthpolicy.usc.edu/article/should-the-government-restrict-direct-to-consumer-prescription-drug-advertising-six-takeaways-from-research-on-the-effects-of-prescription-drug-advertising/

CHAPTER 4

Healthcare Buyers

Negotiating Price

The U.S. Department of Health and Human Services (HHS) reported that, in 2021, $4.3 trillion was spent on national health expenditures in the United States, 83% of which was spent on personal healthcare delivered by hospitals, outpatient providers, pharmacies, and other industry suppliers as covered in Chapter 3. The HHS uses two major categories—out-of-pocket payers and third-party payers—to account for the entities from which healthcare providers receive payments. Out-of-pocket payments, which account for only 10% of all national health expenditures as shown in Figure 1, are those paid directly by the consumer (or *household* per HHS terminology) receiving the healthcare. Third-party payers—the large majority of which are health insurance payers—account for 82% of total national health expenditures and pay healthcare providers on behalf of consumers.

While this HHS accounting approach is useful to understand from whom healthcare providers receive payment (and the powerful role of health insurance as buyers as described in this chapter), it is also misleading. This approach obscures the fact that most consumers pay for not only out-of-pocket expenses but also insurance premiums, which are then used by the health insurance organizations to pay healthcare providers for services. This is significant given that consumer spending on health insurance premiums is much greater than consumer out-of-pocket spending on healthcare. According to a 2020 Bureau of Labor Statistics report, consumer spending on health insurance represented nearly 70% of their healthcare spending as of 2018, with the remaining spending on out-of-pocket expenses for medical services (18%), drugs (10%), and medical supplies (3.5%).

HHS does distinguish between the *payers* and the *sponsors* or funders of those payers and recognizes that consumers fund health insurance in addition to paying out-of-pocket expenses. In their crosswalk table showing which entities fund which payers, HHS also indicates businesses pay for a portion of health insurance for their employees. According to a September 2023 Bureau of Labor Statistics report, employers pay 80% of the health insurance premium expense for single coverage, with employees paying only 20%, and employers pay two-thirds of the premium for family coverage while employees pay one-third. However, this HHS approach

Figure 1   Health Expenditures in the U.S. in 2021 by Buyer Category, Amount in Billions, Percentage of Total (Bar Chart Breakout Shows Buyer Categories Within the Health Insurance Segment)

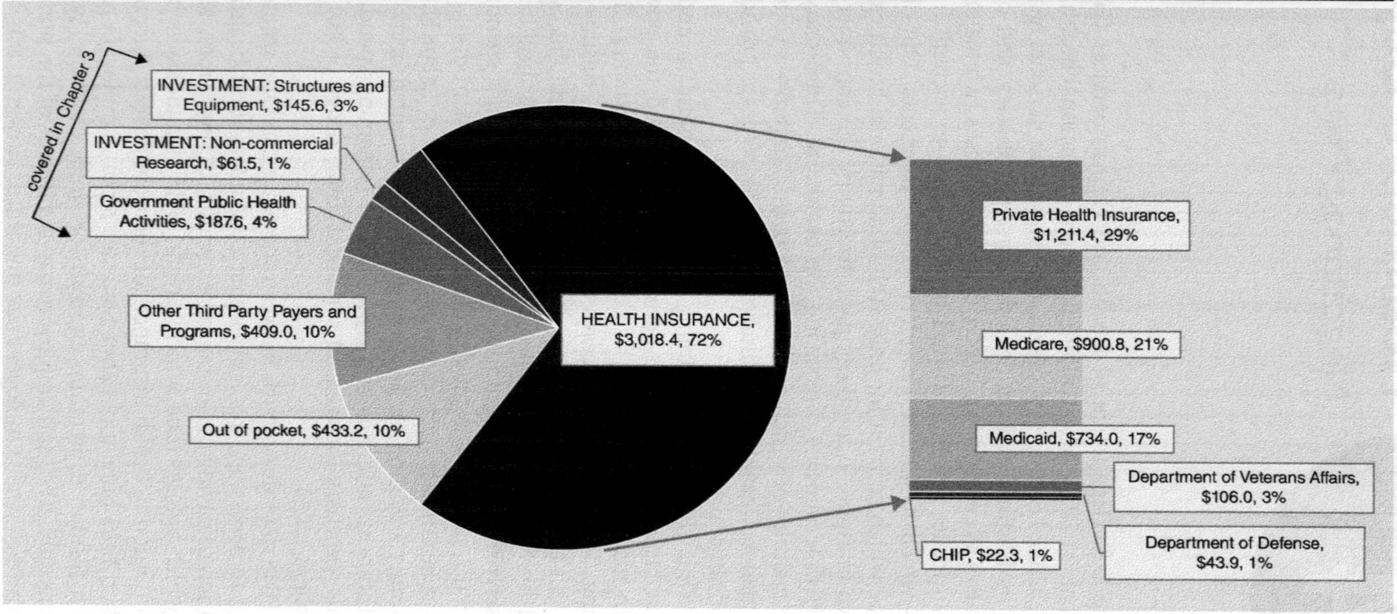

HEALTH INSURANCE, $3,018.4, 72%

Private Health Insurance, $1,211.4, 29%

Medicare, $900.8, 21%

Medicaid, $734.0, 17%

Department of Veterans Affairs, $106.0, 3%

Department of Defense, $43.9, 1%

CHIP, $22.3, 1%

INVESTMENT: Structures and Equipment, $145.6, 3%

INVESTMENT: Non-commercial Research, $61.5, 1%

Government Public Health Activities, $187.6, 4%

Other Third Party Payers and Programs, $409.0, 10%

Out of pocket, $433.2, 10%

covered in Chapter 3

that considers both consumers and businesses as funders of health insurance obscures the real contribution of consumers. Considering that the employer's contribution to an employee's health insurance premium is part of the employee's compensation package, it is the worker who earns and pays for 100% of their health insurance premiums.

Employer-based health insurance increased significantly during World War II as a way for businesses to legally compete for workers when wage increases were capped by the federal government. Thus, it became a substitute for directly paid income. The tax exemption on these health insurance premium expenses increases their value as part of a compensation package. In fact, a Congressional Budget Office analysis indicated reductions in the tax subsidies for employment-based health insurance could reduce the national deficit by $500 to $900 billion over a decade.

Finally, in addition to obscuring the contribution of the consumer in funding the healthcare they receive, the HHS crosswalk between payers and sponsors is misleading in that it entirely obscures the contribution of consumers (and employers) in funding other health expenditures, including healthcare others receive. HHS considers the government, both federal and state, to be a funder of Medicare and Medicaid health insurance, without acknowledging that taxpayers are the primary funders of the government. Taxpayers, both employers and consumers, are primary funders of government-sponsored health insurance, noncommercial research, and public health activities. These taxpayer-funded expenditures impact prices for goods and services consumed across industries.

Table 1 contrasts the HHS approach to categorizing payers and those that fund the payers—which considers only the next intermediate funding source—with the reality of the true healthcare cost burden that falls on consumers and households as the ultimate funding source across all major categories of payer expenditures per HHS. In no other industry is the consumer so burdened with cost while so disconnected as a direct buyer from the products and services they fund.

While the HHS accounting methods obscure the contributions and burdens of consumer households for funding healthcare, these methods are very instructive in documenting the dramatic shift of this contribution from direct consumer control to indirect control via third-party payers (choice of health insurance) and government (choice of elected officials). HHS data indicate that 47% of total national health expenditures were paid directly by consumers out of pocket in 1960. This decreased to 22% by 1980, to 14% by 2000, and to 10% in 2021. Considering the HHS sponsor categories with available data, the private sector, mostly private businesses and households, funded 68% of total national health expenditures in 1987, with government funding the remaining 32%. In 2021, the private sector funded 51%, with 49% funded by government.

HHS "Payers" of Healthcare Bills (% of Total National Health Expenditures per HHS)	HHS Categories of "Sponsors" / Funders of Payers	Ultimate Source of "Sponsor" Funds Obscured by HHS Categories
	Table 1 Consumer/Household Healthcare Expenditure Burden and Sources of Funding Obscured by HHS Sponsors	
Out of pocket (10%)	Household	No source obscured (consumers' income and/or savings pay these expenses directly)
Private health insurance (29%)	Household AND Employer	**Household** ONLY (employer contribution to premium is part of earned compensation; worker/retiree earnings are the obscured funding source behind the employer as "sponsor")
Medicare (21%)	Household AND Employer AND Government	Household AND Employer ONLY (households and employers pay Medicare taxes and premiums and are obscured as the funding sources behind government as a "sponsor")
Medicaid (17%)	Government	Household AND Employers pay for Medicaid insurance for low-income households via taxes and are obscured as the funding sources behind government as the "sponsor" of Medicaid
Government public health activities (4%)	N/A, not included in HHS crosswalk	Household AND Employers fund via taxes
Non-commercial research (1%)	N/A, not included in HHS crosswalk	Household AND Employers via taxes (and private donations)

Key Determinants of the Power of Buyers

Given this great consumer disconnect in the healthcare industry, considerations of the power of buyers requires extension to households and, to a lesser extent, employers as the ultimate funders of healthcare purchasing. Porter identified several factors as key determinants of the power of buyers.

Price sensitivity increases the power of buyers to pressure price reductions. Two variables are key determinants of consumer price sensitivity to health insurance cost in countries where there is competition: age and health status. Across countries, older consumers, and those in worse health, are less price sensitive than younger consumers and those in better health. In addition, consumers in the United States are less price sensitive than those in European countries where there is competition among health plans. Consumer price insensitivity for health insurance drives price insensitivity for healthcare providers, fueling continuous increases in expenditures in the United States. Because of this price insensitivity combined with the market power of hospital and physician suppliers, the only policy approach that would significantly reduce what commercial health insurance companies pay healthcare providers would be capping the level of price growth, while price transparency and increased competition would result in only small reductions in prices paid.

Where there are few buyers or large-volume buyers, the buyers have increased power, particularly when suppliers have high fixed costs and low marginal costs. To the extent that consumers continue to purchase their health insurance through their employers, consumers have little power as the options are limited by the employer. Given that large employers are large-volume buyers, they have more power. However, to recruit and retain employees, they need to ensure the options offered are competitive and meet current and prospective employee expectations within the context of overall compensation packages. Heath insurance companies typically then steer members to in-network providers to ensure sufficient volume to negotiate lower prices with those providers. The health insurance buyer volume holds greater power with hospitals and pharmaceutical suppliers due to their high fixed costs and low marginal costs. Hospitals must maintain high tech facilities and equipment and specialized staff regardless of how many patients are admitted. Pharmaceutical companies incur major costs to develop a new drug, while the production of each successful new drug is quite small.

Buyers who perceive little differentiation among suppliers have more power to select among available vendors. In healthcare, buyers' perceptions of provider reputation—both via word of mouth and quality ratings—can shift significant power from buyers to suppliers. Buyers have more power when switching costs are lower. While there are not fees for switching health insurance or providers (as long as the providers are in their health plan's network), there is the cost of time in completing paperwork and in recounting medical history. Too often medical record systems still do not share health data, so patients who switch to a new provider risk losing important health information, including test results, medication history, and history of conditions. While technology is available to solve this problem, adoption and sustainability have been challenging.

Buyers who can credibly threaten to integrate backward—that is, produce the product or service themselves rather than buy it—have more power. While individual consumers cannot credibly do this, health insurance companies can and have done this. For example, UnitedHealth grew as a health insurance company for many decades before integrating into the provider space. UnitedHealth's care delivery arm—Optum Health—now employs more physicians than any other organization in the nation. UnitedHealth has brought together all aspects of healthcare into its fold: patients, providers, and payers.

Health Insurance Payers

Unlike virtually every other type of insurance, most health insurance has evolved to include coverage of everyday, generally predictable, relatively small expenses instead of only protecting the insured from infrequent, unpredictable, very large, or catastrophic expenses. This means that health insurance organizations make payments for the large share of healthcare provider bills for services received by consumers, resulting in consumers not having a compelling reason to know or care about cost even though they fund so much of it. The power of each HHS category of buyer to negotiate, or at least influence, healthcare prices is broken down in the following sections.

Private Health Insurance

Accounting for more than $1 trillion in health expenditures (29% of total expenditures), private health insurance covers more than half of the United States population as reported by the Kaiser Family Foundation (KFF) in 2021: 48.5% via employer-based plans and 6.1% via nongroup or individually purchased plans in 2021. The total percentage covered by private insurance has changed little since the passage of the Patient Protection and Affordable Care Act of 2010 (ACA), also known as Obamacare, which includes employer mandates for health insurance.

Employer-based plans include those offered by insurance companies that accept all of the risk of insuring the beneficiaries (fully insured plans per HHS) as well as plans offered by employers that accept risk insuring their employees. The latter (self-insured plans per HHS) will often purchase stop-loss reinsurance to protect them from the losses beyond a certain limit. Self-insured employers sometimes administer the health plans themselves and sometimes outsource this administration to a health insurance company.

That employers are increasingly insourcing this risk with self-insured plans rather than outsourcing it is an indication of the profitability of the health insurance sector. According to KFF, 44% of covered workers were enrolled in a self-insured plan in 1999 compared to 65% in 2022. This practice is much more common in larger employers with 1,000 or more employees, among which 88% of covered workers were in self-insured plans in 2022. However, this practice has also increased among employers with fewer than 200 employees, among which 20% of all workers were in self-insured plans in 2022.

Despite the CBO's pessimism about the likelihood that price transparency will make any meaningful dent in reducing what commercial health insurance companies pay healthcare providers, federal policy has mandated it. This *transparency in coverage* rule requires health insurers (including employers that are self-insured) to disclose estimates of the consumer's cost-sharing liability for covered items or services by provider and to make this information available on the internet, so consumers have a better understanding of their out-of-pocket expenses and can be smarter shoppers. This rule also requires health insurance companies to disclose their in-network provider negotiated rates, historical out-of-network charges and payments, and prescription drug pricing information. This rule follows a previous rule requiring hospitals to publicly post their prices, effective January 1, 2021.

Prior to these transparency mandates, health insurance companies and healthcare providers negotiated prices in secrecy and did not make the rates available to the public. In an analysis of IBM's MarketScan database of deidentified fully adjudicated closed paid healthcare claims from private health insurers across the United States, Nisha Kurani and colleagues found that prices paid for the same service varied widely between geographical regions. For example, in 2018, the average joint replacement surgery price paid (including payments by the health plan and out-of-pocket costs by the beneficiary) ranged from $23,170 in the Baltimore-Columbia-Towson Metropolitan Statistical Area known as Central Maryland to $58,193 in the New York-Jersey City-White Plains Metropolitan Statistical Area. While some variation between geographical regions may be caused by differences in labor costs, there was also significant variation within regions. For example, in the San Diego-Carlsbad Metropolitan Statistical Area, the 25th percentile price paid was $20,305 while the 75th percentile was $51,995.

In 2019, Zack Cooper and colleagues also found significant variation in prices paid by employer-sponsored health insurers both across and within regions using claims from three of the five largest commercial health insurers in the nation. They found that prices paid to monopoly hospitals—those with no competitors within a 15-mile radius—were 12% higher than areas with four or more competitors. Conversely, where insurance markets were concentrated, hospital prices were lower. These findings demonstrate how prices vary based on whether suppliers (healthcare providers) or buyers (private health insurers) have more bargaining power. Cooper's team also found significant variation within hospitals that is unexplained by patient variables, even for apparently undifferentiated services, an indication that individual insurers have differing bargaining power within a local market.

The Transparency in Coverage rule went into effect July 1, 2022, designed to pressure lower prices to be negotiated and paid to healthcare providers by health insurers, which should then translate to lower health insurance premiums for consumers. In 2022, Haque and colleagues reported that less than 6% of more than 5,000 hospitals were fully compliant with the hospital transparency rule 6 to 9 months after the effective date. They noted that acute care hospitals in more concentrated markets (i.e., where there are fewer competitors) were less likely to be fully compliant with the hospital price transparency rule. That same year, Kona and Corlette reported fines for hospitals in violation represented only 0.04% of their net patient revenue. They noted that fines for insurers in violation of the newer rule are much higher and that most insurers are complying. However, while insurers are complying with the technical requirements of the rule, the information posted is not usable to consumers or others without the significant expertise and resources needed to decipher it. States have several levers that can be used to improve compliance with price transparency rules and usability of the posted information through local-level regulations as well as existing oversight of healthcare facilities and insurers.

Medicare

Sponsored by the federal government, Medicare provides health insurance for those age 65 and older, those younger than age 65 with certain disabilities, and all those with end-stage renal disease. Total enrollment in Medicare has increased from 52.4 million beneficiaries in 2013 to 65.1 million beneficiaries in 2022. Medicare covered 14.3% of the U.S. population as of 2021, a reflection of the demographic shift to an older nation and significant increase from 10.9% in 2008.

While private health insurance is the largest health insurance category in terms of expenditures per HHS, it represents a group of insurers. In contrast, Medicare is the single largest health insurer in the United States and accounts for 21% of total national health expenditures per HHS. Also, in contrast to private health insurance, which pays providers based on negotiated prices, Medicare does not negotiate prices. Medicare starts with a base payment and adjusts for geographic and provider factors. Hospitals may also qualify for outlier payments from Medicare to cover a portion of the hospital's costs that exceeds a certain limit on an individual patient. On average, commercial insurance prices paid to hospitals have been more than double those paid by Medicare. Within hospitals, Zack Cooper and colleagues found very low correlations between procedure-specific per beneficiary prices paid by employer-sponsored health insurers and those paid by Medicare.

Medicare is funded through two trust funds that can only be used for Medicare. The Hospital Insurance Trust Fund is funded by payroll taxes paid by employers, employees, and the self-employed as well as income taxes on Social Security benefits, interest earned on the trust fund investments and premiums paid for Part A benefits. Medicare Part A covers hospital stays, skilled nursing facility stays, and hospice care. Most people do not have to pay premiums because they worked long enough—generally 10 years— while paying Medicare taxes. The Supplementary Medical Insurance Trust Fund funds Part B and D benefits and receives funds appropriated from Congress and from premiums paid by those enrolled in Medicare Part B (Medical Insurance) and Medicare Part D (drug coverage). Most people pay premiums based on income level for Part B and Part D coverage, as well as penalties if they do not enroll when first eligible. Part B covers physician services, durable medical equipment, outpatient laboratory tests, ambulatory surgery centers, and other medical services. Part D covers retail prescription drugs.

Medicare Part C—the Medicare Advantage program—is the private plan managed care alternative to traditional fee-for-service Medicare insurance. It is funded through the same two trust funds, but Medicare outsources the insurance risk by paying private health insurers a per beneficiary amount per month for their coverage, an amount that is adjusted based on the beneficiary's demographics, health status, and county of residence. The beneficiary must be enrolled in Part B and continue to pay Part B premiums along with any Part C premiums. Private health insurers must meet certain requirements of coverage to offer a Medicare Advantage, Part C plan, but can also add benefits and coverage not offered by traditional fee for service Medicare.

The solvency of Medicare is a significant concern. As reported by Cubanski and Neuman, in 2021, only 15% of the Medicare trust revenues were from premiums. General revenue appropriated from Congress accounted for 46% of Medicare funds, with 34% coming from payroll taxes. The current Medicare funding models are projected to be insufficient to cover the current benefits, so the options are to reduce benefits, increase taxes, or increase premiums. Demographic and economic trends affect solvency—particularly the proportions of the population that are Medicare-eligible versus working (and paying into Medicare) as well as economic growth versus contraction (which affects availability of tax revenue from consumers and employers). As of 2021, Medicare spending accounted for 10% of the federal budget.

Medicaid and CHIP

CMS also oversees Medicaid and the Children's Health Insurance Program (CHIP), both of which provide health insurance to eligible low-income populations and are jointly sponsored by federal and state governments.

While Medicaid covers eligible adults and children, CHIP covers children who are not eligible for Medicaid because their family income is higher than the Medicaid cutoffs. Medicaid accounts for 17% of total national health expenditures while CHIP accounts for 1%. Administered by the states according to federal requirements, Medicaid provides insurance to more than 87 million people nationwide and CHIP to more than 7 million, as of April 2023. In 2021, KFF reported that as a percentage of the total United States population, combined enrollment in Medicaid and CHIP had increased significantly from 13.4% in 2008 to 21.1% in 2021. State funds for Medicaid are matched by federal funds, with states having significant flexibility to design their own health plans. The federal match for CHIP is generally around 15% higher than for Medicaid to encourage states to expand their coverage programs for children.

States are required to provide mandatory benefits, such as hospital and medical services, to core populations, including those with low income, to participate and receive the federal match for Medicaid. They may also receive federal matches for optional services such as dental care and for broader populations such as those with significant medical care needs who have higher incomes. The percentage of costs paid by the federal government for Medicaid varies based on the specific service provided and type of enrollee. The Medicaid formula is designed so the federal government pays a higher portion of the costs in states with lower per capita income, generally ranging from 50% to 78% across states. Hospitals that serve a large number of Medicaid and uninsured low-income patients receive *disproportionate share hospital* (or "DSH") payments from Medicaid. Federal DSH payments are capped for each state and facility and must be matched by state funds. DSH payments to hospitals were approximately $17 billion in 2021.

A major challenge for the Medicaid program has been the low reimbursement provided for physician services, which averages only 72% of Medicare payments nationwide, though rates vary by state with a few paying a bit more than Medicare. The relative power of physicians as suppliers of healthcare services to pressure Medicaid payers is seen in their lower rate of acceptance of new Medicaid patients. In a national survey of physicians who were accepting new patients, Holgash and Heberlein reported a significantly lower percentage (70.8%) were accepting new Medicaid patients compared to 85.3% accepting new Medicare patients and 90% accepting new patients with private insurance. Physicians reported insufficient payment was the primary reason for not accepting new Medicaid patients. This was confirmed in an analysis of rates across states, where there was a nearly 1% increase in new Medicaid patient acceptance rates for each 1% increase in the Medicaid-to-Medicare fee ratio.

Expansion of the Medicaid program to cover all adults with income below 138% of the federal poverty level was a key goal of the Patient Protection and Affordable Care Act of 2010. The federal government incentivized states to expand Medicaid eligibility by paying those expanding an enhanced federal match rate, and only ten states have not expanded as of July 2023. According to Brian Blase's 2021 analyses, Medicaid expansion has resulted in approximately 15 million additional enrollees, with nearly 4 million of those enrolled because marketing efforts reached those who were previously more eligible, not because of the expanded eligibility. However, Blase also reported that more than 2 million people enrolled under Medicaid expansion were not actually eligible, a problem he suspects was exacerbated during the pandemic and reflects failures in verification procedures.

Federal law limits what states can charge Medicaid enrollees for premiums and copays, including limiting out-of-pocket spending to 5% of family income. However, some states have applied for and received approval of waivers of these limits to help foster personal responsibility or enhance sustainability. Numerous studies indicate that this low-income population for whom Medicaid was designed is highly price sensitive. In 2021, Guth and colleagues published a review of the research on the effects of this price sensitivity and found charging enrollees premiums for Medicaid insurance is associated with reduced coverage and increased disenrollment, particularly among healthier people. In addition, higher out-of-pocket costs are associated with reduced healthcare utilization and prescription refills, including among those with higher healthcare needs, and with worse health outcomes. Guth and team also examined available data from states that had obtained waivers and found that many Medicaid enrollees failed to pay premiums and, as a result, lost coverage or were subjected to debt collection. The enrollees reported that the premium policies were confusing and that the premiums were not affordable. Given the added administrative burden of charging premiums and the low payment rate, it is unclear whether premiums enhance or undermine Medicaid sustainability.

Departments of Defense and Veterans Affairs

TRICARE is the federal government–sponsored health insurance provided for active and retired military members and their families and survivors. TRICARE allows beneficiaries to receive care at military facilities as well as via a network of civilian healthcare providers. The Veterans Affairs (VA) healthcare system is one of the largest healthcare providers in the United States, with 172 medical centers and more than 1,000 outpatient clinics. Veterans' eligibility and costs for care provided by the VA system are determined based on discharge status, service connection, or income. Free healthcare at the VA is provided for any illness or injury they determine is connected to the veteran's military service. According to the Government Accountability Office (GAO), as of 2023, approximately 9 million veterans were enrolled in the VA's healthcare system, and the system continues to face challenges meeting the demand. These challenges include ensuring timely access to care through its own clinics and facilities or via community providers, effective identification and treatment of mental health and substance use disorders among veterans, quality care for veterans in long-term care facilities, and modernization of electronic health record systems. Combined, the Department of Defense TRICARE insurance and the Veterans Affairs healthcare system account for 4% of total national health expenditures. KFF reported that as a percentage of the total U.S. population, 1.3% have health insurance coverage through these military plans as of 2021, and this percentage has changed very little since 2008.

Other Third-Party Payers and Programs

This miscellaneous category of third-party payers and programs accounts for 10% of total national health expenditures. This includes programs like worksite health care provided by employers for their employees and school health programs, including nursing services, hearing and vision tests, and clinical services provided to students in primary and secondary public and private schools. Philanthropic donations for healthcare and the medical portion of property and casualty insurance are also included in this category.

Federal programs may fall under this category, including the Substance Abuse and Mental Health Services Administration, which provides public health services and funding to support treatment for mental health and substance use disorders, and the Provider Relief Fund, which provided funds for lost revenue to healthcare providers due to the COVID-19 pandemic. Federal, state, and local governments also combine to provide subsidies for hospitals, home health, and other facilities owned by state or local governments.

Specialized federal and state services also make up a portion of this spending with programs like the Indian Health Service, which provides healthcare to American Indians and Alaska Natives; maternal and child health programs, jointly sponsored by federal and state governments to improve access to prenatal and postnatal care for women as well as to children with special medical needs, particularly among low-income populations; and a variety of programs like vocational rehabilitation for those with physical and mental impairments. Some regions also have general assistance programs offered by state and local governments, independent of federal programs, to provide healthcare, including medications and services, for those who are in financial need but are not eligible for federal programs.

Consumers

According to HHS, considering the total national health expenditure relative to the population, per capita spending on healthcare was nearly

$13,000 in 2021. Based on HHS calculations, households sponsored 26.9% of the cost, including employee—but not employer—contributions to premiums for private health insurance, employee payroll taxes and premiums for Medicare Part A, medical portion of property and casualty insurance premiums, and out-of-pocket payments. At this rate, the per capita annual household healthcare cost burden is $3,474. The HHS per capita amount simply divides the total national health expenditure by the total population in the United States and then applies the percentage share HHS attributes to households as sponsors.

Another approach to analyzing healthcare cost from the consumer perspective is provided by the Consumer Price Index (CPI). The CPI methodology is based on surveys of urban households over time, asking consumers about their daily living expenditures for a representative sample of products and services. Healthcare expenditures are included in the CPI survey and include out-of-pocket payments as well as health insurance premiums covered by the consumer. The CPI average total annual expenditures were $66,928, with healthcare expenditures accounting for 8.1% of this total at $5,452 ($3,704 for health insurance). This amount spent on healthcare was 76% less than the amount spent on housing, 50% less than that spent on transportation, 34% less than that spent on food, and 31% less than that spent on combined personal insurance (e.g., premiums for life insurance and personal liability insurance) and pension (i.e., contributions to social security and retirement). Given these relative costs, consumers are likely to be more price sensitive in shopping for those categories of higher spending than for healthcare.

Table 2, which compares the two methods of considering costs, demonstrates that in both methods, consumers spend more on health insurance

Table 2 Annual Household Costs for Healthcare in 2021, HHS Versus CPI Method		
Type of Cost	HHS per Capita Household Healthcare Cost = $3,474	CPI per Household Cost = $5,452
Health insurance premiums, excluding employer contributions	41.6%	67.9%
Out-of-pocket spending	38%	32.1%
Other	20.4% (employee payroll taxes and premiums for Medicare Part A, medical portion of property and casualty insurance premiums)	

premiums than they spend out of pocket buying healthcare products and services directly. This is in stark contrast to other areas of consumer spending as shown in Table 3, which compares healthcare to the cost of owning a home or car. The premiums paid for homeowners insurance and auto insurance are less than 20% of the total cost of owning a home or car, which means the consumer is directly purchasing the majority of maintenance, repairs, and other costs.

Given the higher cost, consumers have a stronger incentive to shop for health insurance than they do for healthcare products and services. In addition, because of the relatively larger percentage of the healthcare category spent on insurance premiums and because healthcare insurance premium costs are higher than automobile or homeowners insurance on average, consumers are likely to be relatively more price sensitive to health insurance premiums.

Given the financial impact of health insurance shopping on consumers, in 2017, Bhargava and colleagues examined employee choices in the selection of health insurance. They used data from a large national company for which the plans varied only in the extent of cost-sharing, including deductible, copayment, and out-of-pocket maximum. They found that more than half of employees selected health plans that were financially worse than other available plans and could have saved $372 per year by choosing a plan with the same benefits but a higher deductible. They also

Table 3   Percentage of Total Annual Cost Households/ Consumers Spent on Insurance for Healthcare, Home, and Auto for Latest Available Year

Type of Cost	Average Annual Cost per Consumer	Insurance Premiums (% of Annual Cost)
Housing (cost of owned dwelling), 2020	$7,473[1]	$1,311[2] (17.5%)
Transportation (cost of owning an automobile), 2021	$9,666[3]	$1,342[4] (13.9%)
Healthcare, 2021 HHS per capita CPI per consumer unit	$3,474 $5,452	$1,445 (41.6%) $3,704 (67.9%)

[1] https://www.bls.gov/news.release/cesan.nr0.htm
[2] https://content.naic.org/sites/default/files/publication-hmr-zu-homeowners-report.pdf
[3] https://www.bts.gov/content/average-cost-owning-and-operating-automobilea-assuming-15000-vehicle-miles-year
[4] https://newsroom.aaa.com/wp-content/uploads/2021/08/2021-YDC-Brochure-Live.pdf

found that employees earning less than $40,000 per year, older employee and employees with chronic conditions were more likely to choose pla that were guaranteed to be worse for them in terms of total annual cost.

Bhargava and colleagues aimed to better understand these findings b conducting additional research in which participants chose among hypo thetical plans. They found that participants made the same poor choice from a total cost perspective whether presented with complex options (more plans with less ease of comparison) or simple options (few plans displayed for easy comparison). The researchers then compared participant choices when additional information about the financial consequences of their choices was provided. The additional clarifications reduced poor choices from 48% to 18%. They also found that less than 2% of partici- pants who tested high on measures of insurance knowledge made poor health plan choices. This research points to the importance of health insur- ance literacy in improving shopping decisions.

Given these challenges with health insurance literacy and that consumers are the ultimate funders of much more than just the 26.9% of total national health expenditures HHS credits them with in their crosswalk between payers and sponsors, it is likely that many if not most consumers cannot readily and adequately digest complex healthcare policy options. This makes it difficult for them to know whom they should elect for office to direct the 49% of total national healthcare expenditures consumers have entrusted to be spent by their governments (34% federal, 15% state and local).

Impact of Federal Health Insurance Laws on Consumers as Buyers

The establishment of the Medicare and Medicaid programs in 1965 marked the most significant changes to health insurance law in United States his- tory. According to estimates by Cohen and colleagues, the percentage of the population of age 65 or older who had hospital insurance increased from 46% in 1959 to 96% in 1968, and the percentage under age 65 increased from 69% to 79%. At over 900 pages, the Patient Protection and Affordable Care Act (ACA) of 2010 made the most significant changes to health insur- ance law since 1965 and included significant changes to the private health insurance market.

The ACA requires most of the population to have health insurance that meets certain standards (the penalty for not having such insurance was eliminated in 2017, effective in 2019) and requires employers with 50 or more employees to offer health insurance that meets affordability standards and provides minimum essential benefits or pay a penalty. Employers must

also pay a penalty if one or more employees purchases subsidized insurance. The ACA sets lifetime limits and annual limits on coverage and prohibits health plans from requiring cost sharing for certain evidence-based prevention services and refusing coverage or charging higher prices for those with a pre-existing condition.

It also established an online health insurance exchange that offers four categories of plans with essential benefits and different cost sharing—bronze (lowest premiums, highest cost sharing), silver, gold, and platinum (highest premiums, lowest cost sharing)—to individuals, as well as a catastrophic plan category with low premiums and very high deductibles with the same essential benefits to individuals under age 30. All new health plans must meet one of the four metal levels, and all health plan information must be displayed in a standard format to allow consumers to compare plan options online. Any health plans offered on these exchanges must meet certain standards regarding marketing, provider networks, and quality measures. Under the ACA, states can form compacts that allow health insurance companies to sell policies more easily in any state participating in the compact as long as the plans meet the standards of plans offered on the exchanges.

The ACA allows coverage for dependent children up to age 26 and expanded eligibility for Medicaid insurance to all those under the age of 65 who are not Medicare eligible and have incomes up to 138% of the federal poverty level. The Supreme Court made this expansion optional for states, and as of March 2023, all but 10 states had implemented the Medicaid expansion. Subsidies were also made available to purchase health insurance for those who are not Medicaid eligible, are not working for an employer that offers health insurance meeting certain standards and have incomes up to 400% of the federal poverty level.

The primary impact of the ACA on coverage has been that a greater percentage of the population now has Medicaid health insurance. According to a 2021 report by the KFF, the percentage of the population that is uninsured has decreased from 15.2% in 2008 to 8.6% in 2021. There is also evidence that the ACA has made it easier for consumers to shop for individual health insurance. In 2019, Hero and colleagues surveyed customers of a large nonprofit health insurance company who purchased individual insurance via the ACA federal exchange Marketplace versus traditional sources (off-Marketplace). Overall, those who purchased health insurance on the Marketplace were less likely to report difficulty finding the best or most affordable plan (36%) compared to those who purchased off-Marketplace (49%).

However, among those with low health insurance literacy, there was no difference between those who bought insurance on or off the Marketplace in terms of difficulty finding the best or most affordable health plan. In addition, those with low literacy who bought insurance on the

Marketplace were significantly *more* likely to report that they wished they had had help choosing a plan. It is possible that those who purchased on the Marketplace were more likely to do so with the hopes of getting help choosing and were disappointed. Given that those with low literacy were more likely to have been younger, had lower household incomes, and bought insurance on the Marketplace, more work is needed to achieve the ACA goals by improving the consumer-friendliness of shopping for health insurance.

In the decade before the ACA, high-deductible health plans—often referred to as consumer-driven or consumer-directed plans—were introduced by private health insurance companies to provide consumers with more opportunity to shop for products and services directly (via a higher deductible) while saving money on lower insurance premiums. This option began gaining in popularity in 2003 when federal legislation was passed to allow consumers who are covered by a high deductible health plan the option to open a health savings account (HSA). Thus, high deductible health plans became known as HSA-eligible plans.

The HSA option has significant financial advantages to consumers. Specifically, the individual can contribute to their HSA, as can their employer. The individual's contribution is tax deductible, any employer contribution is not taxed as income, and the interest earned is not taxed. The account funds can be used to cover health expenses, and the unused amounts can be carried over indefinitely with the account growing tax-free. Beginning at age 65, the accumulated savings can continue to be used for medical expenses and can also be used for any purpose without penalty but with taxes paid as with other retirement investments. Given these advantages, HSA-eligible plans are particularly beneficial to younger, healthier consumers, who tend to be more price sensitive.

Despite the promise of HSA-eligible plans, several concerns have dampened enthusiasm for these plans. First, there is some evidence that those who choose these plans tend to avoid getting preventive care. In a review of studies on this in 2019, Mazurenko and colleagues reported that nine of the more rigorously controlled contemporary studies found a reduction in the use of preventive services while seven found no differences. Second, reports of consumers who were unable to pay medical bills because of the high deductible without sufficient savings to cover them (in an HSA or otherwise) have resulted in some companies eliminating these plans as an option for their employees.

Given that the ACA prohibits health plans from imposing cost sharing requirements for important preventive services, Shafer and colleagues in 2023 examined patterns in use of these services among nonelderly adults in IBM's MarketScan large national database of employees who chose a high-deductible health plan from 2008 (before the ACA) through 2016 (after the ACA). They found that enrollment in these plans increased from

3% to more than 20% across the time span. The percentage who used any preventive services increased over time both among those with (56.6% to 62.1%) and without (58.8% to 63.6%) a high deductible health plan. Given the gradual small increase, it is unclear whether the ACA was the cause of the increased use of preventive services across health plans. The researchers found that the increase in use of six specific preventive services (out of 17 total)—wellness visits, lipid disorder screening, diabetes screening, sexually transmitted infections, and flu shots and other immunizations— was smaller among those with a high deductible health plan compared to those without this type of plan.

It is unclear why the use of preventive services would not be higher in all health plans after the ACA prohibited cost sharing (e.g., copays or other out-of-pocket costs) for these services, particularly given the health risk to the beneficiaries for not using these services. It is possible that at least some consumers were unaware of the ACA's cost sharing prohibition given the well-documented problem of low health insurance literacy and complexity of the ACA law. For those with a high deductible health plan, they might have had concerns that the free screenings could result in a diagnosis that would require treatment that is not free. It is noteworthy that there were no differences between those with and without a high deductible health plan in the increase in use of screening for any of the four types of cancer included in the free preventive screening services. It is possible that fear of cancer is a stronger motivator for prevention than other conditions. It is also possible that health plans, healthcare providers, and public health organizations are more aggressive in promoting the importance of cancer screenings.

From 2005 to 2012, the percentage of employers offering an HSA-eligible high deductible health plan steadily increased from less than 4% to 26% among employers offering health benefits. The percentage has varied from 17% to 26% from 2013 through 2022. Among companies with 200 or more employees, 51% offered an HSA-eligible high deductible health plan in 2022, compared to 24% among smaller companies. The lower premiums for these plans are a key reason.

There appears to be a tradeoff between premium cost and plan satisfaction, with those in a high deductible health plan less likely to report satisfaction with their plan (52%) relative to those with a traditional plan (66%) according to the Employee Benefit Research Institute (2023). However, there is a greater increase in plan satisfaction over time for those with a high deductible health plan relative to those with a traditional plan. Only 32% of those who have had a high deductible health plan for less than a year reported satisfaction with the plan compared with 58% of those who were in the plan for three or more years. While 56% of those in a traditional plan were satisfied in the first year, satisfaction increased to 71% for those who were in the plan for three or more years.

The Employee Benefit Research Institute found that more than one third of those with a high deductible health plan did not know that preventive care was covered with no cost sharing, while 45% reported that preventive care coverage had a great impact on their decision to select a high deductible health plan. Nearly two-thirds of those with a traditional plan indicated they would be likely to choose a high deductible health plan if preventive care were covered without cost sharing. Those with a high deductible health plan were more likely to use employer-provided tools to make a decision relative to those who chose a traditional plan. Among those with a health savings account, 39% indicated they would be more likely to accumulate and invest funds if they received an annual statement of their balance, and nearly one third indicated they would be more likely to do so if they received information about the account benefits and instructions via email.

Consumers have significant knowledge gaps about the insurance plans they choose, but many are eager to learn and make better choices. As prices increase, so do motivations to improve shopping acumen, particularly for more price-sensitive consumers. Apart from the period from 2022 to 2023, when overall inflation was at historic highs, healthcare inflation has generally been higher than inflation for other consumer goods and products. As reported by Rakshit and colleagues, from 2000 to 2023, the cost of medical care has increased 114% compared to 81% for all goods and services. Not surprisingly, given the differences in buyer power, inflation for private health insurance payers has increased faster than for public payers. From 2014 to 2023, prices for private insurance health services increased 25% compared to 17% for Medicaid and 14% for Medicare. The slow but steady traction of consumer-directed health plans may be approaching the point at which market share growth will accelerate along with consumer buying power.

REFERENCES

Bhargava, S., Loewenstein, G., & Sydnor, J. (2017). Choose to lose: Health plan choices from a menu with dominated option. *The Quarterly Journal of Economics, 132*(3), 1319–1372. http://doi.org/10.1093/qje/qjx011

Centers for Medicare & Medicaid Services. (2023, September 6). *National health expenditure data.* U.S. Department of Health and Human Services. https://www.cms.gov/research-statistics-data-and-systems/statistics-trends-and-reports/nationalhealthexpenddata

Cohen, R. A., Bernstein, A. B., Bilheimer, L. T., Makuc, D. M., & Powell-Griner, E. (2009). Health insurance coverage trends, 1959–2007:

Estimates from the National Health Interview Survey. *National Health Statistics Reports*, (17), 1–25. https://www.cdc.gov/nchs/data/nhsr/nhsr017.pdf

Cooper, Z., Craig, S. V., Gaynor, M., & Van Reenen, J. (2019). The price ain't right? Hospital prices and health spending on the privately insured. *The Quarterly Journal of Economics, 134*(1), 51–107. https://doi.org/10.1093/qje/qjy020

Cubanski, J., & Neuman, T. (2023, January 19). *What to know about Medicare spending and financing.* Kaiser Family Foundation. https://www.kff.org/medicare/issue-brief/what-to-know-about-medicare-spending-and-financing/

Employee Benefit Research Institute and Greenwald Research. (2022). *Consumer engagement in health care survey.* https://www.ebri.org/docs/default-source/cehcs/2022-cehcs-report.pdf?sfvrsn=da56392f_2

Employee Benefit Research Institute and Greenwald Research. (2023, April 6). *What leads to greater satisfaction with health plan coverage?* https://www.ebri.org/docs/default-source/fast-facts/ff-463-cehcs7-6apr23.pdf?sfvrsn=c599392f_2

Guth, M., Ammula, M., & Hinton, E. (2021, September 9). *Understanding the impact of Medicaid premiums and cost sharing: Updated evidence from the literature and section 1115 waivers.* Kaiser Family Foundation. https://www.kff.org/medicaid/issue-brief/understanding-the-impact-of-medicaid-premiums-cost-sharing-updated-evidence-from-the-literature-and-section-1115-waivers/

Haque, W., Ahmadzada, M., Janumpally, S., Haque, E., Allahrakha, H., Desai, S., & Hsiehchen, D. (2022). Adherence to a federal hospital price transparency rule and associated financial and marketplace factors. *JAMA, 327*(21), 2143–2145. https://doi.org/10.1001/jama.2022.5363

Holgash, K., & Heberlein, M. (2019). *Physician acceptance of new Medicaid patients: what matters and what doesn't.* Medicaid and CHIP Payment and Access Commission. https://www.macpac.gov/wp-content/uploads/2019/01/Physician-Acceptance-of-New-Medicaid-Patients.pdf

Kaiser Family Foundation. (2021). *Health insurance coverage of the total population.* https://www.kff.org/other/state-indicator/total-population/

Kominski, G. F., Nonzee, N. J., & Sorensen, A. (2017). The Affordable Care Act's impacts on access to insurance and health care for low-income populations. *Annual Review of Public Health, 38*, 489–505. https://doi.org/10.1146/annurev-publhealth-031816-044555

Kona, M., & Corlette, S. (2022). *Hospital and insurer price transparency rules now in effect but compliance is still far away.* Georgetown

University Center on Health Insurance Reforms. https://chirblog.org/hospital-and-insurer-price-transparency-rules-in-effect/

Kurani, N., Rae, M., Pollitz, K., Amin, K., & Cox, C. (2021, January 13). *Price transparency and variation in U.S. health services.* Peterson-KFF Health System Tracker. https://www.healthsystemtracker.org/brief/price-transparency-and-variation-in-u-s-health-services/

Mazurenko, O., Buntin, M. J. B., & Menachemi, N. (2019). High-deductible health plans and prevention. *Annual Review of Public Health, 40,* 411–421. https://doi.org/10.1146/annurev-publhealth-040218-044225

Rakshit, S., Wager, E., Hughes-Cromwick, P., Cox, C., & Amin, K. (2023, July 26). *How does medical inflation compare to inflation in the rest of the economy?* Peterson-KFF Health System Tracker. https://www.health-systemtracker.org/brief/how-does-medical-inflation-compare-to-inflation-in-the-rest-of-the-economy/

Shafer, P. R., Dusetzina, S. B., Sabik, L. M., Platts-Mills, T. F., Stearns, S. C., & Trogdon, J. G. (2023). High deductible health plans and use of free preventive services under the Affordable Care Act. *Inquiry: A Journal of Medical Care Organization, Provision and Financing, 60.* https://doi.org/10.1177/00469580231182512

U.S. Bureau of Labor Statistics. (2020, November). *How have healthcare expenditures changed? Evidence from the Consumer Expenditure Surveys.* https://www.bls.gov/opub/btn/volume-9/how-have-healthcare-expenditures-changed-evidence-from-the-consumer-expenditure-surveys.htm

U.S. Bureau of Labor Statistics. (2023, September 21). *Employee benefits in the United States.* https://www.bls.gov/news.release/ebs2.toc.htm

FURTHER READINGS

Congressional Budget Office. (2022, January). *The prices that commercial health insurers and Medicare pay for hospitals' and physicians' services.* https://www.cbo.gov/system/files/2022-01/57422-medical-prices.pdf

Congressional Budget Office. (2022, September). *Policy approaches to reduce what commercial insurers pay for hospitals' and physicians' services.* https://www.cbo.gov/publication/58541

Emerson, J. (2023, February 16). *Meet America's largest employer of physicians: United Health Group.* Becker's Healthcare. https://www.beckerspayer.com/payer/meet-americas-largest-employer-of-physicians-unitedhealth-group.html

Hero, J. O., Sinaiko, A. D., Kingsdale, J., Gruver, R. S., & Galbraith, A. A. (2019). Decision-making experiences of consumers choosing individual-market health insurance plans. *Health Affairs (Project Hope)*, *38*(3), 464–472. https://doi.org/10.1377/hlthaff.2018.05036

Kaiser Family Foundation. (2013, April 25). *Summary of the Affordable Care Act*. https://www.kff.org/health-reform/fact-sheet/summary-of-the-affordable-care-act/

Kaiser Family Foundation. (2019). *Medicaid-to-Medicare fee index*. https://www.kff.org/medicaid/state-indicator/medicaid-to-medicare-fee-index/

Pendzialek, J. B., Simic, D., & Stock, S. (2016). Differences in price elasticities of demand for health insurance: A systematic review. *The European Journal of Health Economics*, *17*, 5–21. Patient Protection and Affordable Care Act of 2010. https://www.govinfo.gov/content/pkg/PLAW-111publ148/pdf/PLAW-111publ148.pdf

Rudowitz, R., Drake, P., & Tolbert, J. (2023, March 31). *How many uninsured are in the coverage gap and how many could be eligible if all states adopted the Medicaid expansion?* Kaiser Family Foundation. https://www.kff.org/medicaid/issue-brief/how-many-uninsured-are-in-the-coverage-gap-and-how-many-could-be-eligible-if-all-states-adopted-the-medicaid-expansion/

Williams, E., Rudowitz, R., & Burns, A. (2023, April 13). *Medicaid financing: The basics*. Kaiser Family Foundation. https://www.kff.org/medicaid/issue-brief/medicaid-financing-the-basics/

CHAPTER

5

Alternative Healthcare
The Threat of Disruption From Substitutes

J ust as Porter cautions that the threat of new entrants is often overlooked by incumbents who are focused on navigating the landscape of current competitors, he also urges organizations across industries to pay attention to the threat of substitutes. Potential substitutes may be even more easily overlooked than potential new entrants because substitutes might appear vastly different from the industry's current product. According to Porter, a substitute product or service is one that performs the current product's function by another means. In a classic example, to transport people, substitutes for horses include automobiles and trains, which in turn can be substituted by planes. Even easier to overlook are products that are substitutes for transportation itself, such as videoconferencing.

In the healthcare industry, as in so many others, the internet has been a key tool for creating many substitutes for traditional services, with the likelihood of many more substitutes to come. However, healthcare industry complexities, including federal and state regulations as well as billing requirements, have slowed progress. It took the COVID-19 pandemic to push telemedicine—the delivery of medical services from a distance via telecommunications technology—to the tipping point of adoption, primarily because of regulatory changes that removed restrictions and increased demand by patients. According to the Office of the National Coordinator for Health Information Technology, telemedicine was used by only 15% of office-based physicians before the pandemic, with no change from 2018 to 2019. In 2021, the usage was 87%. Most physicians reported being satisfied with the use of telemedicine, and a majority reported that patient difficulty using the technology is the most common barrier.

The ability to offer medical services remotely has allowed at least some physicians to expand their practices more easily. For example, once X-ray images moved from film to digital storage, radiologists were able to read and interpret them from anywhere. This is particularly beneficial in acute care settings when fast turnaround is needed for optimal care (e.g., time-sensitive treatment decisions for stroke patients) and more efficient care (e.g., shorter lengths of stay in the hospital). Today, it is common for hospitals to outsource at least some of their radiology services to remote radiologists.

Traditional healthcare providers who do not offer telemedicine as an option are at risk of being substituted by those who do. The internet has also inspired substitutes for medical care itself both with traditional in-person care and via telemedicine, but while the internet is a powerful tool for creating a vast array of healthcare substitutes, the threat of substitutes is not solely from technology. Porter noted that customers may substitute by forgoing a product or service altogether, performing that service or producing the product themselves, or buying the product used rather than new.

There is already a market for many of the current alternatives to existing healthcare services and products, with trends indicating the potential to create new substitutes. Porter's primary recommended defense against the threat of substitutes is ensuring clear and compelling differentiation from the substitutes in terms of value. According to Porter, the threat will be high if the substitute offers a relatively good value—quality for the cost—compared to the industry's product. Also factoring into the value equation is the switching cost. If the buyers' cost of switching to the substitute is low, the threat of them doing so is higher. To the extent that buyers of healthcare are dissatisfied with its value, that is, with the rising costs for the quality, the threat of substitutes is significant.

The Ripple Effect of Substitutes

In the healthcare industry, there is evidence of a ripple effect of substitutes, wherein organizations offering current products or services adapt to defend against substitutes and in doing so become a substitute threat to another current segment in the industry that then attempts to respond in defense. While so much of healthcare is service based, prescription medications represent the primary category of products used by consumers. The threat of substitutes for prescription medications purchased in retail settings (which account for approximately 10% of total national health expenditures) is significant. In this scenario, the ripple effect starts with the threat of prescription medication substitutes, which creates a chain of substitute threats ending with the threat of substitutes for primary and urgent care clinics.

An example of buying used as a substitute in healthcare is prescription medication sharing, when a patient who has been prescribed a medication gives some of it to someone else, whether paid or not. This substitute is fairly common despite the associated risks. In some cases, this sharing is for recreational use, in which case it is a substitute for buying recreational drugs or alcohol. However, nonrecreational sharing is a substitute for buying a new prescription medicine. In their 2014 systematic review of the research, Kebede Beyene and colleagues reported that 5% to 54% of the populations sampled reported nonrecreational prescription medication sharing (either as the sharer or the shared with) and that the practice was more common among younger samples. Across studies, the most common reasons for sharing were having leftover medication and wanting to be helpful to others. Participants also reported being more willing to share their prescription medications if asked by a family member, friend, person with a similar health problem, person taking a similar medication, or in an emergency situation. In Richard Goldsworthy and Christopher Mayhorn's 2009 study of adolescents, 75% of recipients of the shared medications reported they took it to avoid a medical visit to receive a prescription for medication rather than getting it secondhand. More than one-fourth of those avoidant recipients reported seeing a healthcare provider anyway when the shared medication failed to resolve the problem.

Perhaps a much greater threat of substitute and consumer harm is purchasing medications from an unlicensed vendor, typically an online fraudulent pharmacy selling counterfeit prescription medications. According to the National Association of Boards of Pharmacy, as of 2022, there were more than 40,000 domain names operating illegal online pharmacies, 96% of which do not require a valid prescription, 85% of which offer medications not authorized by the FDA, over half of which offer controlled substances, and none of which are licensed by any state in the United States. Many of the products they sell are contaminated with dangerous toxins such as mercury, lead, and arsenic, and many contain no active ingredient. In addition to selling substandard counterfeit medications, selling them without a prescription puts the patient at risk due to lack of clinical oversight that is part of the prescription process.

According to the Organisation for Economic Co-operation and Development (OECD), international trade in counterfeit pharmaceuticals reached $4.4 billion in 2016, an estimate that does not include domestically produced and consumed counterfeits. The OECD reported that China and India are the primary producers of fake medications and the primary target markets are Africa, Europe, and the United States. The burden of counterfeit medications is particularly hard on low- and middle-income countries where weak supply chain controls and low regulatory barriers make it more difficult for consumers to differentiate between the real product and the fakes. In a systematic review of studies of the problem across low- and middle-income countries, Sachiko Ozama and colleagues found the prevalence of substandard or fake medications was 13.6% overall, with prevalence highest in Africa at 18.7%. The estimates of total market size ranged from $10 to $200 billion.

The Alliance for Safe Online Pharmacies (2021) conducted a national survey of American consumers and found use of online pharmacies had increased as of 2021, largely resulting from perceptions of better convenience and cost, and those who reported awareness of the risks of online pharmacies has also increased. One-fourth of the respondents indicated they would accept higher risk in exchange for convenience and cost savings—an example of the kind of price-performance tradeoff that Porter warns increases the threat of substitutes. Consumers' assessment of the trade-off as attractive may be based on underestimating the risks, so a potentially effective defense by legal pharmacies is a compelling educational campaign. The survey found that nearly half of American consumers falsely believe that all online pharmacies offering medications in the United States have been approved by the FDA or state regulators. Among those who have previously purchased prescription medications from online pharmacies, 59% have this misconception.

As a relatively new entrant to the online pharmacy market, Amazon is positioned to differentiate itself from fraudulent online pharmacies. Amazon Pharmacy is licensed in all 50 states and is a National Association of Boards of Pharmacy Accredited Digital Pharmacy. These credentials add to a long history of consumer experience with Amazon's convenient online shopping that includes trust managing customer credit card and other payment information. For most consumers who want the convenience of an online pharmacy without the risks, Amazon offers a compelling differentiated choice to protect itself against the threat of fraudulent substitutes. However, Amazon and other legitimate online pharmacies are not protected from the threat of consumers seeking to avoid getting a valid prescription. If Amazon can leverage its telemedicine service to make it more convenient to get a valid prescription, it can gain market share while further protecting consumers from the risks of fraudulent online pharmacies.

While legitimate online pharmacies need to protect themselves from the threat of being substituted by fraudulent online pharmacies, these legitimate pharmacies, and particularly Amazon Pharmacy, are a substitute threat that physical retail pharmacies must protect against. According to a J.D. Power survey published in 2022 of customers who filled a prescription within the past 12 months, 66% of physical pharmacy customers have an Amazon Prime account. Among the 48% of respondents who reported being aware of Amazon's pharmacy, 14% have used Amazon's PillPack service, among which 38% report they will definitely switch pharmacies in the next 12 months. As an alternative to going to a physical retail pharmacy to get prescriptions filled, Amazon offers a shopping experience and track record already well known to customers, the option to get their medications delivered in customized PillPack doses, and the ability to speak to Amazon's on-call pharmacist by phone 24/7.

To differentiate from Amazon Pharmacy and other legitimate online pharmacies, physical retail pharmacies are expanding in areas that leverage physical location and are building relationships with local communities. They are providing vaccines, health screenings, and other services that require a physical location. While these products and services could be substituted (e.g., with the development of self-administered vaccines), they provide protection from being substituted by online-only pharmacies currently. According to the Centers for Disease Control and Prevention (CDC), as of August 2023, retail pharmacies across the United States have administered more than 307 million doses of COVID vaccines as part of the Federal Retail Pharmacy Program, which represents nearly half of all vaccines administered in the United States as of the CDC's final report in May of 2023.

As both Walgreens and CVS have added a variety of primary and urgent care services to their retail pharmacy locations, many consumers are welcoming the change. JD Power's survey found that consumers who use the health and wellness services offered by their pharmacy were more likely to report they will not switch pharmacies and to express other signs of greater loyalty. In addition, the survey found that consumers who use their pharmacy's mobile app to order and track prescriptions reported being more satisfied with the pharmacy and less likely to switch pharmacies than those who do not use an app. This approach allows physical pharmacies to provide in-person services supported by user-friendly technology and the option for medication delivery as a defense against being substituted by online-only pharmacies. This approach also exacerbates the threat of substitutes to current primary and urgent care clinics by providing an attractive alternative to getting medical care in a traditional clinic, including valid prescriptions. While this threat to traditional primary and urgent care is the end of the ripple effect in this example, the effect can extend far beyond in ways that continuously challenge and shape the industry as healthcare consumers and buyers demonstrate what they value through the price-performance trade-off decisions they make.

Traditional, Complementary, and Alternative Medicine as Substitutes

While in-person office visits can be described as traditional healthcare service delivery compared to technology-supported telemedicine, the terms traditional or herbal medicine are often used to refer to ancient cultural practices that are generally based on experiential knowledge such as Ayurvedic medicine, which originated in India, and traditional Chinese medicine. In contrast, conventional medicine is based on scientific methods. The terms complementary medicine and alternative medicine are also frequently used to describe herbal medicine, dietary supplements, acupuncture, and other therapies that are used in addition to (i.e., complementary medicine) or instead of (i.e., alternative medicine) conventional treatments. Collectively, these are often referred to as traditional, complementary, and alternative medicine (TCAM). Integrative medicine typically refers to efforts to intentionally combine TCAM with conventional science-based medicine.

The National Institutes of Health has an entire division dedicated to testing these nonconventional products and practices: the National Center for Complementary and Integrative Health. This division provides information to consumers and conventional healthcare providers about the current evidence pertaining to the effectiveness and risks of TCAM approaches. The pharmaceutical industry demonstrates the value of integrative approaches in the search for new drugs, many of which have been developed based on leads from herbal medicine and other cultural practices. The natural environment produces a wealth of resources, such as plants, algae, fungi, and bacteria, which natural products chemists study to identify potential new drugs and other uses of the substances produced by organisms. The pharmaceutical industry has a history of leveraging natural products for drug discovery because of the advantages of these compounds, which have adapted and survived through evolution, in contrast to synthetic compounds. David Newman and Gordon Cragg (2020) monitored the origins of new drugs over nearly 40 years and reported that only 25% of new drugs approved during this period are totally synthetic.

Many consumers turn to supplements as substitutes for prescription or over-the-counter medications and medical care, without understanding the risks and benefits. The distinction between a drug and a supplement is largely a regulatory one. According to the FDA, drugs are substances intended to diagnose, treat, cure, or prevent a disease. Drugs must be determined to be safe *and* effective to be approved by the FDA and marketed for the proposed use. The FDA determines whether a drug requires a prescription by a licensed clinician or may be sold over the counter. Dietary supplements, including vitamins, minerals, and herbs, can have strong biological effects like drugs and may interact with drugs. The FDA does not have an approval process for supplements; rather, they are regulated like food, leaving it up to the company to ensure that their products are safe and accurately labeled. There is no requirement that a supplement be effective for any purpose. However, a company that wants to market a supplement to diagnose, treat, cure, or prevent a disease must go through the FDA drug approval process, including testing the substance for safety and effectiveness.

The FDA has several processes for allowing food and dietary supplements to include health-related claims on the label. The claims must be based on scientific evidence and describe a *relationship* (not necessarily cause and effect) between the product and reduced risk of disease or health condition. In contrast, the standard for marketing a drug is scientific evidence that the drug *causes* the desired health effect as determined by controlled trials that rule out other possible causes of the relationship. Thus, the benefits and risks of many dietary supplements are unknown, and those that are known are not easily discernable from drugs with FDA marketing approval by the consumer who does not have scientific and regulatory knowledge.

E. Lyn Lee and colleagues found the prevalence of the use of TCAM was estimated to range from 24% to 71% from 2010 to 2019 globally, with TCAM prevalence in the United States ranging from more than 30% to more than 50%. Across studies over time, prevalence has remained consistent, and methods used have likely resulted in underestimations of TCAM use. In the United States, it is estimated that out-of-pocket spending on TCAM was more than $30 billion per year as of 2016.

According to the Pew Research Center in 2017, while most Americans report positive experiences with their conventional healthcare provider, a majority also report they do their own search for information in addition to listening to their provider before making a treatment decision for a serious health issue. Pew found that 20% of U.S. adults reported using TCAM instead of conventional medicine, and these respondents were less likely to report having a primary care provider or having had a preventive care checkup or flu shot within the past year. Clearly TCAM is a substitute threat to conventional medicine in the United States and globally.

Conventional healthcare providers who integrate the use of TCAM into their practices or at least help consumers sort through the often-confusing information available about the risks and benefits of TCAM may reduce the threat of being substituted by TCAM. However, doing so may require significant changes. For example, current information systems for tracking medication use generally only include prescribed medications, using the electronic prescription process to automatically track a patient's medication list. Typically, these tracking systems also include automatic alerts to the provider when the patient is prescribed drug combinations that might increase risk of harm from drug interactions. To reliably include supplements and over-the-counter medications purchased out-of-pocket in medication information systems, these purchases would need to be tracked, or providers would need to change how they ask about, document, and transmit information about TCAM use by their patients.

Perhaps the bigger challenge to offering integrative medicine services is expanding the conventional provider's knowledge of scientific evidence (or lack thereof) pertaining to TCAM and refining their ability to translate that knowledge into a discussion of treatment options to help guide informed decision making with their patients. The timely dissemination of new scientific evidence about FDA-approved drugs and other treatments and their adoption within medical practice is already a challenge to optimal care. The expectation that physicians and other conventional healthcare providers also stay informed on the state of the science across TCAM products and services is not realistic without appropriate information support systems and training. However, to the extent that conventional healthcare providers differentiate themselves as being science-based, failure to adopt those TCAM practices in accordance with available scientific evidence increases the threat of substitutes.

Healthy Lifestyles as Substitutes

Scientific evidence on the effects of a healthy lifestyle on disease prevention and progression has not been integrated into conventional medicine. The economic engine of healthcare runs on diagnostic tests, prescription drugs, and medical procedures to identify and treat diseases, the most common of which are caused by unhealthy diets, physical inactivity, and tobacco and alcohol use. While the science, technology, and clinical expertise and dedication to diagnosing and treating disease is often inspirational and sensational, the science of prevention is less dramatic, less marketable, and more difficult to sell. The payments clinicians receive for their brief patient visits do not encourage meaningful discussion or coaching about healthy lifestyles. Furthermore, most clinicians (e.g., physicians, nurses, pharmacists) are not sufficiently trained in the nutrition, exercise physiology, stress management, and cognitive behavioral therapies that have been scientifically tested and shown to be safe and effective treatments to prevent and reverse chronic diseases.

Every five years, the U.S. Department of Health and Human Services and the U.S. Department of Agriculture publish an updated *Dietary Guidelines for Americans*. As part of this process, these departments convene a distinguished panel of nutrition and public health experts to serve on the Dietary Guidelines Advisory Committee, which reviews the current relevant scientific evidence and produces a report that informs the development of the updated guidelines. The current guidelines are more similar to the first guidelines published in 1980 than they are different as shown in Table 1.

The differences in the current guidelines reflect research that has demonstrated the health benefits of vegetables, vegetarian proteins, and oils from vegetables, nuts, seeds, and fish that are lower in saturated fats. Specifically, the 2020 Advisory Committee conducted a systematic review of the research and concluded that lower all-cause mortality rates were associated with diets higher in vegetables, fruits, legumes, nuts, whole or nonrefined grains, fish, and unsaturated vegetable oils, and lower in meat, high-fat dairy, refined grains, and added sugars. They also reported these findings were consistent across studies, making the case for these recommendations all the more compelling. The federal report *Make Every Bite Count*, which includes the current guidelines based on the Advisory Committee recommendations, also presents data showing where Americans fall short in adherence to the guidelines. Most noteworthy, only 2 in 10 Americans meet the dietary guideline recommendations for consuming fruits and only 1 in 10 do so for total vegetables, for dairy, and for seafood while virtually none meet the recommendations for consuming whole grains.

Unhealthy diets have been associated with several leading causes of death, specifically cardiometabolic diseases like heart disease, stroke, and

Table 1 Comparison of First and Current U.S. *Dietary Guidelines for Americans*

1980 Guidelines	2020–2025 Guidelines
Eat a variety of foods, including fruits, vegetables, whole grains, dairy, protein foods (meat, poultry, and fish), and legumes	Core elements of a healthy diet: Vegetables Fruits Grains, at least half of which are whole grains Dairy, including those with reduced fat, or fortified soy alternatives for vegetarians Other protein foods, including lean meats, poultry, seafood, and vegetarian proteins Oils, including vegetable oils and oils in nuts and seafood
Maintain ideal weight	Choose nutrient-dense foods—those with lots of nutrition for the number of calories (e.g., vegetables)
Avoid too much fat, saturated fat, and cholesterol	Limit choices that are higher in saturated fats
Eat foods with adequate starch and fiber	[no comparable recommendation]
Avoid too much sugar	Limit choices that are higher in added sugars
Avoid too much sodium	Limit choices that are higher in added sodium
Drink alcohol in moderation or not at all	Limit alcohol

diabetes. In 2017, Renata Micha and colleagues found that nearly half of all cardiometabolic deaths were associated with less-than-optimal diets, specifically 44% of heart disease deaths, 52% of stroke deaths, and 48% of all diabetes deaths. The top specific dietary factors related to deaths were high sodium (9.5% of all cardiometabolic deaths), low nuts and seeds (8.5%), high processed meats (8.2%), low seafood omega-3 fats (7.8%), low vegetables (7.6%), low fruits (7.5%), and high sugar-sweetened beverages (7.4%).

Several structured diets have been tested in randomized controlled trials, much like the way new drugs are tested, comparing them to a minimal intervention control group which is equivalent to a placebo or inactive substance in a drug trial. These tested diets included a low-fat diet, a very low-fat diet, a modified-fat diet, a combined low-fat and low-sodium diet, the Mediterranean diet, the Ornish diet, and the Pritikin diet. In a 2023 systematic review across studies, Giorgio Karam and colleagues found the Mediterranean diet and the low-fat diet were the only diets found to reduce all-cause mortality and nonfatal myocardial infarction (i.e., heart attack). Only the Mediterranean diet was found to reduce cardiovascular mortality and stroke. In a separate systematic review by Edward Hill and colleagues in 2019, the link between diet and Alzheimer's disease was examined, and the Mediterranean diet was found to protect against the devastating brain disease.

The body of scientific knowledge pertaining to the effects of physical activity or exercise is equally compelling as the case for a healthy diet. A systematic review of the research by Pawel Posadzki and colleagues in 2020 found an overall 13% reduction in mortality rates and improvements in quality of life with exercise across studies, both in healthy populations and those with medical conditions. Among the studies that included participants with medical conditions, the largest improvements in quality of life were found among those with mental health conditions, underscoring the links between mental and physical health.

Despite the scientific evidence, most Americans fall short of recommended exercise regimens. The U.S. Department of Health and Human Services also publishes Physical Activity Guidelines for Americans. These include recommending that adults get at least 150 minutes per week of moderate-intensity aerobic exercise, or at least 75 minutes of vigorous-intensity aerobic activity, or some equivalent combination of these. The guidelines also recommend at least moderate-intensity, muscle-strengthening exercise involving all major muscle groups at least twice per week. Americans tend to do a bit better adhering to federal exercise guidelines than to dietary guidelines, though still with much room for improvement. According to a CDC report in 2022, among adults, 47% met the guidelines for aerobic activity, 31% met the guidelines for muscle strengthening activity, and 24% met both sets of guidelines.

Diet and exercise changes should be a compelling substitute threat for healthcare use. No one wants to develop heart disease, have a stroke, or suffer the declines in quality or length of life associated with the myriad of conditions that can be prevented, delayed, or mitigated through a healthy lifestyle. Health as a substitute for at least some healthcare would mean a reduced need for hospital care—the most expensive part of the U.S. healthcare system. However, humans are creatures of habit, and changing those habits takes much more effort than taking a pill and is more complicated. To change diet and activity levels, consumers first need to gain knowledge about what behaviors are likely to improve health outcomes based on the science, then apply that knowledge to assess and change their daily habits. Promoting optimal health requires persistent effort over a significant period of time for the new healthier habits to continue. In addition, if health plans do not cover the costs of their members switching to a healthier lifestyle, these expenses must be paid by consumers. These costs in terms of out-of-pocket expenses, time, energy, and attention are important in consumers' consideration of trading off behavior change today for better health outcomes tomorrow.

There are a variety of healthcare professionals with expertise to help guide consumers through these steps for those who are motivated to do so. Nutrition experts and exercise physiologists can help educate consumers about healthy diet and activity respectively and help design a customized plan. Psychologists work across health-related behaviors (e.g., eating, activity, smoking, stress management, sleep, relationships, mood) to help consumers change old unhealthy habits and adopt new healthier ones using behavior change techniques and therapies that have been found to be safe and effective in controlled studies. Finding these experts, navigating through insurance coverage rules, and coordinating across the care team present additional barriers. Traditional primary care practices do not include this expertise, though increasingly primary care physicians are integrating them into their practice. Those primary care practices without a psychologist leave diagnosing and treating behavioral and mental health conditions to the primary care providers, who have minimal training in these areas.

As with many other healthcare professionals, there is a significant shortage of psychologists, particularly since the pandemic resulted in an increase in the number of those seeking help with mental health. A survey by the American Psychological Association published in 2022 found that 60% of psychologists reported they are not accepting new patients and that, on average each month, psychologists are contacted by 16 people seeking services (excluding their current patients). Given these challenges, some consumers, health insurance companies, and employers are turning to health coaches as a substitute for licensed psychologists, the traditional behavior change experts. Psychologists have a doctoral degree and years of advanced education and clinical training in the science and practice of behavior change; they are also licensed through state boards. In contrast, there are no regulations overseeing those who call themselves health coaches, so they can have any type of training or none at all. The higher cost and significant shortage of psychologists and other licensed mental health professionals have provided an opportunity for alternatives to emerge. Health coaches are just one of the many substitutes for traditional healthcare. According to a 2022 McKinsey research report, the wellness industry is booming at an estimated $450 billion in spending and growing 5% annually. McKinsey identifies six segments within this industry:

1. *Health:* over-the-counter medicine, vitamins, and personal hygiene

2. *Fitness:* fitness clubs, studios, at-home fitness equipment, and fitness wearables

3. *Nutrition:* diet programs, subscription food services, nutrition apps, and juice cleanses

4. *Appearance:* skin care, dermo-cosmetics, hair care, and salon services

5. *Mindfulness:* counseling or therapy, meditation studios, and mindfulness apps

6. *Sleep:* sleep supplements, app-enabled sleep trackers, and other sleep-enhancing products

Half of consumers in the McKinsey survey reported wellness as a top priority. They are increasingly reporting a holistic view of wellness as integration across the six dimensions, rather than focusing on individual dimensions, and are reporting unmet needs for products and services that work. They found that 64% of consumers have incorporated wellness apps into their daily routine, and nearly 70% have incorporated online training and fitness services. Across dimensions, better health was the top priority, with 47% of consumers reporting it a high priority, and better sleep was a close second with 45% reporting it a high priority. In comparison, only 30% reported better appearance as a high priority, the lowest priority across the six dimensions. The same order was reported by millennials, but this generation had the highest percentage of individuals reporting each dimension a high priority, with 52% reporting better health as a high priority, 50% better sleep, and 37% better appearance. Millennials and Gen Z consumers have expressed the strongest interest in wellness products and services, particularly those that use their personal data for customized solutions.

Consumers are increasingly turning to influencers and celebrities to find new brands amidst a rapidly growing and crowded market of wellness products, services, and apps. Although consumers may be swayed by marketing in choosing which products to buy, the McKinsey survey demonstrates consumer interest in and preference for product categories that track with scientific research. For example, as more research links sleep and the microbiome (i.e., the microorganisms that live in the gastrointestinal tract, skin, and other parts of the body) to health outcomes, consumers have shown increased interest in products, services, and apps aiming to help them improve their sleep and the good microorganisms in their bodies.

Some employers have noted the strong demand for wellness and responded by offering a variety of wellness benefits to their employees. McKinsey found that 22% of consumers reported their employer offers flexible scheduling and, among those, 82% report using this benefit extensively or regularly. Healthy food and snacks were reported as an employer benefit by 18% of consumers, and among those, 89% reported using it extensively or regularly. In comparison to these wellness benefits, while 18% of consumers reported their employers offered telehealth healthcare services, among those, only 57% reported using this healthcare benefit extensively or regularly. Thus, as the pandemic demonstrated how rapidly traditional in-person healthcare could be substituted by telehealthcare, the McKinsey survey suggests that the choice of consumers and employers, the major buyers of healthcare, to substitute healthcare with wellness is a growing risk to the healthcare industry.

The Science and Regulation of Healthcare Substitutes

While the McKinsey survey indicated consumers are increasingly seeking wellness products that work as a priority over products that are natural or clean, it is unclear how consumers think about, understand, and make decisions about product effectiveness. Terms like natural are unregulated and have been used heavily in marketing efforts. However, the Federal Trade Commission (FTC) has taken action against companies that claim their products are "all natural" as this is deceptive when the product contains synthetic ingredients. The FTC has issued warnings to more than 600 companies engaged in marketing over-the-counter medications, homeopathic products, dietary supplements, and food products to notify them they are acting unlawfully if they fail to substantiate their claims. The companies receiving this notice include major pharmaceutical companies, consumer product brands, and retailers that are household names. The FTC warnings describe violations including failing to have a reasonable basis, reliable scientific evidence, or a well-controlled human clinical trial as well as misrepresenting the substantiation or the scientific or clinical proof of the claim.

Given that many consumers rely on influencers and celebrities to discover new products, companies also need to be aware of the FTC's (2021) notice on deceptive use of endorsements and testimonials. Product ratings and brand recognition also influence consumer purchasing decisions, perhaps by giving consumers more confidence that the product works regardless of whether it has been tested for effectiveness. Expecting consumers to find, read, and accurately assess the available science on the effectiveness of wellness-oriented products is unrealistic, leaving businesses in a challenging position as they aim to navigate consumer demand for effective products and the FTCs interpretation of what constitutes sufficient scientific evidence to meet their standards for truthful, evidence-based marketing claims.

Keeping up with and accurately assessing the evidence regarding what works is challenging enough for healthcare professionals and dramatically more so for lay consumers. Healthcare professionals are trained in assessing the type of evidence, which ranges from single case study observations (very weak evidence) to randomized double-blind placebo-controlled trials with large sample sizes (very strong evidence). Even with this training, synthesizing evidence across studies is a significant effort. Within the industry, professional organizations often issue treatment guidelines that reflect collective expert reviewers of the relevant scientific evidence in a given area to help guide clinicians in following the best evidence. These guidelines are periodically updated as new scientific evidence becomes available. Furthermore, licensed healthcare professionals are required to complete continuing education to maintain their licenses, providing regular opportunities to learn about the latest research on effectiveness of treatments at conferences and other educational venues. To count toward license renewal, these continuing education activities are regulated by accredited organizations to ensure the education is free from commercial bias.

Primary care professionals have guidance on clinical preventive services from the U.S. Preventive Services Task Force, an independent volunteer panel of experts in disease prevention and evidence-based medicine. The Task Force systematically reviews the scientific evidence and publishes recommendations for clinicians regarding providing screening, counseling, and preventive medication services to their patients across all age groups and major diseases. The Task Force also assigns a grade to help clinicians more easily understand the body of scientific evidence supporting or not the use of the clinical preventive service. The current Task Force (2018) grading system is shown in Table 2.

As of 2023, the most frequent grade is "I," as shown in Table 2, demonstrating how often the available scientific evidence leads to uncertainty about what works. Consumers in search of wellness products, services, and apps outside of the healthcare system lack such a grading system to guide their purchases. The development of a system to support consumer decision making at the point of purchase may help guide consumers to make decisions more aligned with their preference for products that work. An independent scientific evidence of effectiveness grade determined by experts alongside aggregate user star ratings of wellness products and services would provide a more complete picture of the product. This would also put pressure on businesses to shift resources from endorsements by celebrities and influencers to improving the validity of their products to earn a higher certainty of effectiveness grade.

The development of mobile health apps in the era of artificial intelligence holds promise in helping consumers achieve their health goals and reduce the need for healthcare. Yet health apps often operate outside of the regulations that provide protection to patients within the healthcare

Table 2 U.S. Preventive Services Task Force Grade Definitions After July 2012

Grade	Definition	Suggestions for Practice
A	The USPSTF recommends the service. There is high certainty that the net benefit is substantial.	Offer or provide this service.
B	The USPSTF recommends the service. There is high certainty that the net benefit is moderate or there is moderate certainty that the net benefit is moderate to substantial.	Offer or provide this service.
C	The USPSTF recommends selectively offering or providing this service to individual patients based on professional judgment and patient preferences. There is at least moderate certainty that the net benefit is small.	Offer or provide this service for selected patients depending on individual circumstances.
D	The USPSTF recommends against the service. There is moderate or high certainty that the service has no net benefit or that the harms outweigh the benefits.	Discourage the use of this service.
I Statement	The USPSTF concludes that the current evidence is insufficient to assess the balance of benefits and harms of the service. Evidence is lacking, of poor quality, or conflicting, and the balance of benefits and harms cannot be determined.	Read the clinical considerations section of USPSTF Recommendation Statement. If the service is offered, patients should understand the uncertainty about the balance of benefits and harms.

industry. In some cases, an app might not only be ineffective but may also increase the risk of harm. The Organisation for the Review of Care and Health Applications (ORCHA) was founded by United Kingdom National Health Service clinicians in 2015 to improve the safe use of digital health apps globally, offering traditional healthcare providers a bridge to credibly connect them to the booming consumer demand for health apps, which may help them reduce the threat of being substituted by the apps. ORCHA offers app developers an independent review and certification process, which requires that the app meet minimum quality standards and offers healthcare providers a library of apps that have passed the ORCHA tests and can be safely recommended to their patients.

The ORCHA app standards cover clinical or professional assurance, data and privacy, and usability and accessibility. The potential value of the ORCHA standards has been demonstrated in an independent review of apps intended to help with insomnia. In 2017, Simon Leigh and colleagues reported significant differences among the apps across the three basic ORCHA domains and that the app performance in these domains was not correlated with user ratings or number of downloads. Thus, the ORCHA quality standards appear to provide meaningful information that should be relevant to consumer decision making. ORCHA also launched a SAFE APPS campaign to help make consumers aware of the risks and benefits of apps and to help them make better health app choices.

To help app developers, the FTC provided guidance for understanding and complying with relevant federal laws and rules. Their interactive tool allows developers to answer a series of questions to determine if their app must meet federal rules pertaining to protected health information privacy and security, medical devices, and other consumer protections. This is particularly important as the FDA's regulations of medical devices have been continuously updated to address health apps. Whether a health app is regulated as a device depends on its general purpose or function, including its indications for use, that is, for the disease or condition the health app is intended to diagnose, treat, prevent, cure, or mitigate.

For health apps that meet the definition of a device, the FDA specifies that those meeting the minimal risk standard need not submit pre-market review applications or to register and list their software with the FDA. Health apps designed to help consumers self-manage their health condition or disease are considered minimal risk as long as they do not provide specific treatment suggestions. However, as traditional healthcare providers move into the wellness industry, for example prescribing daily regimen of fruits and vegetable consumption as part of the treatment plan, the regulatory lines will be blurred. Other healthcare products such as genetic testing performed by healthcare providers is often not covered by insurance. Companies like 23andMe have given consumers low-cost, direct-to-consumer home testing that puts relevant medical information in consumer hands like never before. After finding itself in regulatory trouble with the FDA, 23andMe Personal Genome Service Genetic Health Risk tests for 10 diseases or conditions became the first direct-to-consumer tests authorized by the FDA to help consumers with health decisions and health discussions with their providers.

The potential for technology to dramatically ease the shortage of healthcare professionals and simultaneously help consumers achieve their health and wellness goals is promising. The path through this transition is challenging and not without risk. While regulations and the nature of some health conditions limit potential substitutes for some hospital and emergency care, many aspects of healthcare face the threat of being substituted. As the buyers of healthcare consider potential performance and cost tradeoffs between current healthcare providers and available substitutes, the pressure is on to improve the value of healthcare.

REFERENCES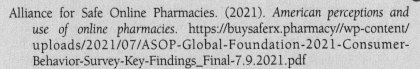

Alliance for Safe Online Pharmacies. (2021). *American perceptions and use of online pharmacies.* https://buysaferx.pharmacy//wp-content/uploads/2021/07/ASOP-Global-Foundation-2021-Consumer-Behavior-Survey-Key-Findings_Final-7.9.2021.pdf

American Psychological Association. (2022, November). *Psychologists struggle to meet demand amid mental health crisis.* https://www.apa.org/pubs/reports/practitioner/2022-covid-psychologist-workload

Beyene, K. A., Sheridan, J., & Aspden, T. (2014). Prescription medication sharing: a systematic review of the literature. *American Journal of Public Health, 104*(4), e15–e26. https://doi.org/10.2105/AJPH.2013.301823

Centers for Disease Control and Prevention. (2023, May). *COVID data tracker.* https://covid.cdc.gov/covid-data-tracker/#vaccination-states-jurisdictions

Centers for Disease Control and Prevention. (2023, August). *Federal retail pharmacy program: A collaboration between the federal government, states and territories, and 21 national pharmacy partners and independent pharmacy networks nationwide.* Centers for Disease Control and Prevention Archive. https://archive.cdc.gov/#/details?url=https://www.cdc.gov/vaccines/covid-19/retail-pharmacy-program/index.html

Federal Trade Commission. (2021). *Notice of penalty offenses concerning deceptive or unfair conduct around endorsements and testimonials.* https://www.ftc.gov/system/files/attachments/penalty-offenses-concerning-endorsements/notice-penalty_offenses-endorsements.pdf

Federal Trade Commission. (2023, April 13). *FTC warns almost 700 marketing companies that they could face civil penalties if they can't back up their product claims.* https://www.ftc.gov/news-events/news/press-releases/2023/04/ftc-warns-almost-700-marketing-companies-they-could-face-civil-penalties-if-they-cant-back-their

Goldsworthy, R. C., & Mayhorn, C. B. (2009). Prescription medication sharing among adolescents: prevalence, risks, and outcomes.

The *Journal of Adolescent Health: Official Publication of the Society for Adolescent Medicine, 45*(6), 634–637. https://doi.org/10.1016/j.jadohealth.2009.06.002

Hill, E., Goodwill, A. M., Gorelik, A., & Szoeke, C. (2019). Diet and biomarkers of Alzheimer's disease: a systematic review and meta-analysis. *Neurobiology of Aging, 76*, 45–52. https://doi.org/10.1016/j.neurobiolaging.2018.12.008

J. D. Power. (2022, July 28). *Innovations at retail pharmacies accelerate as digital competition, health and wellness offerings grow, J.D. Power Finds.* https://www.jdpower.com/business/press-releases/2022-us-pharmacy-study

Karam, G., Agarwal, A., Sadeghirad, B., Jalink, M., Hitchcock, C. L., Ge, L., Kiflen, R., Ahmed, W., Zea, A. M., Milenkovic, J., Chedrawe, M. A., Rabassa, M., El Dib, R., Goldenberg, J. Z., Guyatt, G. H., Boyce, E., & Johnston, B. C. (2023). Comparison of seven popular structured dietary programmes and risk of mortality and major cardiovascular events in patients at increased cardiovascular risk: systematic review and network meta-analysis. *BMJ, 380*, e072003. https://doi.org/10.1136/bmj-2022-072003

Lee, E. L., Richards, N., Harrison, J., & Barnes, J. (2022). Prevalence of use of traditional, complementary and alternative medicine by the general population: A systematic review of national studies published from 2010 to 2019. *Drug Safety, 45*(7), 713–735. https://doi.org/10.1007/s40264-022-01189-w

Leigh, S., Ouyang, J., & Mimnagh, C. (2017). Effective? Engaging? Secure? Applying the ORCHA-24 framework to evaluate apps for chronic insomnia disorder. *Evidence-Based Mental Health, 20*(4), e20. https://doi.org/10.1136/eb-2017-102751

McKinsey & Company. (2022, September 19). *Still feeling good: The US wellness market continues to boom.* https://www.mckinsey.com/industries/consumer-packaged-goods/our-insights/still-feeling-good-the-us-wellness-market-continues-to-boom

Micha, R., Peñalvo, J. L., Cudhea, F., Imamura, F., Rehm, C. D., & Mozaffarian, D. (2017). Association between dietary factors and mortality from heart disease, stroke, and type 2 diabetes in the United States. *JAMA, 317*(9), 912–924. https://doi.org/10.1001/jama.2017.0947

National Association of Boards of Pharmacy. (2022). *Rogue Rx activity report.* https://nabp.pharmacy/wp-content/uploads/2022/10/Rogue-Rx-Activity-Report-Disrupting-Illegal-Online-Pharmacies-2022.pdf

Newman, D. J., & Cragg, G. M. (2020). Natural products as sources of new drugs over the nearly four decades from 01/1981 to 09/2019.

Journal of Natural Products, 83(3), 770–803. https://doi.org/10.1021/acs.jnatprod.9b01285

Office of the National Coordinator for Health Information Technology. (2023 March). *Use of telemedicine among office-based physicians, 2021* [Data Brief No. 65]. https://www.healthit.gov/data/data-briefs/use-telemedicine-among-office-based-physicians-2021

Organisation for Economic Co-operation and Development. (2020). *Trade in counterfeit pharmaceutical products.* OECD Publishing. https://www.oecd-ilibrary.org/sites/a7c7e054-en/index.html?itemId=/content/publication/a7c7e054-en

Ozawa, S., Evans, D. R., Bessias, S., Haynie, D. G., Yemeke, T. T., Laing, S. K., & Herrington, J. E. (2018). Prevalence and estimated economic burden of substandard and falsified medicines in low- and middle-income countries: A systematic review and meta-analysis. *JAMA network open, 1*(4), e181662. https://doi.org/10.1001/jamanetworkopen.2018.1662

Pew Research Center. (2017, February 2). *2. Americans' health care behaviors and use of conventional and alternative medicine.* Pew Research Center. https://www.pewresearch.org/science/2017/02/02/americans-health-care-behaviors-and-use-of-conventional-and-alternative-medicine/

Posadzki, P., Pieper, D., Bajpai, R., Makaruk, H., Könsgen, N., Neuhaus, A. L., & Semwal, M. (2020). Exercise/physical activity and health outcomes: An overview of Cochrane systematic reviews. *BMC Public Health, 20,* 1–12. https://doi.org/10.1186/s12889-020-09855-3

U.S. Department of Agriculture and U.S. Department of Health and Human Services. (2020, December) *Dietary guidelines for Americans, 2020–2025, 9th Edition.* https://www.dietaryguidelines.gov/sites/default/files/2020-12/Dietary_Guidelines_for_Americans_2020-2025.pdf

U.S. Preventive Services Task Force. (2018, October). *Grade definitions.* https://www.uspreventiveservicestaskforce.org/uspstf/about-uspstf/methods-and-processes/grade-definitions

FURTHER READINGS

Federal Trade Commission. (2022, December) *Mobile health app interactive tool.* https://www.ftc.gov/business-guidance/resources/mobile-health-apps-interactive-tool

Nahin, R. L., Barnes, P. M., & Stussman, B. J. (2016). *Expenditures on complementary health approaches: United States, 2012.* National Health Statistics Reports, National Center for Health Statistics. https://www.cdc.gov/nchs/data/nhsr/nhsr095.pdf

Pellegrin, K. L. (2023). Cerebral: Response to service failures in a booming digital mental health market. In *Sage Business Cases*. SAGE. https://doi.org/10.4135/9781071920305

Tang, M., Chernew, M. E., & Mehrotra, A. (2022). How emerging telehealth models challenge policymaking. *The Milbank Quarterly*, *100*(3), 650–672. https://doi.org/10.1111/1468-0009.12584

U.S. Food and Drug Administration. (2020 September 21). *BeSafeRx: Frequently asked questions*. https://www.fda.gov/drugs/besaferx-your-source-online-pharmacy-information/besaferx-frequently-asked-questions-faqs

U.S. Food and Drug Administration. (2023, December 22). *Counterfeit medicine*. https://www.fda.gov/drugs/buying-using-medicine-safely/counterfeit-medicine

World Health Organization. (2023, August 10). *Traditional medicine has a long history of contributing to conventional medicine and continues to hold promise*. https://www.who.int/news-room/feature-stories/detail/traditional-medicine-has-a-long-history-of-contributing-to-conventional-medicine-and-continues-to-hold-promise

Competition

Trends in the Healthcare Industry

G rowth and profitability have made the healthcare industry an attractive opportunity for suppliers and investors while making it a financial burden to the consumers and employers who pay for it. The health plans that make payments to healthcare providers on behalf of consumers insulate the consumer from both the risk of catastrophic expenses and the benefits of being a savvy healthcare shopper. Consumers, however, are increasingly shopping for health and wellness products and services they cannot find within the conventional healthcare system. Meanwhile, employers are increasingly doing it themselves, self-insuring their employees and providing healthcare for their employees, to reduce the cost of the benefits packages they offer to attract and retain employees. Noting the increasing demand for health and wellness, employers are adding these perks to their packages.

The profitability of the healthcare industry will continue to be shaped by the nature of the competition therein. According to Porter, the extent to which rivalry among existing competitors affects profitability depends first on the intensity of the competition and then on the basis of the competition.

Intensity of Competition

The intensity of competition in an industry is determined by several factors, including the number and size of the competitors, the rate of industry growth, exit barriers, and competitor motivation and signaling. In the healthcare industry, consolidation among competitors, growth deceleration, and employers' motivation to reduce the cost of healthcare shape the competition intensity.

Number and Size of Competitors

Where there are many competitors or the competitors are generally equal in size and power, competition intensity is greater. In the healthcare industry, the number and size of the competitors varies by segment. For example, while there are many pharmaceutical companies, they compete globally and range from small startups to giant corporations that have many divisions. In contrast, the many services that can only or optimally be delivered in person like hospitals, medical practices, and pharmacies, including those that are owned by national chains, compete locally, and each local market is different. In some local markets, the providers compete intensely while others are healthcare deserts.

Industry Growth

Intensity increases when growth is slow. After decades of accelerating, healthcare industry growth slowed in the decade prior to the COVID-19 pandemic in the United States and the other 19 countries within the Organisation for Economic Cooperation and Development (OECD) that have data available over a 50-year period, based on analyses reported by Sheila Smith and colleagues in 2022. They found that as a percent of gross domestic product (GDP), healthcare spending grew from approximately 6% in the United States and 5% in the other OECD countries in 1970 to approximately 16% in the United States and 9% in the other countries in 2010. From 2010 to 2019, healthcare spending growth slowed, taking less than an additional 1% of GDP, with the United States healthcare spending at less than 17% of GDP and the other OECD countries at less than 10% as of 2019. Smith and team analyzed real per capita healthcare spending growth from 1970 through 2019 to identify key growth drivers, including the changes driving the deceleration of growth, summarized in Figure 1. Across the 50-year period and the 20 OECD countries, income and medical technologies were the key healthcare industry growth drivers, while insurance and population demographics were much less important. Income played a smaller role in the United States, accounting for 39% of per capita spending growth, compared to 52% of growth in other OECD countries. Medical technologies, defined by the researchers as the set of treatment options, including drugs, devices, and procedures, as well as the organization of care delivery, accounted for a much larger portion of per capita spending growth in the United States (46%) compared to the other OECD countries (33%), estimates which include the effects of both technology and medical price inflation. In the United States, the expansion of insurance played a larger role in per capita healthcare spending growth (6%) relative to other OECD countries (2%). This is, in part, due to the higher portion and smaller changes in the portion of the population covered by insurance in other OECD countries, and thus smaller changes in out-of-pocket spending. Finally, changing demographics, largely aging populations, accounted for only 8.5% of per capita spending growth in the United States and 13% of spending growth in the other OECD countries over the 50-year period.

During the 2010s, when industry growth slowed as a percent of GDP, Smith and colleagues found a somewhat different pattern of growth drivers compared to the aggregate 50-year period prepandemic. Across countries, the income effect as the primary driver of per capita healthcare industry growth has increased, particularly outside of the United States. Growth in income had slowed since 2009 due to the Great Recession. However, this was a temporary and lagged effect. Smith and colleagues noted that the effect of changes in income is delayed because health plans make payments for so much of healthcare spending, which buffers household demand. From 2010 to 2019, the aging population became the second largest driver of growth (accounting for 29% of per capita spending growth in the United States and 35% in the other OECD countries). Smith and colleagues found that the aging of the population will continue to be a driver of growth in healthcare industry spending over the next two decades. In the 2010s, medical technology played a much smaller role in driving per capita growth (23% in the United States and only 3% in the other OECD countries). It is noteworthy that medical price inflation, which is included in the technology estimate, was relatively lower during the 2010s. In the United States, lower price inflation was likely due both to the impact of the Affordable Care Act on reducing payments for Medicare, particularly for hospital care, and to reduced price of capital in hospitals and long-term care facilities.

Even when excluding relative medical price from the estimate (which was 8% in the United States over the 50-year period and 7% in the 2010s), the reduced impact of medical technology as a growth driver is still evident (accounting for 38% of the per capita growth in the United States over the 50-year period and 30% in the 2010s). The declining contribution of medical technology may be due to changes in the nature of innovation within the industry or to constraints on implementation of new medical technologies by the health insurance plans (both private and government payers) that make coverage decisions. Additional analyses by the researchers suggest the trend of declining contribution of medical technologies to the growth of healthcare spending began in 2004 and is largely consistent across countries.

There is also an interaction effect between income and technology, which captures differences in the rates of adoption of and spending on new medical technology as demand for access to these technologies differs based on income within each country's insurance pools. This interaction effect accounted for 23% of the per capita growth in healthcare spending in the United States and 30% of growth in the other OECD countries over the 50-year period. From 2010 to 2019, this income-technology interaction effect accounted for 24% of the spending growth in the United States and 36% in other OECD countries. Assuming that any industry effects from the pandemic are temporary, the drivers of the shift from healthcare spending

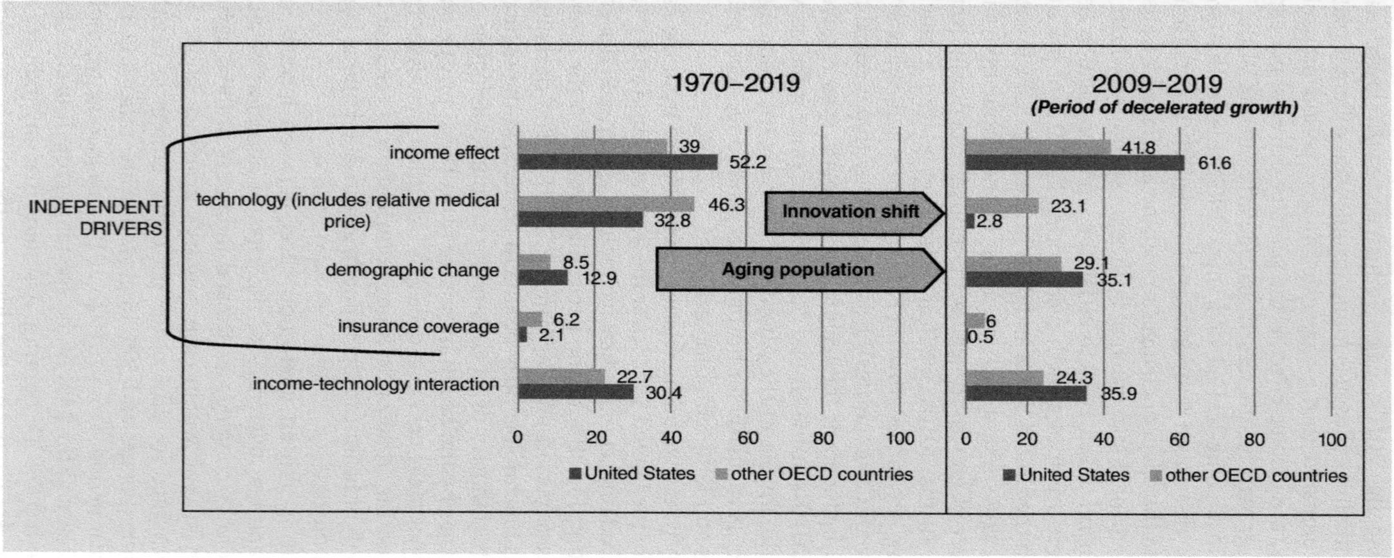

Figure 1   Percent of Growth in Real Per Capita Healthcare Spending Attributed to Key Drivers

growth acceleration over many decades to decelerated growth in the decade leading up to the pandemic will likely persist into the foreseeable future. If this assumption is correct, healthcare industry competition will continue to intensify as will constraints on the adoption of expensive new treatments.

Exit Barriers

Significant exit barriers increase competition intensity by keeping more rivals in the game longer. In the most expensive segment of the healthcare industry, hospital care, the exit barriers are significant due to large investments in specialized equipment and facilities. This is also the case for drug developers and manufacturers. Across the healthcare industry, suppliers of labor (e.g., physicians, nurses, pharmacists, and other healthcare professionals) face significant exit barriers given their substantial investments of time and tuition expenses in these specialized careers.

Competitor Motivation

Intensity increases when competitors are highly committed, aspire to industry leadership, and have goals that transcend performance within the industry. In the healthcare industry, there are at least two significant examples of this. The entrance of global technology companies into the healthcare industry reflects this increasing intensity of competition. While Amazon's history demonstrates high commitment and aspiration for industry leadership, their goals in healthcare go far beyond adding another industry segment to diversify their offerings. If Amazon can alter the healthcare industry, this may have a company-wide effect of reducing labor costs and improving employee health. While corporations involved in the healthcare industry may be focused on profits, state and federal governments that run health plans (e.g., Medicare and Medicaid) and provide services (e.g., Veterans Affairs system, state hospitals) may be more focused on serving the political goals of the elected officials who develop or oversee these systems rather than their performance within the healthcare industry.

Signaling Between Competitors

Intensity increases when competitors cannot easily read each other's signals. To the extent that prices are a key signal, the opacity within the healthcare industry has increased intensity of competition. Efforts to achieve meaningful price transparency may mitigate this effect on profitability by improving market efficiencies. The differing goals among private and public competitors also interfere with market-based signal clarity in the healthcare industry.

Basis of Competition

The dimensions of competition, price based or based on other factors, have an impact on profitability. Where rivals compete on price, profitability is lower. Price competition is more likely when there is little difference between competitors' products and services and when there are low switching costs for buyers. The regulatory requirements to meet certain standards, such as licensure and accreditation requirements and U.S. Food and Drug Administration (FDA) approvals, along with complexities that make it difficult for consumers to accurately judge clinical quality can make differentiation a challenge in the healthcare industry. Price competition is also more likely when fixed costs are high and marginal costs are low, expansion requires large increments to be efficient, and the product or service is perishable. Hospitals and drug manufacturers face all these conditions. The perishability of hospital beds is similar to that of hotels without the same ability to advertise discounted *off-season* rates. Medications also have a shelf life that factors into pricing. As prices become more transparent in the healthcare industry and there is questionable quality for the prices, price competition will likely increase. Providers that can make a compelling case that they are different in ways that matter to consumers will be better able to shift from price to quality competition. The Centers for Medicare and Medicaid Services (CMS) has created quality measures and a composite star rating system to improve comparison shopping. Consumers can use the Medicare Care Compare website to compare star ratings of local hospitals, nursing homes, home health services, hospice, and dialysis facilities. Making these ratings public was a major shift toward transparency in an industry that had historically kept quality matters closely guarded.

If rivals compete on the same dimension, whether price, product feature, service, or brand, profitability tends to decrease. In contrast, in industries where different customer groups have different needs, some price sensitive and others with a variety of preferences for product and service features, rivals can compete on different dimensions, resulting in more customers whose needs are met as rivals segment and target each group. In the healthcare industry, all people are current or, at least, potential customers, so there are opportunities to identify and segment based on the diverse needs, priorities, and preferences of consumers.

Profitability Postpandemic

A 2023 McKinsey & Company report predicted that pandemic-related inflation and staff shortages will affect profitability within the U.S. healthcare industry for several years before returning to prepandemic levels. Thus, they reduced their previously projected overall five-year compound annual growth rate in healthcare industry profitability from 6% to a projection of 4%. However, within the industry, McKinsey projects there will be winners, those segments with expected profitability growth greater than 10%, and losers whom they project will experience negative growth. Overall, the health plan segment is expected to have the greatest growth in profitability. Within this segment, the winners are the commercial private health plans as well as Medicare Advantage plans, the latter of which will grow due to the aging population and their increasing preference for Advantage plans over traditional Medicare. Growth in these health plans is expected to offset the projected negative growth in Medicaid, which is expected to see lower enrollment as eligibility requirements that were paused during the pandemic are again enforced. The projected profitability within the health plan segment will likely accelerate the shift from fully insured to self-insured employers. McKinsey projects that by 2026 total health plan earnings before interest, taxes, depreciation, and amortization (EBITDA) from government plans (dominated by Medicare Advantage profits) will be larger than EBITDA from group and individual plans combined. In the service and technology segment, the winners are projected to be those companies focused on healthcare data analytics, software, and platforms. The key losers are within the provider segment, specifically independent labs within the diagnostic subsegment and skilled nursing facilities within the post-acute care subsegment. Within the pharmacy services segment, retail, and online medication dispensers are projected to be profitability growth losers.

Dimensions of Competition in Customer Segments

Given that the postpandemic world of healthcare is likely to see a continuation of the slower growth seen in the prepandemic decade, competition among rivals will likely continue to intensify. However, given that price and quality information are now more available in a meaningful way, there will likely be more opportunities to compete on these dimensions that target specific customer needs and preferences.

Employer-Driven Competition

Employers are driving competition where health insurance companies have not. Given the current and projected profitability of private health insurance, health plans continue to raise premiums to maintain those profits while healthcare costs escalate. Employers and, ultimately, their employees are the ones who pay for these cost increases with higher premiums and out-of-pocket expenses. To reduce the impact of premiums as a business expense, employers are increasingly opting for self-insurance. In contrast to the health insurance companies that pass along cost increases to premium payers and to consumers who generally lack meaningful information and expertise to be savvy shoppers of high quality, cost-effective care within the complexities of the healthcare industry, employers have begun tackling healthcare as a key business priority.

The Health Transformation Alliance is a nonprofit cooperative that collectively spends more than $27 billion per year on healthcare for its employees among roughly 50 large, self-insured American employers, including JPMorgan Chase, which is led by healthcare transformation advocate Jamie Dimon. With a mission similar to the defunct Buffett-Bezos-Dimon venture, Haven, this cooperative has greater buying power than each employer individually. By aggregating data across employers, they have developed some solutions, including identifying providers and treatments associated with better outcomes as well as consumer technologies to better engage employees in health decisions.

One of the more controversial and risky solutions being used by some self-insured employers is carving out specialty drugs, a category of drugs that are typically very expensive with no generic alternatives and require complex administration and more intensive monitoring such as drugs that treat cancer, rheumatoid arthritis, HIV/AIDS, multiple sclerosis, and hepatitis C. Specialty drugs typically require support from a specialty pharmacy because of complex storage and preparation requirements and are usually administered in a medical office or hospital. Given these requirements, they account for the largest increase in drug spending. According to the U.S. Department of Health and Human Services (HHS), while the total number of specialty drug prescriptions increased less than 1% from 2016 to 2021, total specialty drug spending increased 43% to more than $300 billion, half of the total prescription drug spending, in 2021. However, this analysis does not account for manufacturer rebates, which are often substantial for specialty drugs as an incentive for health plans (and the pharmacy benefit managers they use to control drug spending) to include these drugs on their formulary. There are concerns, however, that the rebated savings are not passed on to consumers directly, though they may be used by health plans to mitigate premium increases.

Employers face a key challenge in considering benefits for specialty drugs, which are critically important to achieving optimal health outcomes for their employees. As the Inflation Reduction Act caps Medicare beneficiary out-of-pocket spending on drugs and limits drug price increases paid by Medicare to the rate of inflation, prices paid through private insurance coverage will continue to grow to subsidize the capped government prices paid. In a carve out, specialty drugs are excluded from the employer's healthcare coverage, and the employer uses an Alternative Funding Program (AFP) service to seek other funding sources. Employees who need these drugs, but do not have coverage for them from their employer health plan because of the carve out, may be eligible for Patient Assistant Programs (PAP). Pharmaceutical companies establish PAPs as charitable foundations for those who do not have coverage for these drugs from private or public sources and have a documented financial need based on income and assets. If the PAP funding request is denied, the employer reimburses the employee for the cost of the drug. If funding is arranged through the AFP, the employer may receive a portion of the savings. This specialty drug carve-out model has received substantial scrutiny for putting patients at risk of delays in receiving the drug and the potential for the AFP to source these drugs from pharmacies outside the United States. In addition, legal and ethical questions have been raised about these practices. Aside from the employee and regulatory risks, the pharmaceutical manufacturers that have PAPs may respond to the loss of specialty drug revenue from employer carve outs by changing how they operate to prevent the use of AFPs.

Pricing and Access to New Prescription Drugs in a Global Market

How U.S. employers and employees respond to not only the increasing cost of healthcare for themselves but also the growing burden on them to subsidize healthcare for others may have significant effects on the cost and availability of treatments globally. According to a 2021 RAND report, the United States overall pays 256% of what 32 other OECD countries pay for prescription drugs. While this estimate does not include rebates and other discounts as these data are not readily available, analyses indicated the results are similar even after adjusting based on estimated discounts in the United States and other countries. Across the 33 OECD countries in the analysis, the United States accounted for 24% of the volume and 58% of the sales of prescription drugs. A key finding in the RAND analysis is that the United States pays even more, 344% of what other OECD countries pay, for brand-name originator drugs (i.e., those manufactured by the company, or its successor, that obtained the first regulatory approval). RAND reported that, in the United States, brand-name originator drugs account for only 11% of prescription drug volume, but 82% of prescription drug spending. While the United States pays over three times more than other OECD countries for these brand-name drugs, the RAND analysis also found that the United States pays less, only 84% of what other OECD countries pay, for unbranded generic drugs.

Given that drug pricing is relatively less controlled by regulation in the United States and given the U.S. market's willingness to pay the premium on brand-name originator drugs, the United States also tends to get access to new drugs faster than other countries. According to the FDA, 68% of new drugs approved in 2022 were approved in the United States first. The FDA has implemented four pathways for expediting drug approvals to address U.S. demand for new treatments.

Fast Track

Drug companies may request the Fast Track designation for a drug they are developing for a serious condition with no current available therapy or if their drug shows some advantage over available therapies. The FDA reviews the request and makes a determination within 60 days. If approved, the Fast Track designation allows for more frequent communication between the company and the FDA, review of the marketing application in sections rather than waiting until the entire application is completed, and potential eligibility for accelerated approval and priority review pathways.

Breakthrough Therapy

When preliminary clinical evidence indicates that a drug in development for a serious condition shows not only some advantage but also clear and substantial advantage over available therapies, the FDA offers the breakthrough therapy designation. The drug company may request this designation, and the FDA may encourage the company to do so based on potential benefits. This designation provides the same advantages as the Fast Track with additional, more intensive FDA guidance and commitment beginning with the early phase of clinical trials.

Priority Review

When the FDA receives an application for a Fast Track or breakthrough therapy, they determine whether the review process should follow the standard 10-month timeline or the six-month priority review timeline. This decision is based on their assessment of whether the drug would offer significant improvement in safety or effectiveness relative to standard applications.

Accelerated Approval

In the standard FDA process, a new drug must show it achieves its intended clinical benefit to receive approval. Because this process can delay approval, the accelerated approval process allows Fast Track and breakthrough therapies to be approved based on a surrogate or intermediate clinical endpoint if there is adequate scientific evidence that the endpoint is likely to predict the intended clinical benefit. This approach may allow faster approval for a new cancer drug based on achieving a target lab result or tumor size rather than waiting for evidence of the drug's intended effect on survival rates over years. The FDA's accelerated approval is contingent upon the company continuing the research to confirm the drug achieves the intended clinical benefit. If the confirmatory trials are successful, the approval converts to a traditional approval. If these trials fail to verify the benefit, the FDA may withdraw approval or require labeling changes to reflect the results.

The accelerated approval process offers the greatest potential reduction in time to approval. It was established in 1992 in response to the demand for HIV/AIDS treatments. According to analyses of FDA data conducted by Ginny Beakes-Read and colleagues in 2022, the accelerated approval process has been used to bring hundreds of new drugs to market over three decades, particularly for infectious diseases and cancer, giving U.S. consumers access to these treatments years earlier than they otherwise would have. Beakes-Read and colleagues conducted their analysis in the midst of criticisms that the FDA's accelerated approval pathway may cut some corners, specifically that the FDA has been too lax in its enforcement of the postapproval follow-up studies to confirm the clinical benefit. In their analysis of the first two decades after implementation of this pathway, Beakes-Read and colleagues found that 88 (79%) of the 111 accelerated approvals from 1992 to 2011 had completed the confirmatory trials and converted the accelerated approval to a traditional approval. The average time to convert was nearly five years. Less than 5% of the drugs with accelerated approvals were still pending confirmatory studies. Of the 16% of drugs with accelerated approval withdrawn, the average time to withdrawal was more than nine years.

From 2012 to 2021, Beakes-Read and colleagues found that the total number of drugs with accelerated approval was more than the previous two decades combined. Given their more recent approval, a greater percent of the drugs from this time frame were still pending confirmatory trials. To examine concerns about potential abuses of this accelerated pathway, Beakes-Read and colleagues analyzed the status of the 30 drugs that had not completed confirmatory trials within the median of 3.2 years after receiving accelerated approval. Of these 30, 10 were on time based on the original milestone; 12 were on time, based on revised milestones; five were under consideration by the FDA for potential withdrawal; and only three were not on schedule.

While this analysis of the FDA's accelerated approval process has demonstrated its success in bringing new drugs to market faster, it also bolsters the case for greater scrutiny of these drug prices. Approved drugs without confirmation of intended clinical benefit might not be covered by health plans, which may then leverage that ability to deny coverage in the negotiation on price until the benefit is confirmed. In particular, the self-insured employers and their employees who subsidize the cost of drugs for others might be effective at challenging pricing of drugs with accelerated approval. Given that all the new drugs approved through the accelerated process in 2022 were specialty drugs, access leverage in price negotiation may be a more promising approach than the risky carve-out strategy.

Hospital Price Transparency in Local Markets

As employers collaborate nationally to push for greater price competition among the global pharmaceutical companies that rely on increasingly high prices paid by private U.S. health plans to cover increasingly heavy discounts to Medicare, Medicaid, and international markets, regional employer groups are taking on the bigger healthcare costs that are nestled within their local markets. With hospital care expenditures adding up to more than twice that of prescription drug expenditures nationwide, the local hospital markets are essential to navigate. A common strategy used by these regional groups is increasing price transparency within these local markets.

The work of the Employers Forum of Indiana (EFI) has not only shed light on prices within Indiana's local hospital markets but also produced a tool that illuminates both price and quality in Indiana and across the nation. In 2017, EFI commissioned its first RAND study to identify prices paid by self-funded employer-sponsored health plans for hospital care in Indiana. To allow easy comparison, the study reported price relative to Medicare's price for the same service at the same facility. Overall, these employers paid more than twice the Medicare price for inpatient care (relative price of 2.17) and more than three times the Medicare price for hospital-based outpatient care (relative price of 3.58). The employers generally paid higher prices to the larger hospital systems. Most importantly, the RAND report included prices by individual provider, giving employers greater leverage in negotiations.

A subsequent report by Christopher Whaley and colleagues in 2022 expanded the analyses to include data from all 50 states. In 2020, across hospital inpatient and outpatient services, employers and private health plans paid more than double the Medicare prices. However, the variation across states was substantial, with prices in some states less than 1.75 times that of Medicare prices and more than 3.1 times that of Medicare prices in other states. EFI-founding CEO, current board member, and economist, David Kelleher, and Dr. Gloria Sachdev, current CEO and pharmacist, have been the driving force behind the RAND reports and price transparency initiative in Indiana, which have gained national attention from employers and politicians alike. EFI has also developed Sage Transparency, a free dashboard that allows users to compare price and quality for hospitals across the United States. Dr. Sachdev has advocated locally and nationally for policy change to improve healthcare affordability, giving employer groups across the nation a voice and call to action.

Competing for the Aging Market

As employers have moved into the health insurance market as a strategy to tackle an important employee benefit and business expense, health insurance companies have shifted to compete for the lucrative and growing aging population of Medicare beneficiaries. McKinsey projects that the health plan profit pool from Medicare Advantage will be 50% greater than the profits from commercial plans by 2026. Medicare beneficiaries may choose traditional fee-for-service Medicare (Parts A and B) or a private managed care Medicare Advantage plan (Medicare Part C) offered by a Medicare-approved insurance company with or without Part D coverage. For each beneficiary who chooses a Medicare Advantage plan, Medicare pays the insurance company a fixed amount per month to provide coverage. In theory, this shifts Medicare's (i.e., taxpayers') financial risk for that enrollee to the insurance company and allows the private sector to compete for beneficiaries with a variety of plan options to meet the market needs. Medicare also pays the insurance company a set amount per beneficiary (referred to as a rebate), $196 per enrollee per month on average, as of 2023, to provide additional benefits (e.g., vision, hearing, dental coverage) not covered by traditional Medicare. This means taxpayers are subsidizing these expanded benefits and the profits the insurance companies make on these expanded offerings.

The Medicare Payment Advisory Commission (MedPAC) is the independent federal agency established to advise Congress on the Medicare program. While they strongly support the inclusion of private plans as an option for beneficiaries, MedPAC reports that reliable information about whether beneficiaries use or value these extra benefits is lacking. According to MedPAC (2023), the average rebate amount paid by Medicare to the insurance companies has more than doubled since 2018, and these rebates account for 17% of the payments health insurance companies receive from Medicare.

The potential savings to Medicare is reflected in MedPAC's report that the average Medicare Advantage plan bid to Medicare for Part A and B benefits is 17% less than the projected spending for these enrollee benefits under traditional Medicare. However, MedPAC reports that Medicare's actual total spending on Medicare Advantage enrollees (which includes the rebate payments to health insurance companies for extra benefits) is 6% higher than it would have been had they been enrolled in traditional Medicare. This is, in part, due to how Medicare sets benchmarks and risk scores for payment and, in part, because healthier beneficiaries tend to choose Medicare Advantage plans over traditional Medicare (and often switch to traditional Medicare when they become sicker), increasing the profits to health insurance companies while Medicare remains at financial risk for the highest-risk beneficiaries. MedPAC reports Medicare has a consistent history of paying more for Medicare Advantage than for traditional Medicare.

MedPAC also criticizes Medicare for providing quality bonus payments to Medicare Advantage plans that are not based on validated quality indicators. In their review of the available research comparing Medicare Advantage and traditional Medicare, MedPAC reported that most study designs are too flawed to reach solid conclusions. They reported that the evidence overall does not suggest that Medicare Advantage actually offers a quality advantage over traditional Medicare, despite the additional cost to Medicare and taxpayers. Furthermore, the Medicare Advantage star ratings that bonus payments are based on are aggregated and might not be reflective of quality in a beneficiary's local community, making these measures less meaningful from the shopper's perspective.

Enrollment in Medicare Advantage plans indicates they offer beneficiaries compelling value or have effective marketing campaigns. According to a 2023 Kaiser Family Foundation (KFF) publication, enrollment in Medicare Advantage plans has increased from 19% of Medicare beneficiaries in 2007 to 51% in 2023, and the average beneficiary now has access to 43 Medicare Advantage plans offered by 9 companies. Two companies, UnitedHealthcare and Humana, account for 47% of Medicare Advantage enrollees nationwide and 75% or more of enrollees in nearly one-third of U.S. counties. Thus, the intensity of competition among companies offering Medicare Advantage plans varies regionally. The competitive landscape is shifting, at least in some markets where hospitals and doctors are dropping Medicare Advantage plans because of low payments for services and other challenges posed by the managed care approaches of these plans. Where these healthcare suppliers have market power, they will either dampen beneficiary enthusiasm for Medicare Advantage plans by further restricting access to local providers or reduce the profitability of these plans by commanding higher payments. Either way, the employers who have been squeezing health insurance companies out through self-insurance and more successfully offering cost-effective health plans for their employees may be well positioned to enter the profitable Medicare Advantage market, particularly for their own retirees.

The competition for the aging population goes beyond Medicare Advantage plans. Aging consumers, including many who have not yet reached the age of Medicare eligibility, are increasingly seeking care from longevity clinics. These clinics typically provide services not covered by health insurance, including full-body scans in patients without symptoms or risk factors, biological age tests, and a variety of supplements and treatments, including many that have not been approved by regulators as safe and effective. These clinics tend to provide a level of personal attention not common in the stressed healthcare system that operates on health insurance. In 2023, the *Wall Street Journal* reported these clinics are responding to consumer demand for this attention and for a focus on wellness and prevention rather than on treating disease, with annual clinic fees ranging from $2,800 to $100,000 per year. They also reported a rapid increase in venture capital investments in longevity clinics, up to $57 million globally in 2022, with 70% of these investments focused on the U.S. market where growth seems most promising.

Competing for the Price-Sensitive Market

Consumers with high discretionary income are not the only segment being targeted for new services in the United States, where a high percent of the population is uninsured relative to other developed countries. While Medicaid insurance is designed for low-income consumers, those who are close but not eligible and do not have insurance through an employer often forgo purchasing individual insurance, particularly as premiums increase. In addition, those with Medicaid may find access to providers more difficult because Medicaid usually pays providers less than Medicare, so fewer of them accept Medicaid patients.

Community health centers serve as the safety net providers for low-income populations. Centers that receive the Federally Qualified Health Center (FQHC) designation qualify for higher reimbursement for Medicaid patients and are required to see any patient regardless of insurance status. Individuals who do not have insurance are charged using an income-based sliding scale fee schedule. FQHC's are also eligible to operate pharmacies under the 340B Program, which gives them access to significant discounts in buying medications. According to the federal Health Resources and Services Administration, the 1,370 community health centers nationwide collected a total of more than $28 billion in patient related revenue serving more than 30 million patients in 2022. Nearly $18 billion of the revenue was from Medicaid, nearly $4 billion from Medicare, more than $5 billion from private payers, and more than $1 billion from self-payers.

These nonprofit community health centers are increasingly facing competition for the price-sensitive consumer from major retail companies. One of the most successful businesses competing for price-sensitive customers, Walmart, has grown its healthcare business from its pharmacy to major health centers. As one of the largest employers in the United States, and despite being one of the nation's largest employers of adult Medicaid enrollees, Walmart spends $6 billion per year on healthcare for its employees.

As Walmart has launched solutions to provide employee healthcare more efficiently, it has become a healthcare provider, expanding many of those offerings to its price-sensitive customers. Walmart Health Centers offer primary care, dental care, and behavioral health services as well as virtual care, and they accept Medicaid insurance. For those without insurance, they provide a good faith estimate for appointments booked at least three days in advance.

In 2022, Walmart announced a 10-year partnership with UnitedHealth Group to further advance its goal to make healthcare more affordable, starting with offering a Medicare Advantage plan for seniors. However, the partnership announcement made clear their intent to better serve Medicaid and commercial health plan members through a focus on affordability. This move follows the establishment of Walmart Insurance Services in 2020 as an insurance brokerage company licensed in all 50 states to help customers select the right Medicare plan for them (e.g., Part D, Medicare Advantage, and Medicare supplement plans) offered by a variety of insurance companies. The partnership with UnitedHealth Group positions Walmart as the low-cost leader and as a health plan and healthcare provider in the nation with the world's most expensive healthcare where, according to Walmart, nearly 90% of the population lives within 10 miles of a Walmart store.

Competing Through Nonmarket Strategies

As the intensity of healthcare industry competition heats up due to slower growth, increasing price and quality transparency will continue to offer new opportunities for organizations to identify and target specific market segments. However, this market competition may not diminish the use of nonmarket strategies for competitive advantage such as strategies focused on political activities and corporate social responsibility to influence the competitive environment. Historically, competition in the heavily regulated healthcare industry arguably has been shaped more by lobbying and legislation than by the value the product delivers to the customer. For example, lobbying has directly impacted legislation regarding price controls and transparency, marketing of drugs and other health products, and scopes of practice among healthcare professionals. The major industry trade groups, including the American Hospital Association, American Medical Association, and Pharmaceutical Research and Manufacturers of America, will continue to lobby for changing healthcare regulations to be more favorable to their members.

Where nonmarket strategies may become more complex and intense is with the entrance of Amazon and other global platform companies into healthcare. Outside of the healthcare industry, nonmarket strategies have been important to the success of these unique companies that have navigated their vast impact on the internet-based economy and society at large. As these companies enter healthcare, issues around data privacy and security will only continue to draw regulatory scrutiny. The discussions about regulating artificial intelligence will also likely encourage nonmarket strategies due to its potential for life-threatening and life-saving impacts in healthcare.

Fraud as a nonmarket strategy will continue to tempt the unscrupulous actors within the healthcare industry. According to the National Health Care Anti-Fraud Association, the financial losses due to fraud are estimated to range from 3% to 10% of total national healthcare expenditures. The most common example is healthcare providers who document false diagnoses or treatments to increase payments from insurance companies. However, one of the more high-profile cases was Theranos, the defunct company founded by CEO Elizabeth Holmes who is serving an 11-year prison sentence for massive fraud. She not only deceived investors with false claims about her company's blood testing technology but also put patient health at risk.

REFERENCES

Assistant Secretary for Planning and Evaluation. (2022). *Trends in prescription drug spending, 2016–2021*. Office of Science and Data Policy, U.S. Department of Health and Human Services. https://aspe.hhs.gov/sites/default/files/documents/88c547c976e915fc31fe2c6903ac0bc9/sdp-trends-prescription-drug-spending.pdf

Beakes-Read, G., Neisser, M., Frey, P., & Guarducci, M. (2022). Analysis of FDA's accelerated approval program performance December 1992–December 2021. *Therapeutic Innovation & Regulatory Science, 56*(5), 698–703. https://doi.org/10.1007/s43441-022-00430-z

Food and Drug Administration. (2023). *New drug therapy approvals 2022*. Food and Drug Administration. https://www.fda.gov/drugs/new-drugs-fda-cders-new-molecular-entities-and-new-therapeutic-biological-products/new-drug-therapy-approvals-2022

Health Resources and Services Administration. (2022). *National Health Center Program Uniform Data System (UDS) awardee data, Table 9D*. https://data.hrsa.gov/tools/data-reporting/program-data/national

Janin, A. (2023, July 10). The longevity clinic will see you now—for $100,000: The clinics cater to a growing number of people obsessed with fighting aging. *Wall Street Journal*. https://www.wsj.com/articles/longevity-clinics-aging-living-longer-2b98e773

Medicare Payment Advisory Commission. (2023). Chapter 11, The Medicare Advantage program: Status report. In *Report to the Congress: Medicare Payment Policy*. Medicare Payment Advisory Commission. https://www.medpac.gov/wp-content/uploads/2023/03/Ch11_Mar23_MedPAC_Report_To_Congress_SEC.pdf

Mulcahy, A. W., Whaley, C., & Tebeka, M. G. (2021). *International prescription drug price comparisons*. RAND Corporation. https://www.rand.org/pubs/research_reports/RR2956.html

National Health Care Anti-Fraud Association. (n.d.). *The challenge of health care fraud*. https://www.nhcaa.org/tools-insights/about-health-care-fraud/the-challenge-of-health-care-fraud/

Ochieng, N., Biniek, J. F., Freed, M., Damico, A., & Neuman, T. (2023, August 9). *Medicare Advantage in 2023: Enrollment update and key trends*. Kaiser Family Foundation. https://www.kff.org/medicare/issue-brief/medicare-advantage-in-2023-enrollment-update-and-key-trends/

Patel, N., & Singhal, S. (2023, January 9). *What to expect in U.S. healthcare in 2023 and beyond*. McKinsey & Company. https://www.mckinsey.com/industries/healthcare/our-insights/what-to-expect-in-us-healthcare-in-2023-and-beyond#/_

Smith, S. D., Newhouse, J. P., & Cuckler, G. A. (2022). *Health care spending growth has slowed: Will the bend in the curve continue?* (No. w30782). National Bureau of Economic Research. http://dx.doi.org/10.2139/ssrn.4336976

Whaley, C. M., Briscombe, B., Kerber, R., O'Neill, B., & Kofner, A. (2022). *Prices paid to hospitals by private health plans: Findings from round 4 of an employer-led transparency initiative*. RAND Corporation. https://www.rand.org/pubs/research_reports/RRA1144-1.html

White, C. (2017). *Hospital prices in Indiana: Findings from an employer-led transparency initiative*. RAND Corporation. https://www.rand.org/pubs/research_reports/RR2106.html

FURTHER READINGS

Clark, B., & Puthiyath, M. S. (2022). *The federal 340b drug pricing program: What it is, and why it's facing legal challenges*. Commonwealth Fund. https://doi.org/10.26099/c4z8-pf65

Cubanski, J., Neuman, T., & Freed, M. (2023, January 24). *Explaining the prescription drug provisions in the Inflation Reduction Act*. Kaiser Family Foundation. https://www.kff.org/medicare/issue-brief/explaining-the-prescription-drug-provisions-in-the-inflation-reduction-act/#bullet02

Fein, A. J. (2022, August 2). *The shady business of specialty carve-outs, a.k.a., alternative funding programs*. Drug Channels. https://www.drugchannels.net/2022/08/the-shady-business-of-specialty-carve.html

Klein, S., & Hostetter, M. (2022, April 1). *Tackling high health care prices: A look at four purchaser-led efforts. Do employers have any leverage to bring down prices?* The Commonwealth Fund. https://www.commonwealthfund.org/publications/2022/apr/tackling-high-health-care-prices-look-four-purchaser-led-efforts

Mathews, A. W. (2023, September 28). These employers took on healthcare costs, and the fight got nasty. *The Wall Street Journal*. https://www.wsj.com/health/healthcare/these-employers-took-on-healthcare-costs-and-the-fight-got-nasty-54674114

Porter, M. E. (1976). Please note location of nearest exit: Exit barriers and planning. *California Management Review*, *19*(2), 21–33. https://doi.org/10.2307/41164693

Siconolfi, M. (2023, May 26). Elizabeth Holmes to report to prison: A history of the WSJ Theranos investigation. *The Wall Street Journal*. https://www.wsj.com/articles/elizabeth-holmes-sentencing-a-history-of-the-wsj-theranos-investigation-11668741222

Wang, P. (2022, November 3). The pros and cons of Medicare advantage. *Consumer Reports*. https://www.consumerreports.org/money/health-insurance/pros-and-cons-of-medicare-advantage-a6834167849/

The Future of the Healthcare Industry

Social Factors

H istorically, healthcare quality has been judged by individual consumers based on their relationship and experiences with individual
providers. Given the extent of public funding for healthcare, societies
are increasingly judging healthcare based on the health of the populations they serve. Life expectancy and mortality rates—among the most
common and definitive indicators of population health—are two sides
of the same coin, with the former being calculated based on the latter.
These measures are tracked over time to determine if population health
is improving or not and to compare health among population group-
ings. Preventable differences in health status among disadvantaged populations compared to others are often referred to as health disparities.
Efforts to close these gaps have become a key focus in societies aiming to
improve health equity.

According to a 2023 Commonwealth Fund report, the United States
has the worst overall health compared to other developed countries, has
the highest healthcare expenditures, and is the only high-income country
without universal health insurance coverage. While life expectancy in the
United States was roughly at the average of the Organisation for Economic
Co-operation and Development (OECD) high-income countries in 1980, it
is the lowest, and a significant outlier at three years lower than the OECD
average in 2020. Similarly, the United States has the highest avoidable
death rate, referring to deaths that could be prevented with better diet and
exercise or with timely healthcare screenings and treatments. The United
States also has the highest rates of obesity and multiple chronic conditions.
In contrast, over the same period, life expectancy in South Korea went from
an extreme outlier at more than eight years lower than the average of the
other high-income OECD countries and more than seven years lower than
the United States to almost two years higher than the average of the other
OECD countries and more than six years higher than the United States.

These population level statistics, along with the pandemic stressors, may be why Americans' perceptions of U.S. healthcare quality have
worsened despite generally positive personal experiences with healthcare
received. According to a 2023 Gallup report, from 2001 to 2021, the annual
percentage of adults surveyed who rated U.S. healthcare quality as *excellent*
or *good* ranged from 50% to 62%. In 2022, it dropped to 48%. Over this

time, a key change was diverging perceptions by age group, with 62% of those age 55 or older rating the quality of healthcare in the United States as *excellent* or *good* in 2022, compared to 42% among those aged 35 to 54 and 34% among those aged 18 to 34. Americans continue to rate the quality of the healthcare they have received themselves higher than they rate U.S. healthcare quality overall. However, the ratings of healthcare received dipped to 72% reporting quality was *excellent* or *good* in 2022, again with a significant divergence by age group, compared to a range of 76–83% from 2001 through 2021.

The relative dissatisfaction of younger generations with the healthcare system in the United States is part of a shift affecting the future of the industry in important ways. In 2023, the Association of American Medical Colleges (AAMC) Center for Health Justice published a national representative poll of adults from Generation Z who were born between 1998 and 2004 to assess their views by political identity. They found majority agreement across groups in an era of political division, with 95% of liberals and 77% of conservatives agreeing that access to healthcare is a basic human right, and 56% of liberals and 74% of conservatives agreeing that a person is ultimately responsible for their own health. Demonstrating more divergent opinions, 25% of liberals and 52% of conservatives agreed that health differences observed between different racial groups are the result of the way people decide to live, not because of racism. The responses to this latter question may be more reflective of the false dichotomy embedded in the question itself than of actual liberal-conservative division on this issue.

The national focus on tackling the complex issues driving health disparities will likely only increase as younger generations enter the workforce, vote, and take action to address their dissatisfaction with the healthcare system. Politics have begun shifting toward healthcare access and equity being a unifying rather than dividing force. After fierce partisan battles over the Affordable Care Act, which barely passed in 2010, the battles over threats to overturn it appear to have ended. As of 2023, many Republican politicians have essentially abandoned their efforts to repeal Obamacare, focusing on a more unifying approach of implementing hospital and insurance price transparency. Generally, both parties have been focusing on the widespread dissatisfaction with the high costs of healthcare, which disproportionately impact lower income Americans, and on the government's role in addressing this problem.

Health equity has become a key priority for the U.S. federal government, and the National Institutes of Health plays a key role in funding health disparities research through its National Institute on Minority Health and Health Disparities (NIMHD). The NIMHD has developed an evolving evidence-based framework for understanding and advancing research in this complex area. The framework identifies biological, behavioral, physical environmental, sociocultural, and healthcare system domains of influence over the life span that impact health outcomes at the levels of the individual, families, organizations, communities, and ultimately populations. Thus, the healthcare system itself is recognized to be only one of the key domains influencing health disparities. This is consistent with the federal Office of Disease Prevention and Health Promotion focus on addressing the social determinants of health and disparities, which include economic stability, education access and quality, healthcare access and quality, neighborhood and built environment, and social and community context.

Poverty has long been recognized as a key factor associated with worse health outcomes. In a 2018 report on the relationship between socioeconomic factors and mortality across the United States, Alexander Long and colleagues demonstrated that county-level median income and percentage of the county population in poverty explained about 50% of the variation in premature mortality across multiple time periods. In 2023, David Brady and colleagues leveraged a national longitudinal survey that used a more complete measure of income that included all income sources (i.e., cash and near-cash transfers, taxes, and tax credits) and adjusted for household size. They tracked current poverty—defined as less than 50% of median income—and cumulative poverty over the previous 10 years and found that current poverty and, even more so, cumulative poverty were significant predictors of mortality. They found that the survival gap between those currently in and not in poverty began around age 40 and grew wider until about age 70 when the gap began to diminish. Cumulative poverty was found to be a greater risk factor for death than obesity. These findings suggest that interventions to address the social determinants of health as root causes of health outcomes may be more successful at improving health and reducing healthcare costs than efforts focused on the healthcare system itself.

In 2011, Paula Braveman and colleagues developed a model documenting the pathways through which educational attainment improves health outcomes. As seen in Figure 1, education leads to knowledge about health and improves literacy and critical thinking, which supports healthier choices. Educational attainment also provides more and better work opportunities, which reduces exposures to hazards and increases income, benefits, and opportunities to live in safer neighborhoods. Finally, educational attainment increases a sense of control and mastery and provides access to a new social network that is similarly knowledgeable about health and supportive of adopting healthy behaviors. A key causal connection across these pathways is that education mitigates chronic stressors that adversely impact health. Education and other social factors affect not only individual health but also the broader economy. In 2023, Thomas LaVeist and colleagues estimated that the economic burden of health inequities based on race, ethnicity, or educational attainment range from $421 to $451 billion per year in the United States, including the value of excess spending on medical care, lost labor productivity, and premature death.

While the healthcare system is not designed to improve educational attainment within the traditional sense of earning a degree, significant

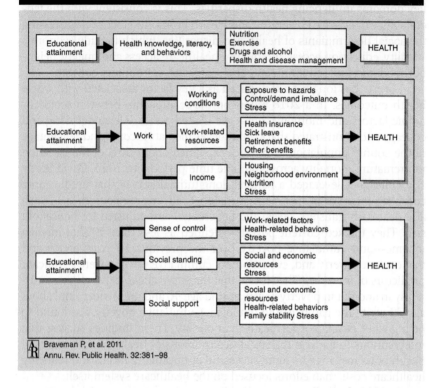

Figure 1   Multiple Pathways Linking Education to Health

Braveman P, et al. 2011.
Annu. Rev. Public Health. 32:381–98

efforts have been made to reduce health disparities by improving health literacy. Interventions such as small group educational sessions, remote video-based education, and social media are promising approaches to enhancing patient knowledge about health and promoting health-related behavior change. Healthcare providers are also increasingly being trained to be more sensitive in how they communicate with patients. This includes avoiding medical jargon, improving listening skills, and checking in with patients to see how much of the clinician instructions they have understood, so misunderstandings can be corrected. This also includes a shift toward patient-centered shared decision making, where clinicians seek to understand their patient's health through the patient's values and preferences. For example, many patients are more focused on quality of life, especially nearer to the end of life, than on clinical factors, such as blood pressure. While informing the patient of the risks and benefits of treatment options, the patient-centered clinician seeks to help the patient weigh the options from the perspective of the patient's values rather than the lab values.

Identifying Health Disparities

Before health disparities can be addressed, they first need to be identified. Federal data collection systems are critically important but often inadequate. A top priority of the Centers for Medicare & Medicaid Services (CMS) health equity framework is to improve collection of standardized individual-level data on race, ethnicity, language, gender identity, sex, sexual orientation, and disability status. The Centers for Disease Control and Prevention (CDC) surveillance system is an important national source of health statistics that can identify disparities as well as progress toward closing health equity gaps. There are also significant weaknesses in this system, particularly regarding how individuals are categorized, which can obscure disparities. The CDC's mortality data are used widely to track population health and disparities. While all-cause mortality is a robust overall health indicator, the CDC system also tracks mortality by cause of death based on medical certification.

Racial and Ethnic Disparities

The federal efforts to standardize data collection on race and ethnicity began in the mid- to late-20th century to enforce civil rights laws requiring equal access to housing, education, employment, and other resources—factors now known to have a substantial impact on health. A key caution documented in the background of the regulations is that the race and ethnicity categories are not based in science, but rather are created based on socio-political constructs to reflect broad groups of the U.S. population. The first set of standardized categories was established in 1977 with updates in 1997 that also allow the selection of more than one race. The standardized categories were established to be the minimum requirements for federal agencies, such that more granular categories could be used if they would aggregate to the standardized categories. However, there have been delays in implementing these standards uniformly, which has impeded progress on identifying and addressing disparities. Figure 2 shows age-adjusted all-cause mortality rates per 100,000 people from the CDC WONDER online database using the race and ethnicity categories available, demonstrating how this data system has helped identify and obscure disparities.

Aggregating Race and Ethnicity Categories

Although the 1977 minimum standards were not available in the CDC mortality data until 1999, the "Other Race" disaggregation to the required minimum 1977 categories of *American Indian or Alaska Native*, *Asian or Pacific Islander*, and *Hispanic Origin* demonstrated significant differences between groups that were not previously visible. Similarly, when the 1997

Figure 2 Age-Adjusted Mortality Rates per 100,000 in the United States by Race and Ethnicity

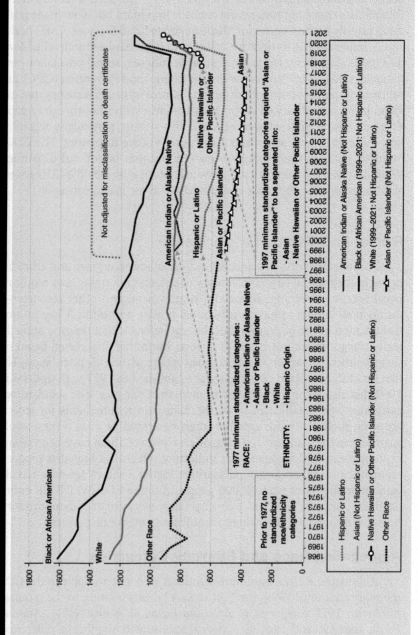

Data source: Centers for Disease Control and Prevention, National Center for Health Statistics. National Vital Statistics System, Mortality 1968–2021 on CDC WONDER Online Database

standard prohibiting the aggregate *Asian or Pacific Islander* category became available in the CDC data in 2018, significant differences in mortality rates between *Asian* and *Native Hawaiian or Other Pacific Islander* were seen nationally. These disparities were already identified based on state-level data, which demonstrated that Native Hawaiians have had significantly lower life expectancy in their homeland since at least 1950. This provided strong justification for the 1997 regulation. This example underscores the importance of states and local communities going beyond the minimum national categories in data collection and advocating for the improvement of the minimum standards at the federal level. Despite the federal regulations, some researchers and public health officials, including those in the National Institute of Minority Health and Health Disparities (NIMHD), continue to use the defunct *Asian or Pacific Islander* category, prompting sharp criticism that this practice is an example of structural biases in datasets that reflect racism when they are used knowingly in violation of the federal standard that was implemented to protect civil rights.

Specifically, the 1997 regulation was implemented after extensive review and despite pressure to avoid adding new categories because the Office of Management and Budget (OMB) determined that Native Hawaiians had provided compelling evidence for the need to disaggregate Asian populations from Pacific Islanders to monitor civil rights and protect against discrimination. The OMB reported that Native Hawaiians represent only 3% of the aggregate Asian or Pacific Islander category, obscuring the social and economic conditions for these indigenous people. In comparison, Native Hawaiians comprise 60% of the Native Hawaiian or Other Pacific Islander category. For the first time in over two decades, the OMB has proposed a change to the minimum categories again, specifically to add *Middle Eastern and North African* (MENA), disaggregating this population from its current categorization as *White*. The OMB recommended this change in 2023 after reviewing evidence that many MENA persons do not identify as White, are not seen as White by others, and have a history and experience that is distinct from White persons of European ancestry.

Misclassification on Death Certificates

In 2016, Elizabeth Arias and colleagues published research on the validity of the CDC's mortality data. The mortality rates shown in Figure 3 were created from a count of deaths as measured by death certificates (the numerator) relative to the count of the total relevant population (the denominator). Inaccuracies in either count can undermine the validity of the rate. The denominator is based on counts of the population from the census data, which includes race and ethnicity information based on individual self-report. However, the race and ethnicity of death certificate data are typically recorded by the funeral director, who should

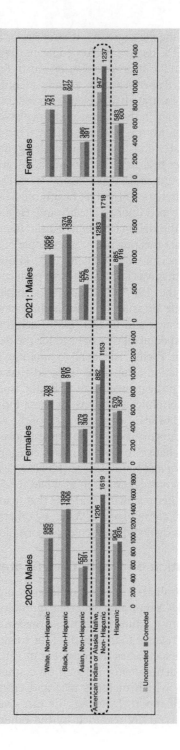

Figure 3 Age-Adjusted Death Rates per 100,000 by Race and Ethnicity, Uncorrected vs. Corrected for Misclassification on Death Certificates, United States, 2020 and 2021

ask available family members and may make the determination based on observation. In a comparison of the individual's self-report of race and ethnicity and that on their subsequent death certificate, Arias and colleagues found a high degree of consistency, nearly 100%, between the two sources for Black and White populations. However, among those who self-identified as American Indian or Alaska Native, nearly half (45–49% over three separately analyzed time periods from 1979 through 2011) were misclassified on their death certificate, and the large majority of those were misclassified as White. Among those whose death certificate reported their race as American Indian or Alaska Native, 72% to 80% had self-identified as such on the survey over the three decades. Among Hispanics, agreement between the survey and death certificate records were approximately 90% across the three time periods. In their 2022 analysis, Jiaquan Xu and colleagues corrected for these misclassifications and demonstrated that the American Indian and Alaska Native mortality rates are substantially higher than all other groups, which have only minor differences between the corrected and uncorrected mortality rates as shown in Figure 3. Thus, the mortality rates reported by the CDC for the American Indian and Alaska Native population in the CDC WONDER data set is a significant underestimation of the actual rate.

The COVID-19 Pandemic

While the significant mortality rate gap between Black and White individuals had been shrinking over the decade before the pandemic, this global health crisis demonstrated how fragile such gains can be. From 1968 to 2005, the annual mortality disparity ranged from about 250 to 350 additional deaths per 100,000 population among Black individuals relative to White individuals as shown in Figure 2. From 2006 through 2019, the gap was under 250, and from 2011 through 2019, it was less than 150. In 2020 and 2021, the gap was back in the 200s. Comparing 2019 to 2021 age-adjusted mortality rates by group, there were 234 additional deaths per 100,000 among Black individuals in 2021, compared to an additional 154 among White individuals. American Indian or Alaska Native individuals fared the worst during the pandemic. Even using the uncorrected CDC data that underestimates mortality rates due to misclassifications on death certificates, there were an additional 327 deaths per 100,000 in 2021 than in 2019 among American Indian or Alaska Native individuals in the United States. Among Native Hawaiian or Other Pacific Islander individuals, there were an additional 245 deaths per 100,000 in 2021 compared to 2019, while among Hispanic individuals, there were an additional 201 deaths per 100,000, among White individuals an additional 154 deaths per 100,000, and among Asian individuals an additional 89 deaths per 100,000.

Combating Racial and Ethnic Health Disparities

Historical and contemporary manifestations of racism are key examples of how the healthcare industry and health disparities have been shaped by broader societal issues. As of 2023, less than 6% of physicians in the United States are Black according to the AAMC, in a nation where nearly 14% of the population is Black. Mistrust of the medical establishment has roots in historical events including the Tuskegee medical experiments conducted by the U.S. government, during which African Americans with syphilis were deceived and deprived of treatment for decades, causing preventable deaths and serious health problems. This mistrust is then reinforced by experiences of discrimination and exacerbates health disparities. Equitable care is also jeopardized when racial and ethnic diversity is not present in the clinical trials the FDA relies on to make drug approval decisions. Racially concordant care, when the healthcare provider is the same race as the patient, helps improve trust and reduce disparities. Thus, increasing the diversity of physicians and other clinicians is one of the ways health equity can be improved.

In just one example of the historical structural barriers to diversity in the healthcare workforce, Black physicians were prohibited from being trained in the municipal hospitals of St. Louis in the early 1900s. This injustice led community members to fight for their own hospital, which eventually was achieved with the construction of the Homer G. Phillips Hospital. Opened in 1937, this hospital provided high quality care for underserved African American patients and excellent training for African American physicians, nurses, and other healthcare professionals. It held a nationally recognized annual conference, drawing attendees from across the United States. In 1955, the mayor of St. Louis implemented a new order requiring patients to be treated at the hospital closest to them rather than one based on their race, resulting in the integration of the city's hospitals. Thus, Homer G. Phillips Hospital became a treatment center for individuals of all races and backgrounds rather than one dedicated strictly to African Americans. This vision of health equity came to a dramatic end in 1979 after a local election resulted in the elimination of funding to continue operating the hospital. After weeks of community protests, the police and National Guard stepped in to ensure its closure. The facility ultimately was converted to an independent-living apartment complex for low-income seniors after surviving threats to tear it down.

In 2022, Hamed and colleagues reported that research on racism in healthcare has increased and documented that racism is a global problem. The body of research reviewed by Hamed and team indicated that experiences of racism result in mistrust of the healthcare system and reduced likelihood of seeking care when needed. Perceptions of racism in healthcare are consistent with findings of healthcare workers having negative attitudes toward members of marginalized races and who provide inadequate care to these persons. Healthcare workers are generally unaware of their racial biases and have difficulty talking about racism. Antiracism training can improve awareness and understanding of the problem and enhance the ability of healthcare professionals to discuss racial discrimination and their interest in further training. However, Hamed and colleagues note that it is unclear whether these changes translate to better care.

Rural Disparities

The health gaps between rural and urban communities have been well documented, and the disparities have been growing. Rurality is generally defined as relatively lower population density. Because the population is less dense in rural areas, if there is healthcare infrastructure, it is often sparse and fragile. Where there is no healthcare, lengthy travel to the nearest facilities sometimes causes life-threatening delays in care.

Data reported from the International Labour Organization (ILO) in 2015 disaggregated rural and urban populations across 174 countries to examine previously invisible rural disparities globally. While there are methodological challenges in measuring rural disparities across countries, the ILO's estimates show vast inequities in many areas. They noted that many of the root causes of the disparities are not within the healthcare infrastructure itself but rather broader societal issues of poverty, lack of economic infrastructure, discrimination, and lack of community empowerment.

The ILO found that 56% of global rural populations lack healthcare coverage compared to 22% of urban populations and 38% of populations overall, a disparity exacerbated by extreme shortages of healthcare workers in rural areas. Africa has the highest percentage of individuals lacking coverage overall (75%), with 83% of rural residents and 61% of urban residents without coverage. The largest gaps between rural and urban populations are found in Asia and the Pacific, where 56% of the rural population and 24% of the urban population are without coverage.

In the ILO research, maternal mortality was used as an indicator of overall health system performance given that most of these deaths are preventable. Among rural populations globally, there are an estimated 29 maternal deaths per 10,000 live births compared to 11 deaths per 10,000 births in urban areas. Africa has the highest rates overall and by area, with 55 maternal deaths per 10,000 live births in rural areas and 29 deaths per 10,000 live births in urban areas.

In the United States, the CDC compared age-adjusted mortality rates in metropolitan (more urban) and nonmetropolitan (more rural) areas by cause of death from 1999 to 2014. Their 2017 publication reported that among the five leading causes of death, mortality rates were higher among nonmetropolitan areas compared to metropolitan areas. For three of the leading causes—heart disease, cancer, and chronic lower respiratory disease—the rural-urban gap grew between 1999 and 2014.

Figure 4 shows the growing gap in all-cause mortality across the United States based on data from the CDC WONDER online database, which

Figure 4   Age-Adjusted Mortality Rates per 100,000 in the United States by Rural and Urban Classification

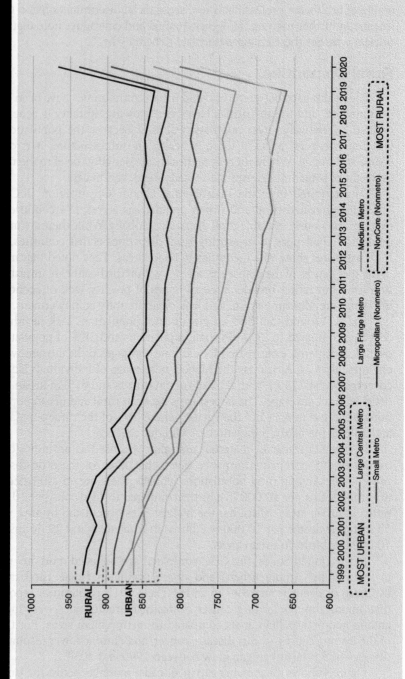

Data source: Centers for Disease Control and Prevention, National Center for Health Statistics. National Vital Statistics System, Mortality 1968–2021 on CDC Wonder Online Database

provides a continuous classification system with six categories from most rural to most urban rather than a dichotomous classification of rural versus urban regions. The two rural (nonmetro) categories have had the highest age-adjusted mortality rates from 1999 to 2020. During that period, mortality rates in the most urban (large central metro) areas and in the suburbs (large fringe metro) of those areas decreased much faster than in the rural areas. Given the importance of socioeconomic factors in explaining variation in mortality rates, in 2018, Alexander Long and colleagues examined rural disparities in age-adjusted mortality at the county level across the United States. After adjusting for the county's median income and percentage of the population in poverty, they found that the rural disparity largely disappeared. Based on this report, another way of understanding the rural disparities in Figure 4 is that level of rurality is a good proxy for level of socioeconomic conditions, and the rural-urban gap in socioeconomic conditions has been growing as a key driver of the growing gap in mortality rates.

The socioeconomic conditions in rural areas add to the challenges of low population density in terms of sustainability of the healthcare infrastructure in these areas. A 2021 study from the U.S. Department of Health and Human Services (HHS) reported that rural areas consistently have a higher percentage of residents who are uninsured and a higher percentage on Medicaid. Thus, providers in these areas face lower reimbursements as well as patients with more complex health needs. These providers also have fewer colleagues and other community resources to whom they can refer patients for specialized medical and social needs. Public health departments in rural areas also face these resource challenges. A 2016 report from Jenine Harris and colleagues indicates that public health offices in urban areas outperform those in rural areas across all core functions. This relative lack of health resources in rural areas compounds the effects of a higher rate of poverty in rural areas, particularly among those who are experiencing racial or ethnic discrimination. In 2023, the Center for Economic Analysis of Rural Health reported on socioeconomic factors as predictors of rural hospital closure among those at risk of financial distress. Among many factors analyzed, including health status, poverty, income, insurance, education, and race and ethnicity, only two variables predicted closure: higher unemployment and higher uninsurance among those under age six. These challenges make recruitment and retention of healthcare workers in rural areas difficult.

Combating Urban-Rural Disparities

One effective approach to addressing the rural healthcare workforce challenge is recruiting students who grew up in a rural area to work in a rural area after completing their training. To improve the healthcare infrastructure in rural areas across the United States, federal subsidies have been implemented in several ways. After many rural hospital closures in the 1980s and 1990s, the Medicare Rural Hospital Flexibility Program was established, which allows states to obtain funding for rural hospital infrastructure support and to designate certain rural hospitals as Critical Access Hospitals (CAHs). Among other criteria, to be certified as a CAH, a hospital must offer 24/7 emergency care services, have no more than 25 acute care inpatient beds, have an annual average length of stay of 96 hours or less for those beds, and be located more than 35 driving miles from any other hospital (with some exceptions for mountainous terrain and other factors). These very small hospitals, once they receive the CAH designation, receive cost-based reimbursement for services provided to Medicare patients. Similarly, to address the physician shortage in rural areas, those clinics that qualify can be designated as a Rural Health Clinic and receive cost-based reimbursement.

Unlike rural hospitals and clinics, retail pharmacies have not received federal subsidies for cost-based reimbursement, and the result has been an increase in the number of closures. In 2022, the Rural Policy Research Institute reported that, in noncore rural areas, the number of retail pharmacies dropped from 5,882 in 2003 to 5,307 in 2021, compared to an increase in pharmacies from 43,810 to 50,417 in urban areas during that same period. The steepest decline occurred after the implementation of Medicare Part D in 2006. While the Part D benefit provided prescription drug coverage to Medicare beneficiaries for the first time, it also created incentives for using mail-order pharmacies and excluded many rural pharmacies from preferred networks. Because pharmacists not only dispense medications but also offer vaccinations and other clinical services, the closure of pharmacies has left many rural communities without a local drug store and, in some cases, without any clinicians. Subsidizing rural pharmacies with cost-based reimbursement, like those provided to Rural Health Clinics and Critical Access Hospitals, would likely eliminate many pharmacy deserts.

As local businesses, those pharmacies, clinics, and hospitals in rural areas not only provide healthcare to community members, but also are integral to fragile rural economies, providing competitive wages that healthcare workers then spend at least partly in their local community. For example, in their 2022 review of research on the economic impact of healthcare in rural areas, Brenton Button and colleagues reported that each physician creates 22 to 26 local jobs, and the healthcare sector itself can account for 20% of jobs outside of farming. Furthermore, in small rural communities where outsiders tend to be less trusted than those who live and work in the community, local healthcare providers may be more successful in encouraging health-related behavior change such as smoking cessation and preventive care. Therefore, consideration of rural healthcare policy options that factor in the broader socioeconomic impacts would improve decision making relative to analyses that only consider cost-effectiveness or efficiencies within the healthcare sector. As such, analysis of policy changes to provide cost-based reimbursement to rural pharmacies would provide a more complete assessment of the benefits to rural communities by including not only the direct cost of the subsidy but also the economic impact on local income, employment, and reduction of other subsidies such as Medicaid and other low-income subsidies for food and housing. Similarly, when subsidies are considered for rural telehealth, the costs and benefits of alternatives such as in-person or local telehealth providers (rather than distant providers) can affect local economies outside the healthcare system. Policies that leverage strengths in local community culture, including the importance of social connectedness and influence of trusted local community leaders, are also likely to be more effective in addressing rural disparities.

If the root cause of the rural disparities is not within the healthcare system itself, but rather the larger socioeconomy, local healthcare jobs that generate spending on goods and services will create other jobs within rural communities and may be at least as important as the healthcare services in improving health outcomes. Adequate access to healthcare is likely to be necessary but insufficient for eliminating the rural health disparities in the United States and globally on its own.

Gender-Based Disparities

In the CDC WONDER mortality database, gender is categorized as either male or female based on information on an individual's death certificate. Examination of these data indicate persistent male disparities. There have been improvements in closing the gap with females apart from the impact of the pandemic, as shown in Figure 5.

In a 2019 comprehensive and global report on the potential reasons for these gender differences, Eileen Crimmins and colleagues identify a complex set of biological, physiological, behavioral, and societal factors that may contribute to higher male mortality. They reviewed data from nearly 200 countries in the World Bank database and found that mortality rates have been decreasing for males and females for over a century in most countries, but rates are higher for males in all countries as of 2016 with a nearly five-year life expectancy advantage for females on average across countries. The gap between males and females differs by country, with a female advantage of eight or more years in several Eastern European countries, and only several months in several Asian countries. They found that among adults aged 45 and older who were born up until 1880, males and females had similar mortality rates. After that time, male mortality rates began to diverge from female rates, largely related to their increased vulnerability to cardiovascular disease and to increased smoking. Across countries and studies, they found that the convergence in mortality rates among men and women was associated with worsening socioeconomic conditions for women and increases in smoking among women. They also found that, over time, when infectious diseases were a larger cause of

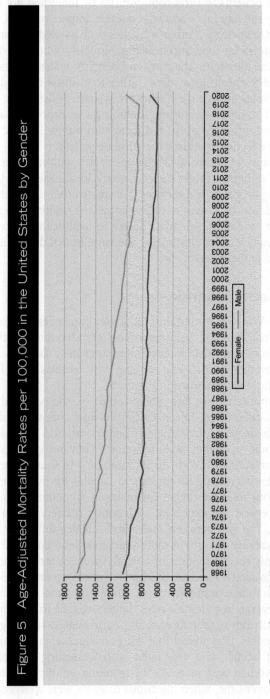

Figure 5   Age-Adjusted Mortality Rates per 100,000 in the United States by Gender

Data source: Centers for Disease Control and Prevention, National Center for Health Statistics. National Vital Statistics System, Mortality 1968–2020 on CDC Wonder Online Database

mortality, male and female mortality rates were more similar. From 1960 to 2016, life expectancy improved overall. During this time, the gap between males and females increased in many countries, and decreased in some, including the United States.

There is relatively very little information available on health outcomes based on sexual orientation and gender identity, though that may change if data systems are modified to accurately collect information and appropriately disaggregate it in reporting outcomes. A 2016 report by Susan Cochran and colleagues compared mortality rates of heterosexual persons aged 18 to 59 with those who are sexual minorities by linking national survey data in the United States with mortality files from 2001 to 2011. After adjusting for demographics and survey cycle alone and after adjusting for these variables plus initial health status except HIV status, they found no significant differences between these groups among women, but a significant difference among men. Men who are sexual minorities had a significantly higher mortality rate compared with heterosexual men. In a subsample of men with HIV testing, after adjusting for demographics, survey cycle, initial health status, and HIV infection status, the mortality rate among men who are sexual minorities was not significantly higher than the rate for heterosexual men, indicating that HIV infection was a primary cause of the higher mortality rate among men who are sexual minorities.

In a study reported in 2023, Sarah Jackson and colleagues, leveraged existing databases representative of the general population in England in terms of age and sex to examine mortality rates among more than 3,000 people with a diagnosis of gender incongruence between 1988 and 2019 compared to a matched group of more than 130,000 cisgender males and females. While acknowledging the limitations of their classification system, the researchers used medical record information regarding sex assigned at birth and gender-related therapies and procedures to group transgender or gender diverse individuals as transfeminine (assigned male at birth), transmasculine (assigned female at birth), or unknown sex assigned at birth. For the latter category, sex assigned at birth was imputed statistically. Mortality rates were adjusted for age, year, race and ethnicity, index of multiple deprivation, smoking status, alcohol use, and body mass index and were calculated based on 100,000 person-years. The all-cause mortality rate was highest for transfeminine persons at 528 deaths per 100,000 person-years, followed by transmasculine persons at 326, cisgender men at 315, and cisgender women at 261. Examination of death rates by cause indicated significantly higher rates of death due to external causes (e.g., suicide, homicide, accidental poisoning) among transgender and gender diverse persons relative to cisgender persons. Much more work is needed to understand and address health disparities based on sex assigned at birth, sexual orientation, and gender identity.

Combined, the evidence indicates that persons assigned male at birth have significant health vulnerabilities across the spectrum of sexual orientation and gender identity.

Combating Gender-Based Disparities

Although males have persistently worse mortality rates, most research on reducing gender-based disparities focuses on reducing bias against females, often focusing on diagnosis and treatment of heart disease, a leading cause of death among males and females. Adhering to science-based treatment guidelines across all patients, not only females, is an important strategy for reducing clinical bias. Interventions specifically designed to reduce gender bias, such as gender-concordant care team programs for women, tend to be successful in reducing gender bias. Enhanced training for medical students and residents is another important way to reduce gender disparities as it improves physician trainee knowledge, confidence, and attitudes pertaining to care for sexual and gender minorities.

Although there is a paucity of research focusing on reducing disparities among males, John Oliffe and colleagues have identified health literacy as a promising target for improving men's health. In their 2020 report reviewing the few studies conducted in this area, they found most studies focused on cancer, primarily prostate cancer. Among these studies prostate cancer support groups were found to advance men's health literacy and proactive behaviors in seeking care. This is important because several studies indicated that often men do not have a knowledge deficit about the importance of cancer screening, but rather are less likely to act on that knowledge to get regular screenings compared to women. The role of social support, including encouragement from peers and family members, is important in men seeking healthcare. The food industry contributes to lower health literacy among males by marketing healthier food choices as more feminine. Oliffe and colleagues concluded that much more research is needed to help address male health disparities and that gender-specific interventions and health promotion programs are needed to help men overcome societal stereotypes and other barriers that prevent them from actively engaging in healthy behaviors.

Geopolitical Disparities

The pandemic demonstrated the intersection of disease and geopolitics with clarity. However, world events other than the spread of disease can have significant effects on health outcomes less directly. Global health was not addressed by the Group of Seven (G7) until after the Cold War after which it became a focus during the first decade of the 21st century.

In a 2022 policy brief, David Fidler, senior fellow for global health and cybersecurity at the Council on Foreign Relations, asserted that the global decline in democracy and increase in authoritarianism since 2010 diffused this health focus and left the G7 nations unprepared to implement a coordinated response to the pandemic. According to Fidler, global health becomes unimportant when the balance of power dominates international relationships. This is evident as debates about how to improve global health and health equity have been abandoned in the wake of the Russian-Ukraine conflict that began in 2022 and the Israel-Hamas war that began in 2023.

The important role of democracy in promoting health is also seen in an analysis of health policy implementation across nations. In 2021, Luke Allen and colleagues reported on factors related to the extent to which countries had implemented population-health policies recommended by the World Health Organization (WHO) to reduce morbidity and mortality from noncommunicable diseases. According to WHO, as of 2023 these diseases—which include heart disease, stroke, cancer, diabetes, and chronic lung disease—account for 74% of all deaths globally. Policy recommendations focus on public health approaches to reduce tobacco use, harm from alcohol, unhealthy diets, inactivity, and exposure to air pollution. Allen and colleagues found that low-income countries and less democratic countries had lower levels of WHO-recommended policy implementation. They also examined corporate permeation—the extent to which corporations are embedded in a country's society—as an indicator of corporate influence and found that countries with higher corporate permeation had lower levels of WHO-recommended policy implementation.

High income countries tend to have lower corporate permeation, which helps protect the public health infrastructure from corporate influence. In the United States, which is in the first quartile of countries with the lowest corporate permeation, health equity is more frequently becoming a business priority for corporations. One major American company, Walmart, has announced a partnership with a managed care organization to address racial inequities among Medicaid and Medicare beneficiaries. Aligned with Walmart's low-cost leader strategy, their retail store–based community health workers aim to assess and address their price-sensitive customers' health and social needs, including access to healthier foods as well as affordable healthcare. With their expanding healthcare services, Walmart is well positioned to compete for the population health business focused on reducing disparities. While threats to democracy continue to distract nations from the pursuit of global health equity, national demand for equity will likely continue to permeate all aspects of the healthcare industry, offering the opportunity for organizations to develop products and services that go beyond addressing individuals' healthcare needs to advance the cause of justice.

REFERENCES

Allen, L. N., Wigley, S., & Holmer, H. (2021). Implementation of non-communicable disease policies from 2015 to 2020: A geopolitical analysis of 194 countries. *The Lancet Global Health, 9*(11), e1528–e1538. https://doi.org/10.1016/S2214-109X(21)00359-4

Arias, E., Heron, M., & Hakes, J. K. (2016). The validity of race and Hispanic-origin reporting on death certificates in the United States: An update. National Center for Health Statistics. *Vital Health Stat 2*(172). 2016. https://www.cdc.gov/nchs/data/series/sr_02/sr02_172.pdf

Boyle, P. (2023, January 12). What's your specialty? New data show the choices of America's doctors by gender, race, and age. *Association of American Medical Colleges. AAMCNews.* https://www.aamc.org/news/what-s-your-specialty-new-data-show-choices-america-s-doctors-gender-race-and-age

Brady, D., Kohler, U., & Zheng, H. (2023). Novel estimates of mortality associated with poverty in the US. *JAMA Internal Medicine, 183*(6), 618–619. https://doi.org/10.1001/jamainternmed.2023.0276

Braveman, P., Egerter, S., & Williams, D. R. (2011). The social determinants of health: coming of age. *Annual Review of Public Health, 32,* 381–398. https://doi.org/10.1146/annurev-publhealth-031210-101218

Button, B. L., Taylor, K., McArthur, M., Newbery, S., & Cameron, E. (2022). The economic impact of rural healthcare on rural economies: A rapid review. *Canadian Journal of Rural Medicine, 27*(4), 158–168. https://doi.org/10.4103/cjrm.cjrm_70_21

Centers for Disease Control and Prevention. (n.d.). CDC WONDER. Centers for Disease Control and Prevention. https://wonder.cdc.gov/

Cochran, S. D., Björkenstam, C., & Mays, V. M. (2016). Sexual orientation and all-cause mortality among US adults aged 18 to 59 years, 2001–2011. *American Journal of Public Health, 106*(5), 918–920. https://doi.org/10.2105/ajph.2016.303052

Crimmins, E. M., Shim, H., Zhang, Y. S., & Kim, J. K. (2019). Differences between men and women in mortality and the health dimensions of the morbidity process. *Clinical Chemistry, 65*(1), 135–145. https://doi.org/10.1373/clinchem.2018.288332

Executive Office of the President, Office of Management and Budget (1997, October 30). *Revisions to the standards for the classification of federal data on race and ethnicity.* Federal Register Notice. https://obamawhitehouse.archives.gov/omb/fedreg_1997standards

Fidler, D. P. (2022, July 28). *Geopolitics, global health, and the group of seven.* Council on Foreign Relations. https://www.cfr.org/article/geopolitics-global-health-and-group-seven

Gunja, M. Z., Gumas, E. D., & Williams II, R. D. (2023, January 31). *U.S. health care from a global perspective, 2022: Accelerating spending, worsening outcomes.* The Commonwealth Fund. https://www.commonwealthfund.org/publications/issue-briefs/2023/jan/us-health-care-global-perspective-2022#:~:text=The%20U.S.%20has%20the%20lowest,nearly%20twice%20the%20OECD%20average.

Hamed, S., Bradby, H., Ahlberg, B. M., & Thapar-Björkert, S. (2022). Racism in healthcare: A scoping review. *BMC Public Health, 22*(1), 988. https://doi.org/10.1186/s12889-022-13122-y

Harris, J. K., Beatty, K., Leider, J. P., Knudson, A., Anderson, B. L., & Meit, M. (2016). The double disparity facing rural local health departments. *Annual Review of Public Health, 37,* 167–184. https://doi.org/10.1146/annurev-publhealth-031914-122755

Jackson, S. S., Brown, J., Pfeiffer, R. M., Shrewsbury, D., O'Callaghan, S., Berner, A. M., Gadalla, S. M., & Shiels, M. S. (2023). Analysis of mortality among transgender and gender diverse adults in England. *JAMA Network Open, 6*(1), e2253687–0e2253687. https://doi.org/10.1001/jamanetworkopen.2022.53687

LaVeist, T. A., Pérez-Stable, E. J., Richard, P., Anderson, A., Isaac, L. A., Santiago, R., Okoh, C., Breen, N., Farhat, T., Assenov, A., & Gaskin, D. J. (2023). The economic burden of racial, ethnic, and educational health inequities in the US. *JAMA, 329*(19), 1682–1692. https://doi.org/10.1001/jama.2023.5965

Lazaro, E., Ullrich, F., & Mueller, K. J. (August 2022). *Update on rural independently owned pharmacy closures in the United States, 2003–2021* (Brief No. 2022-3). Rural Policy Research Institute Center for Rural Health Policy Analysis. https://rupri.public-health.uiowa.edu/publications/policybriefs/2022/Independent%20Pharmacy%20Closures.pdf

Long, A. S., Hanlon, A. L., & Pellegrin, K. L. (2018). Socioeconomic variables explain rural disparities in US mortality rates: Implications for rural health research and policy. *SSM - Population Health, 6,* 72–74. https://doi.org/10.1016/j.ssmph.2018.08.009

Megibow, E., Orgera, K., & Piepenbrink, S. (2023, May 1). *Generation Z takes the reins.* Association of American Medical Colleges, Center for Health Justice. https://www.aamchealthjustice.org/news/polling/generation-z-takes-reins

Oliffe, J. L., Rossnagel, E., Kelly, M. T., Bottorff, J. L., Seaton, C., & Darroch, F. (2020). Men's health literacy: A review and recommendations. *Health Promotion International, 35*(5), 1037–1051. https://doi.org/10.1093/heapro/daz077

Rhoades, C. A., Whitacre, B. E., & Davis, A. F. (2023 January). *Community sociodemographics and rural hospital survival analysis* [Policy brief]. Center for Economic Analysis of Rural Health, University of Kentucky. https://cearh.ca.uky.edu/sites/cearh.ca.uky.edu/files/Community_Sociodemographics_Rural_Hospital_Survival_CEARH_policy_brief_JAN_23.pdf

Saad, L. (2023, January 19). Americans sour on U.S. healthcare quality. *Gallup News.* https://news.gallup.com/poll/468176/americans-sour-healthcare-quality.aspx

Scheil-Adlung, X. (2015). *Global evidence on inequities in rural health protection: new data on rural deficits in health coverage for 174 countries.* International Labour Organization. https://www.ilo.org/secsoc/information-resources/publications-and-tools/Workingpapers/WCMS_383890/lang--en/index.htm

Turrini, G., Branham, D. K., Chen, L., Conmy, A. B., Chappel, A. R., & De Lew, N. (2021, July). *Access to affordable care in rural America: Current trends and key challenges* [Research Report No. HP-2021-16]. Office of the Assistant Secretary for Planning and Evaluation, U.S. Department of Health and Human Services. https://aspe.hhs.gov/sites/default/files/2021-07/rural-health-rr.pdf

World Health Organization. (2023, September 16). *Noncommunicable diseases.* https://www.who.int/news-room/fact-sheets/detail/noncommunicable-diseases

Xu, J. Q., Murphy, S. L., Kochanek, K. D., & Arias, E. (2022). *Mortality in the United States, 2021.* NCHS Data Brief, no 456. Hyattsville, MD: National Center for Health Statistics. https://doi.org/10.15620/cdc:122516

FURTHER READINGS

Braveman, P. (2023). *Social determinants of health and health disparities.* Oxford University Press, Incorporated.

Cooper, R. L., Ramesh, A., Radix, A. E., Reuben, J. S., Juarez, P. D., Holder, C. L., Belton, A. S., Brown, K. Y., Mena, L. A., & Matthews-Juarez, P. (2023). Affirming and inclusive care training for medical students and residents to reduce health disparities experienced by sexual and gender minorities: A systematic review. *Transgender Health, 8*(4), 307–327. https://doi.org/10.1089/trgh.2021.0148

Madureira Lima, J., & Galea, S. (2019). The Corporate Permeation Index - A tool to study the macrosocial determinants of non-communicable disease. *SSM - Population Health, 7,* 100361. https://doi.org/10.1016/j.ssmph.2019.100361

Russell, D., Mathew, S., Fitts, M., Liddle, Z., Murakami-Gold, L., Campbell, N., Ramjan, M., Zhao, Y., Hines, S., Humphreys, J. S., & Wakerman, J. (2021). Interventions for health workforce retention in rural and remote areas: a systematic review. *Human Resources for Health, 19*(1), 103. https://doi.org/10.1186/s12960-021-00643-7

Taparra, K., & Pellegrin, K. (2022). Data aggregation hides Pacific Islander health disparities. *Lancet (London, England), 400*(10345), 2–3. https://doi.org/10.1016/S0140-6736(22)01100-X

U.S. Census Bureau. (n.d.). *Measuring race and ethnicity across the decades: 1790–2010.* https://www.census.gov/data-tools/demo/race/MREAD_1790_2010.html

Venable, H. P. (1961). The history of Homer G. Phillips Hospital. *Journal of the National Medical Association, 53*(6), 541–551. http://www.ncbi.nlm.nih.gov/pmc/articles/pmc2642069/

Walters, R., Leslie, S. J., Polson, R., Cusack, T., & Gorely, T. (2020). Establishing the efficacy of interventions to improve health literacy and health behaviours: a systematic review. *BMC Public Health, 20*(1), 1040. https://doi.org/10.1186/s12889-020-08991-0

The Future of the Healthcare Industry

Environmental Factors

I n September of 2021, amid the historic COVID-19 pandemic with infections surging due to the delta variant, more than 200 medical and public health journals, including some of the world's top-ranked journals, simultaneously published a *Call for Emergency Action*. This call was not about the pandemic; rather, it was a call to limit the global temperature increase and restore biodiversity to protect human health not only from direct environmental impacts (e.g., heat-related illness and death, loss of food and water supplies) but also from socioeconomic and geopolitical instability related to the environment. The authors noted that the risk of harm from the environmental crisis disproportionately affects those who are most vulnerable to health threats, including populations with health disparities. The pandemic demonstrated the potential for governments to rapidly invest massive resources to protect health, the authors argued that an emergency response was also necessary to make fundamental societal changes to rapidly reduce emissions and reverse the current environmental trajectory. The authors also called on all healthcare professionals to join the effort to make health systems sustainable by 2040, noting that this will require changing clinical practice. In this remarkable demonstration of consensus, the journal editors wrote:

> The greatest threat to global public health is the continued failure of world leaders to keep the global temperature rise below 1.5° C and to restore nature . . . We, as editors of health journals, call for governments and other leaders to act, marking 2021 as the year that the world finally changes course. (Atwoli et al., 2021)

This level of consensus on the idea that planet health and human health are inseparable is new, but the concept of One Health is more than a century old. Rudolph Virchow is often considered the first modern thought leader of this approach. Virchow was a physician who founded the field of cellular pathology, shifting medicine from the treatment of symptoms to more accurate diagnosis by examining cells and allowing the development and application of more precise and effective treatments. He was the first to identify leukemia, to find cells in bone and connective tissue, and to explain the process of pulmonary thromboembolism. He also coined the term *zoonosis* to indicate diseases spread between animals and humans. He was a strong advocate for public health measures to prevent disease transmission and recognized that social and economic factors affect health. In 1964, veterinarian Calvin Schwabe coined the phrase One Medicine in a call for human and veterinary medicine to collaborate in the fight against zoonotic disease. In 2004, the Wildlife Conservation Society convened human and animal health experts to develop priorities for an international and interdisciplinary approach to health called One Health, One World.

One Health Concept

In the 21st century, One Health moves beyond a more singular focus on zoonotic diseases and incorporates a broader focus on the health of the planet's ecosystems, recognizing inseparable connections between human behavior and the health of all living things. The parallel rapid acceleration of both the growth of the human population and the change in the environment since the mid-20th century is unique in human history, and as such, biological adaptation of humans and animals cannot keep pace with environmental changes, making human behavioral adaptation essential to survival. One Health is an approach that proposes seeking the health of humans, animals, and the environment through integrated mutualism. Rather than working on each of these issues in isolation, One Health encourages simultaneous advancement through integrated practices.

The level of cooperation and collaboration across disciplines and sectors that is the foundation of the One Health approach is not the routine approach to solving problems. In the typical approach, distinct disciplines, professions, and stakeholders focus on solving the problems of their respective, specific interests. Whether in government, industry, academia, or communities, these distinct groups are organized within units (e.g., departments, agencies, associations, organizations, etc.) focused on the specific interest, receive funding to advance that interest, and hold conferences or other meetings to share information about that interest. As an area of interest advances, the knowledge and practices become too voluminous for any individual to master, so fields divide into specialties and with more advances in knowledge and practices, subspecialties. This approach has led to innumerable successes in solving important problems in many different specific fields, including advancements in the treatment of diseases, the development of communication and information systems, and the production of high-yield food systems. While there is a compelling need for specialization in science, there are also unintended consequences, including specialized scientists often having no easy pathways to interact with those outside of their specialty, scientific silos impairing the ability of scientists to understand issues outside of their specialty, and scientific monopolies developing and impeding progress even within a specialty. Thus, the specialization that has effectively solved so many specific problems simply cannot solve the grand challenges facing the world.

The grand challenges that One Health aims to tackle are sometimes referred to as wicked problems, those issues that are particularly complex and critically important and for which specialized solutions often cause new problems. While specialization has created highly efficient food systems as solutions to meet the demands of a growing population, it has caused unintended consequences, including overuse of antibiotics in farm animals, increasing the risk of drug-resistant bacteria. It has also led to pesticide contamination of the environment, polluting water resources and harming bees, which pollinate $15 billion worth of crops each year in the United States, according to the USDA. Solutions to these problems can add costs to food production resulting in higher food prices, which disproportionately affect those who are most socioeconomically disadvantaged, which exacerbates health disparities. The number of infections from a deadly fungus, an environmental mold *Aspergillus fumigatus*, have increased, leading the fungus to develop resistance to triazoles, a class of antifungal medications. This increase in infections correlates with an increase in the use of triazoles fungicides in agriculture. In a 2022 report, Johana Rhodes and colleagues confirmed that the dangerous fungus infecting humans developed its resistance to triazoles in the environment, most likely from exposure and adaptation to the agricultural fungicides. This wicked problem is being addressed with a multidisciplinary, multistakeholder One Health approach.

While the need for specialists remains critically important, specialists alone cannot solve grand challenges. Researchers in the social sciences have made progress in identifying some of the factors that may facilitate cooperation and collaboration across disciplines to tackle wicked problems more effectively. In a 2018 report, Kara Hall and colleagues reviewed the research on the science of team science to shed light on what makes research teams more effective. They found that teams that cross the boundaries of the typical organizational or geographic units (e.g., departments, institutions, nations) tend to be more effective, both in terms of productivity and scientific impact, relative to solo scientists or those teams working within their units. Similarly, teams that cross the typical silos of specialization to include experts or representatives from different disciplines, professions, and other stakeholder groups (e.g., research or clinical specialty, community members, policy makers) are more effective compared to teams working within an area of specialization. In particular, experts whose disciplines are by nature cross-cutting, such as example data scientists or other generalists, can help bridge communication across specialties to support effective problem-solving. Organizational factors, such as establishing cross-disciplinary centers, facilitating cross-disciplinary meetings and other communication, and providing seed funding for cross-disciplinary projects, can improve the quality and quantity of scientific work of multidisciplinary teams. Hall and colleagues also found that complex teams tackling complex problems require more intensive resources to effectively manage the team, noting the need for more time and effort to allow collaborators to gain a working understanding of the different disciplines involved as they relate to the problems being tackled. Additional resources are also needed to navigate different cultures, policies, and procedures across units and geographic areas involved and to deploy tools designed to support effective cross-disciplinary cross-unit collaborations.

The Healthcare Industry in a One Health World

The global call to protect human health by protecting the environment will undoubtedly change the healthcare industry. The healthcare professions are already increasingly working in interprofessional teams in which physicians, nurses, pharmacists, psychologists, social workers, and many others collaborate to integrate their expertise into a care plan that advances the patient's health. Accreditors of health profession educators require that students receive training in interprofessional team-based care, skills that align with and can be adapted to advance the One Health approach to problem solving. The Joint Commission, the primary accreditor of healthcare providers in the United States, requires hospitals to have an antibiotic stewardship program that meets certain standards designed to reduce the risk of infection and death from drug-resistant bacteria. These standards could be adapted to animal health and agricultural practices.

Two years after the journal editors' call for urgent environmental action, The Joint Commission has identified environmental sustainability as one of their top priorities and announced a voluntary Sustainable Healthcare Certification program for hospitals, effective in 2024. Certification requires that a hospital collect baseline emissions data for three greenhouse gas emission sources, have an action plan to reduce the emissions, and demonstrate reduction. The Joint Commission provides suggestions for reducing emissions in healthcare transportation, buildings and energy use, anesthetic gases, and waste.

To encourage hospital participation in their voluntary Sustainable Healthcare Certification program, The Joint Commission lists several benefits, including regulatory compliance and risk mitigation as well as new regulations and standards that are likely ahead. In addition, organizations that achieve this certification can leverage it in their marketing and public relations efforts. Improved health outcomes and cost savings are also listed among the benefits as The Joint Commission reports that better health for healthcare workers as well as patients can result from less exposure to chemicals and less air pollution, and that cost savings may be achieved with improvements in energy efficiency and potentially through tax incentives. However, for many hospitals, even if they could identify a firm path to return on investment, the more immediate challenges of dealing with staff shortages, rapidly increasing expenses, and inadequate reimbursement make it difficult to consider investing resources in environmental sustainability.

According to Fierce Healthcare, The Joint Commission originally planned to make these standards for sustainability a requirement, but hospital leaders pushed back. Responses to an open comment period on the proposed new standards were mostly negative and from senior leaders who reported being overwhelmed by other challenges. Potentially adding to those challenges, younger clinicians have expressed support for the standards. Given the need to address clinician shortages, failing to participate in sustainability initiatives may put hospitals at a competitive disadvantage in shoring up their workforce recruitment and retention efforts.

At least some hospitals have embraced sustainability goals, including creating new leadership positions such as medical director for sustainability, which focuses on clinical practices. Organizations representing more than 15% of hospitals in the United States have signed the White House and Department of Health and Human Services (HHS) Health Sector Climate Pledge to reduce organizational emissions by 50% by 2030, using a 2008 or later baseline; to achieve net-zero production of greenhouse gases by 2050; to publicly account for progress on these goals annually; to designate an executive responsible for overseeing the organization's emissions reduction initiatives; and to develop a climate resilience plan to mitigate operational risk and address the needs of those most vulnerable to climate-related harm. The organization Health Care Without Harm, which has advocated for making The Joint Commission sustainability standards mandatory, offers resources and tools to help support healthcare organizations in their sustainability efforts. These include an energy and health impact calculator, a list of priority chemicals of concern along with safer alternatives, and access to additional resources through their membership organization Practice Greenhealth.

There are also toolkits available to support sustainability efforts in primary care settings. In a 2023 report, Sonja Wicklum and colleagues reviewed the literature and evaluated 11 toolkits, which ranged from simple checklists to tools with more comprehensive breadth and depth. Most of the toolkits focused on administrative practices, such as energy use, waste management, and procurement of office supplies. A few included a clinical component, such as medication prescribing and disposal. Most toolkits included educational materials for healthcare professionals and their patients. The toolkits that included adaptation and implementation guides would likely be most useful to primary care clinics to help them overcome barriers to action. The available literature indicated these toolkits differed in their adaptability to primary care settings and outcome measures but that they are still in their infancy and their effectiveness has not yet been formally evaluated. Toolkits and other interventions may be helpful to address climate-related mental health issues.

Climate Anxiety

Climate anxiety, sometimes referred to as eco-anxiety, results from environmental threats, and is most common among younger generations who, simply based on age, will be more likely to experience the consequences of an ailing planet. In an international survey of 10,000 children, adolescents, and young adults conducted by Caroline Hickman and colleagues in 2021, 59% reported being very or extremely worried about climate change, and nearly half indicated that their feelings about climate change adversely affected their daily life and functioning. In addition, a higher level of climate anxiety was associated with perceptions that government response is inadequate and feelings of betrayal. Hickman and colleagues also found that negative beliefs related to climate change included 39% who reported being hesitant to have children, 56% who believe humanity is doomed, and 83% who believe that people have failed to take care of the planet. Youth in two countries were particularly pessimistic about humanity, with 74% in India and 73% in the Philippines believing humanity is doomed. Regarding attitudes toward government, only 31% of respondents in the international sample believed governments can be trusted, and 64% believe the government is lying about the effectiveness of the actions they are taking. While the concept of climate-related anxiety is not defined consistently across studies, there is a positive association between these worries and engagement in activities to help address environmental threats. These range from changing daily habits to policy activism. These active coping mechanisms are associated with reduced stress and increased hope.

Trust in Businesses and Demand for Corporate Social Resonsibility

As awareness and anxiety about climate risk increases, to the extent that the world has lost trust in governments to address the risk or to accurately report the effectiveness of its responses, there is an opportunity for other entities to take the lead. The 2023 Edelman Trust Barometer report included survey results from more than 32,000 respondents across 28 countries who were asked whether they trust various institutions *to do what is right*. Globally, 62% of respondents trust businesses, which is more than those who trust nongovernmental organizations (trusted by 59%), governments (trusted by 51%), and the media (trusted by 50%). In over half of the countries, there was a double-digit trust gap favoring businesses over government. South Africa had the biggest gap, with 62% reporting trust in businesses and only 22% reporting trust in government. There were only two countries, Singapore and Saudi Arabia, with a double-digit gap favoring government. Overall average trust in institutions was higher among those in the top 25% of income (64% trusting) versus the lowest 25% of income (49% trusting) across countries. In terms of trust in people, government leaders were least trusted at only 41% compared to scientists, the most trusted at 76%.

The Edelman survey also found that 63% of respondents said they buy or advocate for brands based on their beliefs and values and 69% said that having a societal impact is a strong expectation or deal breaker when considering a job. In questions asking about whether businesses are overstepping or not doing enough to address societal issues, respondents overwhelmingly said businesses are not doing enough to address climate change, economic inequality, energy shortages, and healthcare access. Among the 48% of respondents who said it is possible for businesses to address societal issues without being seen as politicized, the most recommended way to achieve this is by being a trustworthy information source, followed by basing actions on science. Across 17 industry sectors, healthcare was the fourth most trusted, with 70% of respondents reporting trust in the sector, behind the food and beverage sector and education sector at 71%, and the technology sector at 75%. The least trusted sector was social media at 44%.

Thus, businesses in the healthcare industry, and the educators, scientists, and clinicians within the industry, have an opportunity to leverage the trust placed in them by demonstrating the responsible leadership the public expects. Because it is not feasible for all healthcare leaders to become experts in environmental sciences, collaborating with credible partners who have this expertise is a pathway that aligns with One Health concepts. Businesses outside of the healthcare industry can also play a role by credibly aligning the health and wellness benefits they offer to employees as part of compensation packages with the health of the environment. For example, as healthcare price and quality become increasingly transparent in the United States, employers can also disclose the environmental impacts of the health plans they offer. The key caveat is that businesses—whether in the healthcare industry or not—need to be careful to ensure the accuracy of the information they provide or risk losing their credibility. Businesses engaged in greenwashing, making misleading or false statements about their environmental friendliness, risk the loss of their reputation and regulatory action for deceiving consumers.

As consumer expectations for activism collide with political polarization, it becomes increasingly difficult for businesses to choose a side on issues. When engaging in corporate political activism, it is important that businesses are clear and consistent regarding their values when navigating how and when to take a stand on societal issues. In 2006, Michael Porter and Mark Kramer provided guidance on aligning corporate social responsibility efforts with strategies to achieve competitive advantage. This starts with the recognition that organizations cannot solve all the world's problems, but they can focus resources where they will most benefit society and the organization's strategic goals. Organizations can achieve this by identifying how they intersect with the communities where they operate (e.g., supply and quality of local workforce) and assessing the socioeconomic conditions of those communities (e.g., poverty, crime, environmental risks). Organizations can then prioritize issues and effectively use resources that align with their goals. Leaders of healthcare organizations of any size and within any sector can apply these concepts to ensure that efforts around environmental sustainability are synergistic with their mission rather than a distraction or an empty slogan. For example, local pharmacies can serve as a drug take-back site, collecting unused or expired prescriptions and over-the-counter medications for safe disposal. In doing so, they can educate their local community members about risks of diversion and environmental contamination with inappropriate disposal of medications. This may attract and retain customers as well as support employee recruitment and retention. Similarly, hospitals located in areas with greater air pollution can focus community education on risk reduction strategies and establish clinical services specializing in treating lung diseases caused or exacerbated by air pollution, while working on reducing emissions from hospital operations. Pharmaceutical companies can support research on the use of biological approaches to rehabilitating ecosystems that have been contaminated by pharmaceutical compounds.

Carbon Footprint of the Healthcare Industry

In addition to focusing on the environmental issues affecting the local communities where healthcare organizations operate, understanding how an organization fits within the global industry-wide environmental impact can facilitate strategic alignment. In their 2019 report on OECD countries plus China and India, Peter-Paul Pichler and colleagues found that the healthcare industry has the largest service sector carbon footprint in most countries and is comparable to the food industry in size. Based on data from 2014, they found that healthcare accounts for 5% of the total national carbon footprint, on average across countries. Figures 1 and 2 demonstrate the variation across nations, both in the

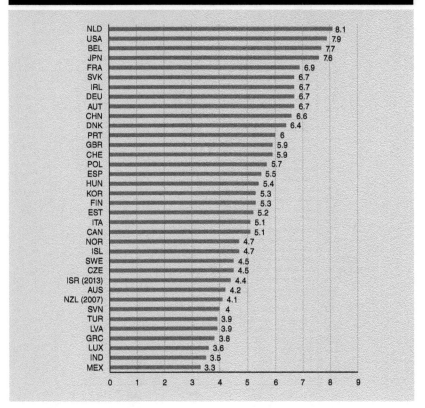

Figure 1   Healthcare Carbon Footprint: % of National tCO$_2$ in 2014, Except Where Noted

NLD	8.1
USA	7.9
BEL	7.7
JPN	7.6
FRA	6.9
SVK	6.7
IRL	6.7
DEU	6.7
AUT	6.7
CHN	6.6
DNK	6.4
PRT	6
GBR	5.9
CHE	5.9
POL	5.7
ESP	5.5
HUN	5.4
KOR	5.3
FIN	5.3
EST	5.2
ITA	5.1
CAN	5.1
NOR	4.7
ISL	4.7
SWE	4.5
CZE	4.5
ISR (2013)	4.4
AUS	4.2
NZL (2007)	4.1
SVN	4
TUR	3.9
LVA	3.9
GRC	3.8
LUX	3.6
IND	3.5
MEX	3.3

Source: Pichler et al. (2019)

percentage of the national total metric tons of carbon dioxide (CO$_2$) emissions accounted for by healthcare and in the healthcare CO$_2$ emissions per capita.

Pichler and colleagues reported that, within healthcare, retailers and other providers of medical goods (e.g., pharmacies and suppliers of durable medical equipment and pharmaceuticals) account for the largest share of the healthcare carbon footprint on average at one-third of the total healthcare CO$_2$. Hospitals come in second at 29%, followed by ambulatory care providers at 18% on average. Across settings, 38% of healthcare CO$_2$ emissions are associated with heating, water, and electricity generation, 22% are associated with transportation, and 10% with pharmaceutical and chemical sectors. Thus, a key target for healthcare organizations to reduce their

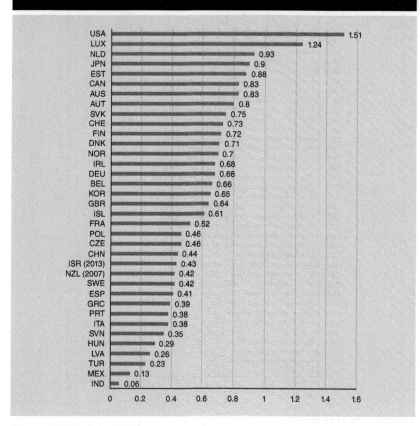

Figure 2   Healthcare Carbon Footprint: CO_2 per Capita in 2014, Except Where Noted

USA	1.51
LUX	1.24
NLD	0.93
JPN	0.9
EST	0.88
CAN	0.83
AUS	0.83
AUT	0.8
SVK	0.75
CHE	0.73
FIN	0.72
DNK	0.71
NOR	0.7
IRL	0.68
DEU	0.68
BEL	0.66
KOR	0.65
GBR	0.64
ISL	0.61
FRA	0.52
POL	0.46
CZE	0.46
CHN	0.44
ISR (2013)	0.43
NZL (2007)	0.42
SWE	0.42
ESP	0.41
GRC	0.39
PRT	0.38
ITA	0.38
SVN	0.35
HUN	0.29
LVA	0.26
TUR	0.23
MEX	0.13
IND	0.06

Source: Pichler et al. (2019)

carbon footprint is reducing energy demand, for example, with energy efficient building standards, lighting, and equipment operating protocols.

Pichler and colleagues also found that domestic energy systems explain a greater portion of the variation in healthcare CO_2 per capita than do healthcare expenditures; some countries achieved a reduction in their healthcare carbon footprint while healthcare expenditures were increasing. This suggests that a more potent solution to reducing the healthcare carbon footprint would be to focus outside of the healthcare industry on decarbonization of domestic energy systems. Furthermore, focusing resources on reducing the carbon footprint within the healthcare industry could shift resources away from improving healthcare access to impoverished communities worldwide, exacerbating health inequities. In alignment with One

Health concepts, Pichler and colleagues recommend advancing integrative research to better understand the relationships between healthcare carbon footprints, healthcare system performance, and health outcomes, including health disparities.

Measuring Environmental Impacts on Health

In the United States, America's Health Rankings is an effort to integrate the many complex factors that affect health by leveraging multiple data sources and weighting them to create a composite measure of health defined more holistically. This state ranking system was created by the United Health Foundation, the philanthropic arm of UnitedHealth Group, the nation's largest health insurance company and one of the largest corporations in the United States. The ranking system recognizes four categories of influence on health outcomes: behaviors (e.g., diet, exercise, sleep, sexual behaviors, smoking and tobacco use), physical environment (e.g., air and water quality, climate risks and policies, renewable energy, energy use), social and economic factors (e.g., community and occupational safety, state funding for public health, poverty, income, unemployment, education, disparities, segregation, volunteerism, voter participation), and clinical care (e.g., access to care, availability of healthcare providers, preventive care, quality of care). The indicators comprising the composite measure and the weight applied to each indicator have evolved over time as new information on health risk factors and more data become available for comparison. Based on their overall composite measure from 2022, the healthiest state is New Hampshire, and the least healthy is Louisiana. Among the indicators, the level of economic hardship—New Hampshire with the lowest and Louisiana with nearly the highest—had the biggest impact on rankings for both states. This reflects the effect of the weighting of each category of indicators, with social and economic factors weighted at 30% of the composite, double that of the clinical care category, weighted at 15%, and three times that of the physical environment category, weighted at 10%, for their annual report in 2022.

The ability to examine both the overall composite measure and the individual weighted factors allows healthcare leaders to understand their relative strengths and weaknesses at a more granular and actionable level. For example, leaders interested in focusing on the environmental category of indicators can see where they stand relative to other states to help with action planning and monitoring improvements. Table 1 shows all the indicators in the physical environment category for 2022, along with the weight of each in the overall composite measure, the data source for each measure, and the states with the best and worst ranking on each measure.

Measure[1] (weight[2])	Description[1]	Source[1]	Best / Worst State(s) in 2022[3]
Air and Water Quality			
Air pollution (1.429%)	Average exposure of the general public to particulate matter of 2.5 microns or less, measured in micrograms per cubic meter.	U.S. EPA	Hawai'i / California
Drinking Water Violations (1.429%)	Percentage of population served by community water systems with a serious drinking water violation during the year.	U.S. EPA, Enforcement and Compliance History Online, Safe Drinking Water Information System	California, Delaware, Hawai'i, Iowa, Kentucky, Massachusetts, Maryland, Maine, North Carolina, North Dakota, Rhode Island, South Carolina, Utah / West Virginia
Non-smoking Regulation (Not included)	Percentage of population covered by 100% smoke-free laws for restaurants, bars and non-hospitality workplaces.	American Nonsmokers' Rights Foundation	Arizona, California, Colorado, Connecticut, Delaware, Hawai'i, Iowa, Illinois, Kansas, Massachusetts, Maryland, Maine, Michigan, Minnesota, Montana, North Dakota, Nebraska, New Jersey, New Mexico, New York, Ohio, Oregon, Rhode Island, South Dakota, Utah, Vermont, Washington, Wisconsin / Florida, New Hampshire, Nevada, Oklahoma, Pennsylvania, Tennessee, Virginia

Measure[1] (weight[2])	Description[1]	Source[1]	Best / Worst State(s) in 2022[3]
Risk-screening Environmental Indicator Score (1.429%)	Estimated human health-related risk from exposure to toxic chemicals based on emission data of more than 600 chemicals, with higher scores denoting elevated risk.	U.S. EPA, Toxic Release Inventory National Analysis	Vermont / Texas
Water Fluoridation (1.429%)	Percentage of population served by community water systems that have fluoridated water.	CDC, Water Fluoridation Reporting System	Kentucky / Hawai'i
Climate Change			
Climate Change Policies (Not included)	Number of the following state policies in place: legally binding electricity portfolio standards, carbon pricing policies, climate change action plans and economy-wide greenhouse gas emission targets.	Center for Climate and Energy Solutions	California, Connecticut, Delaware, Massachusetts, Maryland, Maine, New Jersey, New York, Rhode Island, Virginia, Vermont, Washington / Alaska, Alabama, Georgia, Idaho, Indiana, Kansas, Mississippi, North Dakota, Nebraska, Oklahoma, South Dakota, Tennessee, Utah, West Virginia, Wyoming
Transportation Energy Use (Not included)	Amount of energy (in trillion British thermal units) consumed by the transportation of people and goods per 100,000 population.	U.S. Energy Information Administration, State Energy Data System	Rhode Island / Alaska

(*Continued*)

Table 1   (Continued)

Measure[1] (weight[2])	Description[1]	Source[1]	Best / Worst State(s) in 2022[3]
Housing and Transit			
Drive Alone to Work (1.429%)	Percentage of workers ages 16 and older who drive alone to work.	U.S. Census Bureau, American Community Survey	New York / Mississippi
Housing With Lead Risk (1.429%)	Percentage of housing stock with potential elevated lead risk due to age of housing.	U.S. Census Bureau, American Community Survey	Nevada / New York
Severe Housing Problems (1.429%)	Percentage of occupied housing units with at least one of the following problems: lack of complete kitchen facilities, lack of plumbing facilities, overcrowding or severely cost-burdened occupants.	U.S. Department of Housing and Urban Development, Comprehensive Housing Affordability Strategy	West Virginia / Hawaiʻi

[1] https://assets.americashealthrankings.org/app/uploads/ahr_2022annualreport_measurestable.pdf

[2] https://www.americashealthrankings.org/about/methodology/measures-weights-and-direction

[3] https://www.americashealthrankings.org/explore/measures/reports/annual

Within the One Health concept, healthcare leaders are challenged to effectively demonstrate appropriate understanding of the holistic concept of health and the current state of the evidence. Researchers, Wayne Gao and colleagues from Taiwan and Australia, caution that some environmental advocates and leaders, in particular those at the World Health Organization (WHO), have stepped dangerously beyond the evidence in efforts to shift attention and resources to environmental issues. One claim supported by some WHO leaders, which became rapidly popularized by the media, is that air pollution is as harmful to health as smoking. Gao and colleagues, in their 2020 report, methodically compared the global disease burden from outdoor air pollution and tobacco use from 1990 through 2017. They reported that the effects of tobacco use, including second-hand smoke, led to many more deaths and much lower life expectancy than the effects of outdoor air pollution.

In comparing the effects on disability over time, Gao and colleagues reported that loss of disability-adjusted life years (DALY, a statistic used by the WHO to allow comparison of disease burden by causes of premature death that have differing levels of disability before death) has been lower globally for air pollution than for tobacco use since 1990. They also found that the loss of DALY has decreased more rapidly for air pollution than for tobacco use since 1990, with loss of DALY due to air pollution in 2017 under 2,000 per 100,000 compared to loss of DALY due to tobacco use above 2,700 per 100,000. They report the most dramatic improvements in loss of DALY due to air pollution have been seen in low-development countries, from approximately 8,000 per 100,000 in 1990 to approximately 3,000 per 100,000 in 2017. In contrast, high-development countries started much lower with a loss of DALY due to air pollution just above 1,000 per 100,000 in 1990, which decreased to under 1,000 per 100,000 by 2017. Loss of DALY from tobacco use remains much higher in high-development countries, decreasing from over 5,000 per 100,000 in 1990 to under 3,500 per 100,000 in 2017, compared to low-development countries, which decreased from approximately 3,000 to 1,700 per 100,000 during the same period. Middle-development countries saw relatively little improvement in loss of DALY from air pollution or tobacco use during this period compared to low-development countries. As of 2017, loss of DALY in middle-development countries was approximately 1,700 per 100,000 due to air pollution and approximately 2,800 per 100,000 due to tobacco use. Gao and colleagues concluded that the misleading claims made by WHO leaders and others undermine the credibility of environmental health advocates and risk furthering harm to human health by undermining tobacco control efforts.

In 2022, Richard Fuller and colleagues reported that tobacco use remains a greater health risk than outdoor air pollution, with about twice the number of deaths attributable to smoking and second-hand smoke as those to outdoor air pollution. Even when combining outdoor air pollution with household air pollution from cooking with open fires or other hazardous methods, tobacco use is more deadly. However, when combining all sources of pollution (i.e., total air pollution, total water pollution, and occupational pollution), pollution is estimated to cause approximately 9 million deaths, 16% of all deaths per year globally, which is about the same as tobacco use.

Applications to Patient Care

Clinicians can consider how One Health might be applied to their daily patient care, both to support active coping among their patients who experience climate anxiety and to advance health literacy among their patients more broadly. For example, clinicians can incorporate both environmental and behavioral components of health into patient educational materials and messaging in a way that is both accurate and actionable, such as demonstrating how lung health can be improved by monitoring local air quality reports in areas prone to pollution and by stopping smoking. They can also use patient education as an opportunity to share what the healthcare provider is doing to reduce pollution and to correct misleading information in the media. For any patient who smokes, helping them stop will typically be the top health priority for intervention based on science, and helping them understand the health risks from smoking relative to other risks may increase their motivation to stop. Clinicians who understand health more holistically will also be better able to prioritize their effort and resources to improve health outcomes based on science. For example, while evaluating clinic practices for evidence-based emissions reductions, clinicians can review whether their smoking-cessation services are adequately prioritized and aligned with the evidence for effectiveness.

Clinicians can also consider learning more about the links between food and health for themselves, their patients, and the planet. In the highly specialized healthcare industry, most clinicians are not well trained on the topic of nutrition, much less its environmental impact, yet food can optimize human health and safeguard environmental sustainability. Consistent with the One Health approach, the EAT-Lancet Commission convened a global panel of experts from different fields in human health, agriculture, political science, and environmental sustainability with the goal of achieving planetary health diets for 10 billion people by 2050. While nations and health organizations have previously produced evidence-based dietary guidelines for human health, the EAT-Lancet Commission published the first dietary guidelines for both human and planet health in 2019. They are similar to dietary guidelines that focus exclusively on human health in that half of each plate is filled with vegetables and fruits but differ in that they specify that most protein should be plant based, with a minimal amount from animal sources.

Relative to baseline diets globally, the Commission reported that adoption of a planetary health diet would require more than doubling consumption of healthy plant-based foods, specifically fruits, vegetables, whole grains, nuts, seeds, and legumes and cutting consumption of red meat and starchy vegetables by more than 50%. Importantly, the gaps between baseline and planetary health diet vary substantially by region. While underconsumption of fruits, vegetables, whole grains, nuts, seeds, and legumes is more common worldwide, overconsumption of animal proteins, a dietary pattern associated with higher rates of chronic disease, is particularly high in North America. Specifically, the EAT-Lancet Commission reported that the North American diet included 638% of the planetary health diet recommendation for red meat, 234% of the recommendation for poultry, and 268% of the recommendation for eggs.

The EAT-Lancet Commission recognized that the shift to a worldwide healthy diet for both the planet and people will require immense international cooperation and collaboration. The healthcare industry, and particularly the clinicians who are trusted to advance health and healing, are well positioned to be a major force in this effort to save lives. The Commission estimated that worldwide adoption of the planetary diet would prevent approximately 11 million adult deaths from diet-related disease per year, which would represent 19% to 24% of all adult deaths.

Along with their dietary guidelines for human health, the EAT-Lancet Commission has established the first set of science-based guidelines for food production systems that align human and planet health. These guidelines set upper limits or boundaries, including ranges of uncertainty. If global food production systems stay within these limits, they can reduce the risk of irreversible and catastrophic harm to the planet. Specific boundaries are set for greenhouse gas emissions, cropland use, water use, nitrogen application, phosphorus application, and the extinction rate. The Commission reported that global food production, using a 2010 baseline, has almost reached the guideline boundary for cropland use and water use and has exceeded the boundaries set for all other categories. The 2010 baseline phosphorus application was more than double the guideline boundary, and the baseline extinction rate is at least ten times the guideline boundary. Without any changes in human dietary patterns or food systems, the safe boundaries will be exceeded in all categories by 2050.

The EAT-Lancet Commission report reflects the complex challenges involved in achieving the goal of meeting the food production system guidelines. If humans adopt the recommended dietary changes, which is no small feat, the Commission projects that greenhouse gas emissions would be reduced sufficiently to meet the guideline boundary by 2050. However, the boundaries would be exceeded in all other categories. To stay within the boundaries or at least within the range of uncertainty for the boundaries in all categories by 2050, adoption of the human dietary guidelines will need to occur along with two key food system changes: halving food loss and waste and significantly improving food production.

In addition to securing international, multisector, cross-industry commitment to facilitate the adoption of the human dietary guidelines, the EAT-Lancet Commission identifies additional critical strategies to achieve the food system transformation needed to achieve planet health. To achieve planet and human health, agricultural priorities would need to shift from maximizing the production of food volume to producing a diversity of healthy foods. With reductions in human consumption of animal proteins, there is a reduction in the need for crops to feed those animals. Production methods need to sustainably improve yields from croplands through improved water and nutrient management, greater biodiversity within agricultural systems, and improved energy efficiency. In addition, land and ocean governance improvements are necessary to prevent the expansion of agricultural land, protect the Earth's intact ecosystems, and sustainably manage the supply of healthy food from the ocean. Finally, to cut food loss and waste in half, technical improvements will be needed throughout the food supply chain along with changes in food policies and consumer behavior.

In their 2023 publication analyzing the short-term impact of the EAT-Lancet Commission report, Ayesha Tulloch and colleagues found that it had stimulated substantial research and debate across disciplines, including publications on additional modeling, case studies, interventions, tool development, and commentary in scientific journals. Among the articles that critiqued the Commission's work, opinions were more positive than negative on average across all disciplines, including the life sciences, health and medical sciences, and social sciences. Themes from the negative critiques of the Commission's report focused on inadequate consideration of socioeconomic factors, such as the importance of respecting cultural values and consumer preferences that would require substantial local adaptations, the impact of unaffordable food on those with low incomes or already in poverty, and the impact of food production changes on the livelihoods of those who are already vulnerable. Critiques also included questions of feasibility and the challenges of coordinating across governments and supply chains. Concerns were also raised about nutritional inadequacies in the dietary guidelines, particularly the potential for micronutrient deficiencies and about the environmental challenges in shifting agricultural production.

Tulloch and colleagues found that the most common positive themes were that the Commission's report helps in guiding science-based policy change, may improve human and planet health, raises public awareness, and enhances progress toward holistic food system transformation. They also found frequent positive comments about the benefits of establishing science-based measurable targets and about the effectiveness of the Commission in synthesizing the scientific evidence. In particular, the scholarly community has commended the Commission for articulating a singular goal: to achieve planetary health diets for 10 billion people by 2050. The Commission's report has been cited in thousands of scientific journal articles worldwide. Outside of this academic sector, the work of the EAT-Lancet Commission may be considered an invitation to the global healthcare industry to become part of a One Health industry.

REFERENCES

America's Health Rankings. (2022). *Annual report*. United Health Foundation. https://assets.americashealthrankings.org/app/uploads/ahr_2022annualreport.pdf

Atwoli, L., Baqui, A. H., Benfield, T., Bosurgi, R., Godlee, F., Hancocks, S., Horton, R., Laybourn-Langton, L., Monteiro, C. A., Norman, I., Patrick, K., Praities, N., Rikkert, M., Rubin, E. J., Sahni, P., Smith, R., Talley, N., Turale, S., & Vázquez, D. (2021). Call for emergency action to limit global temperature increases, restore biodiversity, and protect health. *PLoS Med 18*(9): e1003755. https://doi.org/10.1371/journal.pmed.1003755

Edelman Trust Institute. (2023). *Edelman Trust Barometer global report*. https://www.edelman.com/sites/g/files/aatuss191/files/2023-01/2023%20Edelman%20Trust%20Barometer%20Global%20Report.pdf

Fuller, R., Landrigan, P. J., Balakrishnan, K., Bathan, G., Bose-O'Reilly, S., Brauer, M., Caravanos, J., Chiles, T., Cohen, A., Corra, L., Cropper, M., Ferraro, G., Hanna, J., Hanrahan, D., Hu, H., Hunter, D., Janata, G., Kupka, R., Lanphear, B., Lichtveld, M., ... & Yan, C. (2022). Pollution and health: a progress update. *The Lancet Planetary Health, 6*(6), e535–e547. https://doi.org/10.1016/S2542-5196(22)00090-0

Gao, W., Sanna, M., Hefler, M., & Wen, C. P. (2020). Air pollution is not 'the new smoking': comparing the disease burden of air pollution and smoking across the globe, 1990–2017. *Tobacco Control, 29*(6), 715–718. https://doi.org/10.1136%2Ftobaccocontrol-2019-055181

Hall, K. L., Vogel, A. L., Huang, G. C., Serrano, K. J., Rice, E. L., Tsakraklides, S. P., & Fiore, S. M. (2018). The science of team science: A review of the empirical evidence and research gaps on collaboration in science. *American Psychologist, 73*(4), 532. https://doi.org/10.1037/amp0000319

Hickman, C., Marks, E., Pihkala, P., Clayton, S., Lewandowski, R. E., Mayall, E. E., Wray, B., Mellor, C., & Van Susteren, L. (2021). Climate anxiety in children and young people and their beliefs about government responses to climate change: a global survey. *The Lancet Planetary Health, 5*(12), e863–e873. https://doi.org/10.1016/s2542-5196(21)00278-3

Pichler, P. P., Jaccard, I. S., Weisz, U., & Weisz, H. (2019). International comparison of health care carbon footprints. *Environmental Research Letters, 14*(6), 064004. https://doi.org/10.1088/1748-9326/ab19e1

Porter, M. E., & Kramer, M. R. (2006, December). Strategy and society: The link between competitive advantage and corporate social responsibility. *Harvard Business Review, 84*(12), 78–92. https://hbr.org/2006/12/strategy-and-society-the-link-between-competitive-advantage-and-corporate-social-responsibility

Rhodes, J., Abdolrasouli, A., Dunne, K., Sewell, T. R., Zhang, Y., Ballard, E., Brackin, A. P., van Rhijn, N., Chown, H., Tsitsopoulou, A., Posso, R. B., Chotirmall, S. H., McElvaney, N. G., Murphy, P. G., Talento, A. F., Renwick, J., Dyer, P. S., Szekely, A., Bowyer, P., Bromley, M. J., . . . & Fisher, M. C. (2022). Population genomics confirms acquisition of drug-resistant Aspergillus fumigatus infection by humans from the environment. *Nature Microbiology, 7*(5), 663–674. https://doi.org/10.1038/s41564-022-01091-2

Tulloch, A. I., Borthwick, F., Bogueva, D., Eltholth, M., Grech, A., Edgar, D., . . . & McNeill, G. (2023). How the EAT–Lancet Commission on food in the Anthropocene influenced discourse and research on food systems: A systematic review covering the first 2 years post-publication. *The Lancet Global Health, 11*(7), e1125-e1136. https://doi.org/10.1016/s2214-109x(23)00212-7

United States Department of Agriculture. (n.d.). *Honeybees.* https://www.usda.gov/peoples-garden/pollinators/honey-bees#:~:text=Beehives%20are%20often%20important%20elements,fruits%2C%20nuts%2C%20and%20vegetables.

Wicklum, S. C., Nuique, K., Kelly, M. A., Nesbitt, C. C., Zhang, J. J., & Svrcek, C. P. (2023). Greening Family Medicine clinic operations and clinical care, where do we start? A scoping review of toolkits and aids. *Family Practice, 40*(3), 473–485. https://doi.org/10.1093/fampra/cmad006

Willett, W., Rockström, J., Loken, B., Springmann, M., Lang, T., Vermeulen, S., Garnett, T., Tilman, D., DeClerck, F., Wood, A., Jonell, M., Clark, M., Gordon, L. J., Fanzo, J., Hawkes, C., Zurayk, R., Rivera, J. A., De Vries, W., Majele Sibanda, L., Afshin, A., . . . & Murray, C. J. L. (2019). Food in the Anthropocene: the EAT-Lancet Commission on healthy diets from sustainable food systems. *Lancet (London, England), 393*(10170), 447–492. https://doi.org/10.1016/S0140-6736(18)31788-4

FURTHER READINGS

Casadevall, A., & Fang, F. C. (2014). Specialized science. *Infection and Immunity, 82*(4), 1355–1360.

Costa, F., Lago, A., Rocha, V., Barros, Ó., Costa, L., Vipotnik, Z., Silva, B., & Tavares, T. (2019). A review on biological processes for pharmaceuticals wastes abatement—a growing threat to modern society. *Environmental Science & Technology, 53*(13), 7185–7202. https://doi.org/10.1021/acs.est.8b06977

Drexel University Online. (2021, August 26). *Authentic or virtue signaling? Marketing professor breaks down corporate social responsibility* [Video]. https://www.youtube.com/watch?v=FvJXD5BHaIQ

Evans, B. R., & Leighton, F. A. (2014). A history of One Health. *Revue Scientifique et Technique (International Office of Epizootics), 33*(2), 413–420. https://doi.org/10.20506/rst.33.2.2298

Hernando-Amado, S., Coque, T. M., Baquero, F., & Martínez, J. L. (2019). Defining and combating antibiotic resistance from One Health and Global Health perspectives. *Nature Microbiology, 4*(9), 1432–1442. https://doi.org/10.1038/s41564-019-0503-9

Schultz, M. (2008). Rudolf Virchow. *Emerging Infectious Diseases, 14*(9), 1480–1481. https://doi.org/10.3201/eid1409.086672

Travis, D. A., Sriramarao, P., Cardona, C., Steer, C. J., Kennedy, S., Sreevatsan, S., & Murtaugh, M. P. (2014). One medicine one science: A framework for exploring challenges at the intersection of animals, humans, and the environment. *Annals of the New York Academy of Sciences, 1334*(1), 26–44. https://doi.org/10.1111/nyas.12601

Verweij, P. E., Lucas, J. A., Arendrup, M. C., Bowyer, P., Brinkmann, A. J., Denning, D. W., Dyer, P. S., Fisher, M. C., Geenen, P. L., Gisis, U., Hermann, D., Hoogendijk, A., Kiers, E., Lagrou, K., Melchers, W. J. G., Rhodes, J., Rietveld, A. G., Schoustra, S. E., Stenzel, K., & Fraaije, B. A. (2020). The one health problem of azole resistance in Aspergillus fumigatus: Current insights and future research agenda. *Fungal Biology Reviews, 34*(4), 202–214.

Case Studies

A Real-World Glimpse Into the Healthcare Industry

Across every segment of the healthcare industry, the competitive forces described by Porter are driving change, inclusive of increasing global demand for health equity and planet health. This chapter presents six cases that demonstrate how these forces play out as new entrants, incumbents, and for-profit and nonprofit organizations strive to deliver better healthcare value in the United States where growing dissatisfaction echoes the principles of justice and liberty that underpin the nation's regulatory system. Those organizations that proactively monitor and adapt to the ever-changing competitive forces and adopt either low-cost leadership or differentiation as a core strategy based on alignment with organizational comparative strengths and mission will be best positioned for success. As the healthcare industry enters a new era of transparency wherein quality and price information is more meaningfully available to buyers to assess and compare value, opportunities to participate in shaping the products and services offered will grow.

Amazon Acquires One Medical as Primary Care Competition Heats Up

Abstract

Amazon's nearly $4 billion acquisition of One Medical, announced in 2022 just a few years after its purchase of online pharmacy PillPack, put to rest any questions about whether the online retail giant was serious about growing its healthcare business. Although One Medical was not yet profitable at the time it was acquired, the technology-integrated customer-focused primary care provider gave Amazon instant market share with One Medical's 767,000 individual members and 8,000 employer customers spanning both the commercially insured and Medicare market segments. The acquisition gave Amazon the opportunity to better address customer needs through integration of their healthcare and nonhealthcare consumer data. With this data, they can provide personalized health recommendations like suggesting no-salt products as alternatives and offering additional discounts for the healthier options when a customer with high blood pressure puts salty foods in their shopping cart. A more complete picture of customer behavior outside of typical healthcare settings gives Amazon a differential advantage over most primary care providers in promoting health and wellness. This case examines the competitive forces that have driven Amazon into the healthcare industry, that make Amazon's unlimited on-demand healthcare feasible, and that are shaping options for Amazon's next healthcare move.

The Case

Since purchasing One Medical, Amazon has added primary care as an optional service for its Prime members for an additional $9 per month and is cross selling its Prime membership services to One Medical customers who are not already Prime members. According to its website, Amazon's medical services include care for "everyday concerns, chronic conditions, mental health, and more" and "longer appointments so you don't feel rushed." They offer in-person visits that are covered by most major health plans in 17 cities across the United States while virtual care is available without an appointment via app 24/7 in all 50 U.S. states *at no extra cost and without billing insurance.* Amazon's purchase of One Medical complements their previous purchase of PillPack, the online pharmacy known for its customized individualized packaging of medications by dose and acquired by Amazon for its national footprint and advanced software. Prime member benefits already included the optional RxPass, which offers members all of their eligible prescription medications for $5 per month. Now operating as a primary care provider, with discounted fees for Prime members at $9 per month, Amazon accepts most major commercial health plans. Amazon is also marketing its One Medical Seniors program services to Medicare beneficiaries, accepting all those who are on the traditional Medicare plan, with or without supplemental insurance, as well as accepting some Medicare Advantage plans. According to the company's website, Amazon does not accept Medicaid insurance plans because the restrictions in those plans limit care to those providers who are in the Medicaid contract network. Their website indicates Amazon primary care services are available via self-pay for those without insurance, and they offer financial assistance for those who meet certain criteria.

Amazon has arrived late to the primary care game. Though they acquired more than 200 physician offices via One Medical, this number is small compared to CVS's more than 1,000 MinuteClinics and more than 900 HealthHUBS. Amazon's strategic interest in One Medical can help the company figure out the complexities of healthcare pricing to achieve transparency. By better understanding healthcare costs from both the physician and the pharmacy perspectives, Amazon can begin leveraging that information to deliver primary care and pharmacy services in a more consumer-friendly way that customers value. This also puts Amazon in a better position to provide better healthcare value to its own employees and to offer those services to other employers struggling with the rising costs of employee healthcare as a core business expense. This was the intent of Haven, the short-lived nonprofit business venture between Amazon, Berkshire Hathaway, and JPMorgan Chase. Amazon has shown its ability to succeed in the healthcare industry as a for-profit retail giant through their strategy of building economies of scale by satisfying customers. The Healthcare Transformation Alliance (HTA)—a collaboration of major U.S. companies struggling to tame the healthcare costs of their employees—has contracted with Amazon to offer primary care services to 67 employers and their nearly 5 million employees. Amazon's One Medical network of providers is not the only one available to HTA member employers, so Amazon faces competition in providing value to the employers. HTA pays for Amazon's One Medical primary care on a capitated basis, meaning a flat fee per employee covered rather than paying Amazon each time an employee has an office visit or uses the on demand virtual care. This arrangement shifts the financial risk for primary care from the employers to Amazon, which motivates Amazon to keep the employees as healthy as possible through good preventive care and responsive on demand care. The goal is healthier employees and lower healthcare costs. With an online pharmacy and primary care offered in person in 17 cities across the United States and virtually from anywhere, Amazon must consider options for its next strategic investments in the healthcare industry.

Analyzing Amazon's Moves and Impact From Porter's Framework

Amazon's acquisition of One Medical is a classic case of a large buyer of healthcare becoming a supplier of healthcare in response to powerful suppliers. As in any industry, suppliers that get too powerful and use that power too aggressively to demand high prices from large buyers will eventually find that one or more of their buyers (customers) will vertically integrate to become a supplier themselves—either through acquisition of an existing supplier or by building their own supplier. That vertically integrated buyer no longer needs to buy the supplies externally and can then also compete with other suppliers for other buyers. The risk in vertical integration is that the buyer may not know how to adequately manage the new supplier business, which can result in supply costs being higher rather than lower. As of 2023, Amazon has not yet offered One Medical services as a benefit to its employees, suggesting it wants to learn more about the primary care business first.

Significant investments are required to ingest a new line of business whether through purchasing an existing business or through building the business internally. Because organizations (employers) in all industries are buyers of healthcare for their employees as part of compensation packages, and because the cost of that healthcare has rapidly increased as a core business expense, the option to vertically integrate to become a supplier of healthcare has become a compelling option for employers. The trend of more employers self-insuring rather than paying health plans to take on the financial risk of healthcare for their employees is one common example of this vertical integration in big and small organizations. However, this only addresses the cost of the risk, not the cost of each hospitalization, doctor's visit, and medication.

For a business to become a supplier of healthcare is no small investment. Organizations that do so successfully will align their healthcare offering to their own supply needs and unique capabilities. Amazon is only one example of a healthcare buyer that vertically integrated to become a healthcare supplier and was not the first to do so. Other examples include Walmart and UnitedHealth Group. UnitedHealth was already in the healthcare industry, but primarily as a health insurance company. UnitedHealth Group began vertically integrating to provide healthcare in 1998, and then formed Optum in 2011 as a sister company to their health insurance business UnitedHealthcare. Optum delivers healthcare, pharmacy care, and health information technology and data analytics services, which assist UnitedHealth Group's business with managing the financial risk of healthcare. United Health Group is both the largest health insurance company and the largest employer of physicians in the United States. Walmart, competing on a low-cost leadership strategy, entered the primary care market and has expanded availability of healthcare services to its employees. Aligned with its strategy and core market, Walmart offers low-cost services to those self-paying customers without insurance and is partnering to deliver services to those with Medicaid insurance. Amazon, which competes on a differentiation strategy focused on customer-centeredness, began offering primary care to its employees in a pilot before expanding to offer primary care to its customers with their acquisition of One Medical. Amazon has grown its global enterprise by obsessing over the customer experience, a distinct advantage as it enters a healthcare industry that has long struggled to make patient-centeredness a reality rather than a goal.

Amazon's unlimited on-demand virtual healthcare for $9 per month—only available to Prime members—is another way to hook and retain Prime members and their membership fees. These membership fees are set and adjusted to ensure *net* financial benefit to Amazon while also delivering value according to Prime members. Thus, it is possible that the revenue from Prime membership fees does not cover the cost of providing the specific Prime benefits used by members individually or even in aggregate, but that the revenue from the extra shopping by Prime members more than covers the cost of the Prime benefits. Amazon's business model has always been based on growing economies of scale through competitive prices and customer service, including offering Prime's extra services at a price customers are willing to pay. From the time Jeff Bezos opened Amazon for business in 1995 until 2002, Amazon lost money every year (i.e., bottom line, expenses exceeded revenue) but grew its customer base and revenue, often referred to as top line growth. The growing economies of scale that spread fixed expenses over an increasingly large number of sales finally tipped Amazon to an annual profit of $35 million or 8 cents per share in 2003. Since then, Amazon has earned an annual profit most years, with net income of $21.3 billion in 2020, $33.4 billion in 2021, and a net loss of $2.7 billion in 2022. In Amazon's 2022 annual report, CEO Jassy's letter to shareholders noted that its customers pushed the company to expand beyond pharmacy in the healthcare business and that its move into primary care was just a start. As it does every year, Amazon's annual report also included the company's first letter to shareholders from founder Jeff Bezos in 1997 as a reminder of its commitment to its founding mission to use the internet as a platform to transform the shopping experience and its founding operating principles of obsessing over the customer experience as the pathway to reach scale.

The Prime membership started as a way for customers to get unlimited expedited shipping, but the benefits have grown to include video streaming, same-day delivery, extra discounts, and many other benefits that make it easy to continue shopping through Amazon. The benefits include extra discounts on some medications purchased through Amazon pharmacy, which includes a price comparison tool, so consumers can choose another pharmacy if preferred. In addition, each virtual healthcare visit may lead to additional purchases, often through Amazon, such as medication or a follow up appointment with a copay. What might be less obvious are the other strategic reasons this primary care service helps position Amazon for continued growth in the healthcare business. If Amazon wants to lower the cost of providing healthcare to its employees and help other businesses do so too, Amazon needs to understand what drives up costs without improving health (i.e., where the waste is in the system) and what customers want out of healthcare. The more customers and employees use Amazon's healthcare services, the more data they have available to mine to guide them in improving their services.

Amazon is already building partnerships with specialists and hospitals, a key step in understanding the details of total healthcare costs. Given that hospital care is the largest category of healthcare expenditures, driving down those costs by helping to keep customers healthy is a key goal for Amazon. Outright purchase of a national hospital chain would be a much larger investment than the purchase of One Medical but could be a consideration particularly if Amazon is interested in the senior care market. Purchasing a smaller regional hospital system located near One Medical offices where Amazon has a significant number of employees would align Amazon's quest for details of hospital costs and pricing while managing employee healthcare costs as they do with primary care and pharmacy operations. Another key opportunity is in the application of artificial intelligence to improving healthcare value. In 2023, Amazon announced an investment in AI company Anthropic. Anthropic was founded by two former OpenAI executives who left due to concerns about inadequate safeguards in the development of OpenAI's GPT products. Investing in this company may lead consumers to trust Amazon as a steward of patient health data given that Anthropic is building a reputation as the safer and more responsible alternative to OpenAI.

As a relatively new healthcare entrant where competition for market share is intensifying among other retail giants, the threat of new entrants remains. It took many years for Amazon to break into the healthcare market, so entry by industry outsiders is not easy. As an industry outsider, Amazon knows the challenges of breaking in and, therefore, may be better able to defend against the threat of entry compared to the traditional incumbents who did not take Amazon (or other outsiders like Walmart) seriously as potential threats. Amazon may look to other large technology companies as threats of entry. Apple, for example, has already made inroads to healthcare through its devices that track consumer vital signs and other health and fitness metrics, and Meta is using its virtual reality tools to help train doctors. While Meta's Facebook and other social media companies have been criticized for causing declines in mental health, there are opportunities for these companies to benefit from correcting these problems. For example, they could develop products and tools to identify early warning signs of mental health problems, intervene, and connect users to mental health care.

Perhaps the biggest threat of entry to Amazon is its new customer HTA. As a big and powerful supplier of healthcare, Amazon must use that power wisely to deliver good value to its healthcare customers. Otherwise, HTA could pool the collective resources of its major employer members to build or buy their own healthcare supplier. As growth in the healthcare industry slows, the threat of new entrants may be weakening, but projected industry profitability and the healthcare expense burden on consumers and employers will continue to motivate outsiders who want in.

The key to Amazon's healthcare strategy via One Medical acquisition is not likely to be so much in growing its primary care market share through One Medical, but rather in building out and growing the number of users of its healthcare platform to create network effects that serve as a powerful barrier to entry. Amazon has become a retail giant not by selling its own products but by successfully building a retail platform that attracts and connects buyers and sellers, increasing access to a wide variety of products and allowing easy comparison of products and prices. Improvements in access and transparency of quality and cost comparisons are at the heart of the demand for change in the healthcare industry, and Amazon has advanced its position to become the leading healthcare platform that meets this demand.

As a powerful platform company, Amazon can leverage its tools and technologies to develop more customized support services for other healthcare businesses the way it supports growth for other businesses. For example, physician practices and pharmacies could pay a fee to use the Amazon platform, offering tools for telehealth services and streamlining scheduling, billing, and electronic medical records, while giving Amazon greater insights into the healthcare market. As a platform company, Amazon could offer to serve as a more customer-centric health insurance exchange or Marketplace, which is available in every state to help consumers shop for the best health plan to meet their needs.

If Amazon's healthcare strategy is successful, One Medical clinics will just be one among many healthcare services available via Amazon's healthcare platform. By connecting patients and healthcare providers in more user-friendly ways via a healthcare platform, small solo and group practices may be able to thrive rather than be acquired or die off. Home healthcare services, physical therapy and rehabilitation services, health insurance plans, and a myriad of other healthcare products and services could be easily compared and purchased via a healthcare platform. If Amazon is successful in building such a platform, Amazon wins when its healthcare buyers and sellers win, regardless of its own market share from One Medical primary care customers. Senior vice president of Amazon Health Services Neil Lindsay confirmed this strategy stating, "We don't need to do everything ourselves . . . Sixty percent of everything sold on Amazon is sold by a third party."

REFERENCES

Amazon. (n.d.). Prime now offers medical care. https://health.amazon.com/prime

Amazon. (2022). Annual report. https://www.annualreports.com/HostedData/AnnualReports/PDF/NASDAQ_AMZN_2022.pdf

Japsen, B. (2023, October 9). Amazon's One Medical to add more health services in existing markets. *Forbes*. https://www.forbes.com/sites/brucejapsen/2023/10/09/amazon-clinics-and-pharmacy-are-opportunities-to-make-things-easier-for-people/?sh=46ef7a0e5c62

FURTHER READINGS

American Hospital Association. (2023). *5 things to know about Amazon's recent One Medical acquisition.* https://www.aha.org/aha-center-health-innovation-market-scan/2023-03-07-5-things-know-about-amazons-recent-one-medical-acquisition

Jennings, K. (2023, November 8). Amazon Prime's new $9 primary care subscription undercuts Amazon's other health services. *Forbes.* https://www.forbes.com/sites/katiejennings/2023/11/08/amazon-primes-new-one-medical-discount-undercuts-amazon-clinic-prices/?sh=494be18230d6

Landi, H. (2022, July 25). What Amazon's $4B One Medical play reveals about its healthcare ambitions. *Fierce Healthcare.* https://www.fierce-healthcare.com/health-tech/how-amazons-one-medical-deal-could-boost-its-healthcare-ambitions-and-heat-competition

Landi, H. (2023, February 22). *Amazon closes $3.9B One Medical deal as it builds out healthcare strategy.* https://www.fiercehealthcare.com/providers/amazon-closes-39b-one-medical-deal-build-its-ambitions-healthcare-player

Perez, J. C. (2004, January 8). Amazon records first profitable year in its history. *Computerworld.* https://www.computerworld.com/article/2575106/amazon-records-first-profitable-year-in-its-history.html

Wilson, R. (2023, June 1). 50 things to know about UnitedHealth Group. *Becker's Payer Issues.* https://www.beckerspayer.com/payer/50-things-to-know-about-unitedhealth-group.html

For-Profit HCA Healthcare Inc. Competes for Charity Care

Abstract

Despite heroic efforts taking care of the most critically ill patients and the infusion of federal funding to keep them afloat during the pandemic, hospitals have faced significant post-pandemic pressure on both quality and cost issues. Nonprofit hospitals have been criticized for operating much like for-profit hospitals without paying taxes, and for-profit hospitals have been criticized for being for profit. A bipartisan group of senators has called for an investigation into the tax exemptions for nonprofit hospitals, and a bipartisan inquiry was launched to investigate the impact of private equity on the quality of hospital care. The 2022 *Wall Street Journal* report "Big Hospitals Provide Skimpy Charity Care Despite Billions in Tax Breaks" found that for-profit hospitals are providing more charity care as a percentage of total patient revenue than the nonprofit hospitals that have a tax exemption to provide charity care. The *Wall Street Journal* gave a specific example of a community where a nonprofit hospital's percentage of charity care was significantly lower than the two nearest for-profit hospitals'—both owned by for-profit, publicly traded HCA, the largest hospital chain in the United States. This case explores how hospitals compete and how for-profit hospital giant HCA can leverage its strength as a successful competitor for charity care.

The Case

Headquartered in Nashville Tennessee, HCA was founded in 1968 by two physicians—father and son Drs. Thomas Frist Junior and Senior who envisioned the benefits of economies of scale with a chain of hospitals and growth through public markets. HCA filed for an initial public offering in 1969 but went private in 1988 after growing to more than 100 hospitals. HCA went public again in 1992, expanded to the United Kingdom in 1995, and found itself in the center of a U.S. federal criminal investigation into fraudulent Medicare billing in 1997. In 2000, HCA agreed to pay $840 million to settle criminal and civil charges, and its CEO was forced to resign.

HCA demonstrated resilience following their expensive cleanup from the scandal by focusing on markets with high population growth, leveraging its power as a large supplier of hospital care to negotiate higher prices from health plans, and investing billions in improvements in technology and facilities. HCA went private again in 2006, and then public again in 2011. Over the decades, HCA has been the dominant hospital chain in the United States and has leveraged that scale to innovate and spread quality improvements. In 2021, HCA announced a partnership with Google to develop algorithms to improve patient care and efficiencies by leveraging data from HCA's millions of annual patient encounters. Since 2011, HCA's stock price has risen from about $33 per share to consistently trading at more than $220 throughout 2023. HCA is composed of more than 180 hospitals and approximately 2,300 ambulatory care sites, which include physician clinics, urgent care clinics, and ambulatory surgery centers. These outpatient care sites are important feeders to HCA's inpatient care when it is needed. More than 30 of its facilities, including hospitals and outpatient clinics, are located in London and Manchester, with another HCA Healthcare UK hospital scheduled to open in Birmingham. Meanwhile, Nashville, Tennessee, has become known as the healthcare capital of the United States as many other healthcare companies have moved or started there to find synergy with HCA and the healthcare ecosystem it has created there.

In 2023, nearly one-third of the hospitals on the Fortune and Premier Inc. Artificial Intelligence (PINC AI) list of the top 100 hospitals were HCA facilities. To create the list, PINC AI analyzed publicly available data on the 2,644 short-term, acute care nonfederal hospitals in the United States. They use ten measures across domains of patient outcomes, patient experience, operational efficiency, and financial health to create a composite score for each hospital. The composite score was weighted at 50% patient care outcomes (i.e., measures of mortality, complications, and readmissions), 30% operational efficiency (i.e., measures of length of stay and expenses), 10% patient satisfaction ratings, and 10% operating profit margin. Those with the highest composite score made the top 100 list, and the rank within that list was adjusted based on the hospitals' responses (or lack thereof) to a community impact and equity survey. The HCA hospitals on the list of the top 100 demonstrate the diversity of hospitals within the HCA portfolio, including teaching hospitals and large, medium, and small community hospitals.

With this recognition of strong performance, HCA is in a solid position to continue growing as the leader in hospital care. Yet, they continue to spend significant resources on charity care when they do not have to, resources that could otherwise fuel growth into new regions. Operating in 20 U.S. states and two cities (soon to be three) in England as of 2023, HCA has an opportunity to consider where to focus its resources to support growth.

Analyzing HCA's Investment in Charity Care From Porter's Framework

Given that HCA's major competitors have tax exemptions to provide charity care and are being pressured to provide more of it, HCA has an opportunity to shift resources away from providing charity care and invest those resources to expand services or into new locations. However, as a powerful, for-profit supplier in an era of increasing consumer demand for health equity, HCA may be more successful by continuing to compete with nonprofits in the charity care business. To understand HCA's options, it is important to understand how healthcare is different from other industries. In other industries, for example food and housing, for-profit and nonprofit suppliers are generally easy to distinguish and are not in competition with each other. Nonprofit local food banks collect and distribute free food to underserved communities, easily distinguished from for-profit grocery stores and restaurants, and nonprofits like the Salvation Army provide shelter for those in need and displaced from their homes, easily distinguished from for-profit hotels. In the healthcare industry, particularly within the hospital care segment, for-profit and nonprofits are difficult to distinguish, and they often compete intensely for patients covered by commercial health plans that subsidize most other payors. Figure 1 shows the payor mix of the three largest hospital chains in the United States—HCA and two nonprofit chains—based on their respective 2022 annual reports. This highlights how extensively the nonprofit hospitals rely on noncharitable care to stay in business. It is also noteworthy that the nonprofit Ascension's payor mix is more similar to for-profit HCA than to its nonprofit rival CommonSpirit. HCA does have an advantage with a higher percentage of commercial insurance revenue and lower percentage from Medicaid compared to the nonprofits. That translates to better margins, on which they pay taxes, and those taxes help fund the Medicaid insurance program. The nonprofits have the advantage of being tax exempt.

Large hospital chains, for-profit and nonprofit, continue to grow as independent hospitals close or get acquired due to difficulties competing without economies of scale. The target for scrutiny grows with these

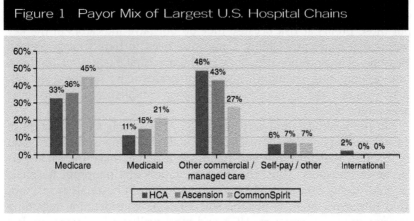

Figure 1   Payor Mix of Largest U.S. Hospital Chains

Source: Zelman, W. N., Pink, G. H., & Matthias, C. B. (2003). Use of the balanced scorecard in health care. *Journal of Health Care Finance, 29*(4), 1–16. Ascension 2022 annual report. https://about.ascension.org/-/media/project/ascension/about/section-about/financials/2023/consolidated-ascension-financial-statements-q4-fy23.pdf

CommonSpirit. (2022). *Unaudited annual report: For the years ended June 30, 2023 and 2022.* https://www.commonspirit.org/investor-resources

HCA Healthcare. (2022). *Annual report to shareholders.* https://s23.q4cdn.com/949900249/files/doc_financials/2022/ar/274375-HCA-Healthcare-Annual-Report.pdf chains, particularly as Medicare faces insolvency in less than a decade and hospital care accounts for the largest category of U.S. healthcare expenditures. The difficulties differentiating for-profit and nonprofit business decisions is increasingly a problem for nonprofits, which face tax penalties if they fail to meet the standards required for their tax exemptions. In their 2023 report of nonprofit hospital operations, the U.S. Government Accountability Office (GAO) identified 30 nonprofit hospitals that reported no spending on community benefits. Based on their analysis, the GAO recommended that Congress be more specific about what nonprofit hospitals need to do to demonstrate the community benefits that earn the tax exemption and that the IRS require greater transparency about those benefits.

This scrutiny of nonprofit hospitals is an opportunity for HCA to wield its power as a supplier wisely to ensure its continued strong performance over the long term. The PINC AI top 100 hospital measurement system, which has 32 HCA hospitals on the list, is based on Kaplan and Norton's (1992) balanced scorecard approach that is used across industries. This evidence-based approach recommends that organizations implement a measurement system that includes nonfinancial measures in addition to traditional financial measures to best achieve their mission. The idea is that financial measures alone (revenue, expenses, and margins), especially short term, cannot help guide strategy implementation toward long-term financial success. Companies that measure performance solely by profitability put those profits at risk because they do not have indicators of the key factors that cause profitability. Companies need to have strategy-aligned measures of organizational learning and human capital (e.g., organizational culture, employee retention), internal processes (e.g., supply chain efficiency, market share, innovation, regulatory compliance), and customer perceptions of value.

In the healthcare industry, the PINC AI system is an application of the balanced scorecard approach to hospitals and demonstrates the broad expectation that for-profit and nonprofit hospitals have the same performance measures. Thus, the IRS expectation that nonprofit hospitals provide charity care while HCA and other for-profit hospitals are exempt from this expectation is not the sole strategic consideration regarding investments in charity care. HCA and most well-run businesses understand the value of building goodwill as an asset, and providing charity care when they do not have to is a potent way for HCA to grow their goodwill. This is important for demonstrating commitment to local communities and to federal policy makers, and goodwill with these stakeholders is a key nonmarket strategy that indirectly facilitates growth in their target markets long-term. As HCA learned from their high-profile scandal decades ago, reputation matters. Thus, rather than shifting resources away from charity care to support direct market growth, HCA might consider establishing percentage of charity care as a key measure in their balanced scorecard of strategic measures. HCA might also consider setting a goal of always beating their competitors, for profit and nonprofit, in the percentage of charity care provided. As a company in the hospital business much longer than most others, adding this as a key performance measure on its balanced scorecard may help ensure HCA's continued growth in the long term.

To continue investing in charity care, HCA needs to ensure strong performance on other measures. While HCA is a powerful supplier, it faces increasingly powerful buyers, particularly employers, who are demanding better healthcare value. HCA has already partnered with a big technology company, which may help it realize greater efficiencies through AI. However, this is not enough as HCA is not competing on a low-cost leader strategy. As a company that competes on differentiation, specifically quality patient outcomes, their primary focus is leading in areas such as federal measures of these outcomes that are used by Medicare and in the ranking systems like the PINC AI top 100 hospitals.

HCA's experience in operating teaching hospitals gives them advantages with opportunities to participate in research on the development of new treatments to improve care that can be disseminated across all their facilities, potentially more rapidly than other hospitals can disseminate new treatments and best practices. Clinical innovation and improvement are important competences that are part of HCA's history and culture. However, concerns about healthcare in the United States is increasingly centered on cost. One potential approach would be for HCA to focus greater attention on identifying the service lines within each HCA hospital that can be strengthened as a clinical center of excellence so that it attracts not only local business but regional and potentially national business. For example, Walmart has launched a Centers of Excellence model to provide care for its employees. Walmart contracts with some of the highest quality providers in the nation and pays travel expenses for the employee and a companion to go to these specialized care centers when needed. The increased volume allows the centers to operate more efficiently. If other employers follow Walmart's lead or if Walmart offers health plans with these benefits, the employer-driven center of excellence business could become substantial for hospitals. HCA could also focus on expanding its ambulatory care rather than hospital care services to focus more on wellness, prevention, and keeping patients out of the hospital to lower the cost of care.

HCA may be well positioned to thrive on value in Europe, where per capita healthcare expenditures are generally half or less than those in the United States. There are signs that these lower levels of spending may not be sufficient to deliver the quality expected by European consumers. HCA already has a foothold in the United Kingdom, where private hospitals are few and Britain's National Health Service (NHS) was once revered as a model for tax payer–funded universal healthcare. This model may be collapsing as the wait lists for care provided by the NHS drive up demand for private health care and widen health inequities. Whether as a separate tier of private care that only Britain's wealthy can afford or as a contractor to operate Britain's struggling NHS, HCA is poised to help meet the new demand for better quality care in the United Kingdom, including better quality charitable care.

REFERENCES

Fortune PINC AI. (2023). 100 Top Hospitals. https://cdn.sanity.io/files/dcd4gsuh/production/7db7428df32516f4d30368ebb6c4cb17d884c0b3.pdf

Kaplan, R. S., & Norton, D. P. (1992). The balanced scorecard—measures that drive performance. *Harvard Business Review, 70*(1), 71–79. https://hbr.org/1992/01/the-balanced-scorecard-measures-that-drive-performance-2

Mathews, A. W., McGinty, T., & Evans, M. (2022, July 25). Big hospitals provide skimpy charity care – Despite billions in tax breaks. *The Wall Street Journal.* https://www.wsj.com/articles/nonprofit-hospitals-vs-for-profit-charity-care-spending-11657936777

FURTHER READINGS

CommonSpirit. (2022). *Unaudited annual report: For the years ended June 30, 2023 and 2022.* https://www.commonspirit.org/investor-resources

HCA Healthcare. (2022). *Annual report to shareholders.* https://s23.q4cdn.com/949900249/files/doc_financials/2022/ar/274375-HCA-Health-care-Annual-Report.pdf

Kaplan, R. S., & Norton, D. P. (2015). *Balanced scorecard success: The Kaplan-Norton collection* (4 ebooks). Harvard Business Review.

Mahase, E. (2023). Private providers see surge in demand as PM blames long NHS waiting lists on strikes. *BMJ (Clinical research ed.), 382,* 2126. https://doi.org/10.1136/bmj.p2126

U.S. Government Accountability Office. (2023, April 26). *Tax administration: IRS oversight of hospitals' tax-exempt status.* https://www.gao.gov/products/gao-23-106777#

U.S. Justice Department. (2000, December 14). HCA – the health care company and subsidiaries to pay $840 million in criminal fines and civil damages and penalties – largest government fraud settlement in U.S. history [Press release]. https://www.justice.gov/archive/opa/pr/2000/December/696civcrm.htm#

Zelman, W. N., Pink, G. H., & Matthias, C. B. (2003). Use of the balanced scorecard in health care. *Journal of Health Care Finance*, 29(4), 1–16. Ascension 2022 annual report. https://about.ascension.org/-/media/project/ascension/about/section-about/financials/2023/consolidated-ascension-financial-statements-q4-fy23.pdf

Nonprofit Civica Rx Inc. Addresses the Problem of Medication Supply for Hospitals

Abstract

In 2018, leaders at Intermountain Health in Utah announced their collaboration with HCA and other hospital system leaders to form Civica Rx, the first nonprofit dedicated to supplying hospitals with the medicines they need at sustainable prices. While hospitals, especially large hospital chains, are powerful suppliers of acute care, they are also powerful buyers of medications and other supplies needed to deliver that care. By leveraging their buying power, including working through group purchasers to increase that power, hospitals have been able to purchase generic drugs, used regularly in delivering inpatient care, at a low price. This is important because most hospitals do not get paid based on their costs, but rather receive a fixed payment based on the diagnosis-related group (DRG) for each hospital admission. Thus, keeping their medication costs low is important to hospital sustainability, especially at a time when their labor supply costs have rapidly escalated due to a shortage of physicians and nurses that was exacerbated by the pandemic. More than a decade before the pandemic, hospitals began facing challenges with shortages of critical hospital supplies, particularly life-saving medications. Even when available, some common generic medications came with unusually high prices, often viewed as price gouging.

The Case

In June of 2018, 135 members of U.S. Congress requested an analysis of the drug shortage problem and recommended solutions. The U.S. Food and Drug Administration spearheaded the Interagency Drug Shortage Task Force, which submitted its report to Congress in October 2019, in which it identified three root causes of the shortage.

There is a lack of incentives for companies to produce drugs that are less profitable. This is due in part to the buying power of large healthcare systems and groups purchasing organizations that smaller healthcare providers rely on to negotiate lower drug prices, especially for generics. In particular, hospitals are motivated to negotiate low drug prices because they do not get paid based on itemized expenses but rather a set amount based on the DRG. This results in generic drug manufacturers receiving insufficient revenue to invest in the maintenance of manufacturing facilities and equipment needed to meet regulatory standards. Evidence of this includes that quality issues were the most common cause of drug shortages, accounting for 62% of all shortages from 2013 to 2017, followed by 12% caused by an increase in demand, 5% caused by a natural disaster, and only 3% caused by production discontinuation. For 18% of drug shortages, the cause was unknown.

Because there is a lack of market rewards for manufacturers to improve supply chain management systems to include early detection of production constraints, manufacturers compete only and intensely on generic drug price, not on the reliability of the supply. Similarly, drug manufacturers buy the active pharmaceutical ingredients they use to make the drugs based on price rather than supply reliability.

Markets may struggle to recover after disruptions, leading to additional issues throughout the entire industry. This is particularly problematic as the drug supply chains have become more complex and multinational, including greater reliance on contract manufacturers. These factors mean there are more links in the chain that can break and less manufacturer control over those links. This is particularly problematic as the drug supply chains have become more complex and multinational, including greater reliance on contract manufacturers. These factors mean there are more links in the chain that can break and less manufacturer control over those links.

In summary, the Task Force noted that drug shortages are primarily due to private sector dynamics, but that federal regulations, including FDA requirements and reimbursement policies by Medicare and Medicaid programs affect those dynamics in ways that can contribute to the shortages. As solutions, the Task Force recommended: 1) improving understanding of the practices that lead to shortages and the impact on patients, 2) developing a rating system to encourage manufacturers to improve their supply chain management systems, and 3) promoting private sector contracts to improve the reliability of drug supplies.

Just months after Congress announced its request for analysis of the drug shortage, Civica Rx was launched in Utah by leaders from the renowned Intermountain Healthcare, along with HCA and five other hospital systems dedicated to solving the generic drug shortage that had plagued hospitals and endangered patients for years. As the first nonprofit generic drug manufacturer and distributor, Civica Rx is based on the following operating principles: long-term contracts with its hospital members to reduce uncertainty; transparent, fair, and sustainable prices; and dedicated manufacturing capacity for the most direly needed medications.

In testimony to the U.S. Senate Finance Committee hearing on drug shortages, pharmacist and Senior Vice President for Public Policy Allan Coukell reported that Civica Rx had a solid track record of accomplishments in its first five years in business, including growing membership to 55 hospital systems, delivering more than 80 drugs selected by hospitals due to shortages, and maintaining a six-month buffer supply of all these drugs. The organization also eliminated the middlemen that created instability in prices and supplies; prioritized sourcing drugs from the United States, with second priority from Canada or Europe; implemented rigorous oversight of suppliers; and offered a single cost-plus pricing model for member buyers.

Analyzing Civica Rx Sustainability From Porter's Framework

There are two key competitive forces that have fueled the generic drug shortage problem: the increased power of large buyers and the intense rivalry among generic drugs (or drugmakers), based solely on price. The hospital buyers of medications got so powerful for all of the reasons Porter indicated would matter: price sensitivity (due to inability to pass cost of the medications on to their customers due to fixed DRG payments per patient), just a few large-volume buyers (due to consolidation into hospital chains and the use of group purchasing organizations among smaller systems and individual hospitals), buyers perceiving little to no differentiation among suppliers (due to generics being generic), the cost of switching from one supplier to another being low (due to supplier lack of power to negotiate switching costs in contracts), and buyers credibly threatening to integrate backwards into the suppliers, which is exactly what hospitals did by creating Civica Rx.

The buyers became so powerful that they drove their suppliers out of the market. This may serve as a cautionary note to powerful buyers (including governments). Buying power can be used to drive down prices, but doing so too aggressively may result in suppliers that stop supplying. If the supplies are essential, powerful buyers should be prepared to backward integrate to become the supplier.

In addition to powerful buyers, the competition among rival generic manufacturers, per Porter, was intense in most cases because growth in demand was slow or declining. From the drug manufacturer's perspective, this makes investing in generic drug production and sales a risk without commensurate reward potential as these drugs could potentially be replaced by newer drugs and there are uncertainties around to what extent newer drugs may become standard of care, making the generic drug obsolete. When rivals compete on price, profitability is low, and they are more likely to compete on price when there is little difference between suppliers, which is, by definition, what generic drugs are as FDA regulations require that generics are equivalent. Price competition is also more likely when fixed costs are high and marginal costs are low, expansion requires large increments to be efficient, and the product or service is perishable. All of these factors were in play, resulting in insufficient incentives for the manufacturers to continue to supply the needed drugs.

Because Civica Rx is a nonprofit solution, it has several key advantages that will facilitate its sustainability, not the least of which is that its mission is to ensure the sustainability of its hospital customers. Civica Rx is well positioned to continue to excel in its mission. It has a large membership of buyers committed to the success of the company, a track record of addressing generic drug shortages, and resources dedicated to advocating for supportive public policy. In effect, Civica Rx has shifted the competition for generic drugs from being based on price only to differentiation based on service and quality (i.e., long-term contracts, supply buffers, price transparency, sourcing responsibly, and oversight). However, this more favorable competitive environment may attract new entrants with other differentiated offerings. For example, a new competitor might offer the same mix of products and services with the exception of more flexible sourcing, which allows for a slightly lower price. The price-sensitive hospital customers might be willing to switch to a similar competitor with a lower price. Likewise, a company like Amazon that is already in the pharmacy business could leverage its unique customer-friendly platform that facilitates the elimination of middlemen and improves price transparency to offer a compelling competitor to Civica Rx. To counter this threat, Civica Rx might benefit from partnering with Amazon or another platform company to improve the efficiency of their operations and pass along those cost savings to its hospital customers.

REFERENCES

U.S. Food and Drug Administration. (2019). Drug shortages: Root causes and potential solutions. https://www.fda.gov/media/131130/download?attachment

U.S. Senate Finance Committee. (2023, December 5). *Testimony of Allan Coukell*. https://www.finance.senate.gov/imo/media/doc/1205_coukell_testimony.pdf

FURTHER READINGS

American Hospital Association. (2023, March 28). *Civica Rx gets more backing in effort to reduce drug prices and shortages.* https://www.aha .org/aha-center-health-innovation-market-scan/2023-03-28-civica-rx-gets-more-backing-effort-reduce-drug-prices-and-shortages

Dredge, C., & Scholtes, S. (2023). Vaccinating health care supply chains against market failure: The case of civica rx. *NEJM Catalyst Innovations in Care Delivery, 4*(10), CAT-23. https://doi.org/10.1056/CAT.23.0167

Pfizer Raises Drug Prices as New Federal Legislation Aims to Lower Them

Abstract

While generic drug manufacturers compete intensely on price, those pharmaceutical companies that develop new drugs compete on differentiation. To succeed, they must invest heavily in the high-risk business of discovering new treatments and bringing them to market via the highly regulated and expensive process of testing the drug, up through human trials. Most new drug candidates never make it to market, which means that those that do must generate enough revenue to recoup the cost of all the failures, to invest in future drug development, and to reward shareholders for taking big risks before their patent protections expire. Pfizer, and at least a few of its competitors, have been headed toward a significant patent cliff—a term used to describe the looming revenue decline that occurs when a pharmaceutical company loses market exclusivity because of the expiration of one or more key drug patents, ushering in price competition from generic drug manufacturers. Adding to this challenge, the Inflation Reduction Act of 2022 established regulatory controls on drug prices. To address this challenge, Pfizer has gone on the offensive, using its COVID vaccine cash to acquire companies with imminent new drug approvals, aggressively pricing its COVID vaccines and treatment drug Paxlovid, and vocally challenging the new law.

The Case

While many pharmaceutical companies have criticized the Inflation Reduction Act's new controls on drug prices, Pfizer CEO Albert Bourla's comments made headlines. In reference to the provision in the law authorizing Medicare to negotiate drug prices, Bourla called it "negotiation with a gun to your head" because of the stiff taxes and penalties incurred by companies for not participating, as reported by Fierce Pharma in 2023. The Inflation Reduction Act of 2022 allows Medicare to negotiate prices for certain single-source drugs under Medicare Parts B and D for the first time. The law requires Medicare to negotiate prices for ten high-cost drugs, effective in 2026 and more in subsequent years. The manufacturers of these first ten drugs all agreed to participate in the program, given that the financial consequences of not participating were likely worse than accepting lower prices from Medicare. Simultaneously, several of these pharmaceutical companies have filed lawsuits based on assertions that the law is unconstitutional and infringes on patent protections. There is consensus that this new law will reduce the number of new drugs developed, though plenty of disagreement about to what extent it will harm innovation.

The new law also requires drug companies to pay rebates to Medicare if their drug prices increase faster than inflation. In the year after the Inflation Reduction Act was approved, the average list prices for medications increased by 5.6%, much lower than increases from previous years which were about 10%, according to a 2023 report in the *Wall Street Journal*. Like other healthcare prices, the list price is not what most patients pay for the drug or what the drug company gets paid for the drug. Insurance companies and the pharmacy benefit management companies they used to lower drug prices negotiate drug prices, and now so does Medicare. Thus, it is quite possible, if not likely, that drug companies will respond to the Inflation Reduction Act law by raising new drug launch prices or by increasing drug prices for private insurance to subsidize the expected cuts in revenue from lower drug prices paid by Medicare.

Pfizer is one of the world's largest pharmaceutical companies, and the first to top $100 billion in revenue, more than half of which was from revenue from COVID vaccines and the antiviral treatment Paxlovid. Pfizer has announced that it has substantially raised prices for both products but noted that insurance companies will pay, not patients. However, this argument for raising drug prices overlooks the fact that increasing the cost to health insurance plans is why health insurance premiums continue to rise, which is why employers who pay most of these premiums have stepped in to exercise their buying power. While Pfizer may have good justification for raising the prices, it will likely benefit from focusing on the value of their treatments and advocating for price transparency.

Analyzing Pfizer's Fight Against Price Controls From Porter's Framework

For Pfizer, the major competitive forces are the power of buyers and the threat of substitutes. Prior to the 2022 Inflation Reduction Act, federal laws limited the ability of Medicare to influence drug prices, which substantially weakened the power of the nation's largest buyer of prescription drugs. Unlike most buyers, the federal government has the power to compel drug companies to participate in the price setting process. While the lawsuits work their way through the courts to determine whether the government has overstepped its authority, Pfizer can better position itself to compete in an era of larger and more powerful buyers.

The new Inflation Reduction Act law allows Medicare to negotiate pricing only for certain high-cost drugs that have no generic equivalent. However, these are drugs that generate significant revenue for drug companies. Drugs that have been approved for less than nine years (and biological products that have been approved for less than 13 years) are not eligible for negotiation by Medicare. This provision changes the window of opportunity for a drug manufacturer to recoup its drug development investments and earn sufficient profits to invest in future drug development and reward shareholders for taking risks. Thus, these calculations need to be included in pricing negotiations with all buyers, including for drugs not subject to the new Medicare pricing negotiations, so the revenue generated across products generates sufficient profit.

In the negotiations for each selected drug, the Inflation Reduction Act requires Medicare to consider evidence about therapeutic alternatives (i.e., substitutes). Medicare's 2023 guidance clarifies that Medicare will consider evidence about therapeutic alternatives submitted by all interested parties, including drug manufacturers, Medicare beneficiaries, and scientific and clinical experts. Medicare is required to consider the extent to which the selected drug is an advance relative to the therapeutic alternatives and the costs of the alternatives; the comparative effectiveness of the drug relative to the alternatives, particularly for specific Medicare populations; and the extent to which the drug and its alternatives address unmet medical needs. The selected drug's manufacturer must submit information to Medicare, including research and development costs and the extent to which those costs have been recouped; previous federal financial support received related to the drug's research and development; unit costs of the drug's production and distribution, market data, and revenue; and sales volume in the United States for the drug.

Given the factors that will be considered in the negotiations, Pfizer can consider investing in drug development and company acquisitions focused on distinct medical advances and those more clearly differentiated from potential substitutes (i.e., therapeutic alternatives). Pfizer also has a strong track record of collaborating with other companies on drug development. Their successful collaboration with BioNTech produced one of the world's first COVID-19 vaccines, the first to be fully approved by the FDA in the United States. Pfizer's partnership with Bristol Myers Squib led to one of the most successful drugs in the world: Eliquis. Just a year after winning a court battle to protect its patents from generic manufacturers, this drug was selected among the first 10 for negotiation under the Inflation Reduction Act.

As a drug price increases without additional benefit, the risk of that drug being replaced by a substitute increases as buyers consider the decreased drug value relative to the quality and cost features of alternatives. If Pfizer does not accept the price Medicare considers fair, there is the risk that Medicare will replace its drug, Eliquis, with other direct oral anticoagulants. However, to the extent that Pfizer can differentiate its drug from the others, they have much greater leverage with Medicare and its beneficiaries. While Medicare is a very powerful buyer, it is also subject to the political forces that shape elections. Medicare and its political leadership may be bruised if it removes a popular drug as an option for beneficiaries, regardless of the general bipartisan support for lowering drug prices. Given this bipartisan sentiment supporting reduced drug prices, Pfizer may benefit from leveraging the new era of price transparency to educate consumers and policy makers about the cost of drugs relative to the hospital costs, morbidity, and mortality they avoid.

REFERENCES

Centers for Medicare and Medicaid Services. (2023, March 15). *Medicare drug price negotiation program: Initial guidance.* https://www.cms.gov/files/document/medicare-drug-price-negotiation-program-initial-guidance.pdf

Dunleavy, K. (2023, May 12). *Medicare IRA measure as 'negotiation with a gun to your head.'* Fierce Pharma. https://www.fiercepharma.com/pharma/pfizer-ceo-bourla-calls-medicare-ira-measure-negotiation-gun-your-head

Hopkins, J. S. (2023, February 2). Drug prices increase 5.6% as government ramps up pressure to lower costs. *Wall Street Journal.* https://www.wsj.com/articles/drugmakers-raise-prices-on-nearly-1-000-medicines-but-show-restraint-11675313960

FURTHER READINGS

Cubanski, J., Neuman, T., & Freed, M. (2023, January 24). *Explaining the prescription drug provisions in the Inflation Reduction Act.* Kaiser Family Foundation. https://www.kff.org/medicare/issue-brief/explaining-the-prescription-drug-provisions-in-the-inflation-reduction-act/#

Dunleavy, K. (2023, April 18). The top 20 pharma companies by 2022 revenue. Fierce Pharma. https://www.fiercepharma.com/pharma/top-20-pharma-companies-2022-revenue

Hickey, K. J., Kirchhoff, S. M., & Rogers H. A. (2023, December 8). *Medicare drug price negotiation under the Inflation Reduction Act: Industry responses and potential effects.* Congressional Research Service. https://crsreports.congress.gov/product/pdf/R/R47872

Health Insurer Elevance Re-Brands, Aims to Improve Health Beyond Healthcare

Abstract

Health insurance companies have historically dealt with rising healthcare costs by raising premiums. However, they are experiencing the limits of this approach as more employers move to self-insurance models and new entrants seek a share of the lucrative Medicare Advantage market. One regional health insurance company has re-branded, once again, this time as Elevance to reflect a focus on holistic health as a key differentiator among health plans. While struggling to address lower performance ratings on their Medicare Advantage plans, they continue to seek new acquisitions to expand their Medicare Advantage market share and deal with the threat of new entrants. This case also explores the viability of a large buyer of healthcare that aims to advance health without elevating costs in a market of powerful suppliers.

The Case

Major health insurance organizations have grown and diversified through mergers and acquisitions focused on vertical integration, including UnitedHealth Group's Optum healthcare provider company and Aetna's merger with CVS Health. Anthem's core business remains its Blue Cross Blue Shield health plans in 14 states, but it has also diversified beyond traditional health insurance by acquiring a behavioral healthcare company in alignment with its rebranding as Elevance. The new name is intended to signify a differentiated approach that includes integration of physical, behavioral, and social dimensions of health. As Elevance aims to offer better value through this approach, it strives to address low star ratings on its Medicare Advantage plans. These ratings are critical to the success of health plans as they affect revenue by driving beneficiaries to higher rated plans and by changing the payments they receive from Medicare. Elevance has reported that it expects a

$500 million reduction in Medicare Advantage revenue because of its decline in star ratings according to a Fierce Healthcare report in 2023.

Medicare star ratings are based on a series of measures that include screening and prevention, management of chronic diseases, and customer experience. Medicare modifies the measures based on changes in best practice and in federal priorities, so plans must adapt their services accordingly to prevent loss of revenue. According to a 2023 Medicare report, nonprofit Medicare Advantage plans are more likely to receive higher star ratings relative to for-profit plans. Although for-profit Elevance is currently struggling with its star ratings, it may have key advantages in adapting to new Medicare priorities. First, Medicare is increasing its focus on access to behavioral healthcare not long after Elevance invested in the acquisition of a national behavioral healthcare provider. Elevance is well positioned to ensure its Medicare Advantage plan members have excellent access to these services. Second, Medicare is adding a new health equity index to its star ratings to reward plans for providing excellent care to underserved populations, including those with limited English proficiency, those with low income, and those with disabilities. If Elevance can deliver on its holistic approach, including addressing social determinants of health, the company may have a competitive advantage that helps it achieve higher star ratings. Upcoming changes in the way Medicare pays Medicare Advantage plans based on star ratings will result in cost savings to Medicare, which is revenue loss to these health plans. Plans focused on reducing health disparities among underserved populations stand to gain in star ratings and revenue.

Analyzing Elevance's Holistic Approach From Porter's Framework

With health insurance premiums continuing to take an increasing portion of consumer income and business labor expenses, health insurance companies are increasingly losing the employer market to self-insurance. Meanwhile, the lucrative Medicare Advantage market competition is increasing at a time when Medicare is raising the bar for these plans to receive the highest payments based on star ratings. The threat of new entrants, specifically by large companies like Amazon and Walmart and others that have learned to self-insure, is a significant threat to Elevance and other commercial health insurance companies. New entrants with experience predominantly in private health insurance for employees will be at a disadvantage relative to Elevance, which has significant experience in both Medicare and Medicaid insurance. These government health plans have different requirements, including Medicare's star rating program for Medicare Advantage plans. Elevance may benefit from acquiring companies with significant Medicare Advantage plan membership in a move similar to that of Amazon, which has a track record of gaining industry experience through acquisitions. This may be part of the reason why Elevance has aggressively bid to acquire such companies.

Another strong force Elevance must contend with is powerful healthcare suppliers, some of whom have refused to accept patients with Medicare Advantage plans because they do not pay the providers enough. This pattern may, in turn, reduce the number of beneficiaries who choose a Medicare Advantage plan over traditional Medicare. Elevance maintains an important advantage in behavioral healthcare at a time when there is a significant shortage in the supply of healthcare professionals. The integration of behavioral healthcare may also give Elevance an edge in controlling overall costs as those with behavioral health needs also frequently have higher total medical spending relative to similar patients without behavioral health needs.

In a 2018 report, Milliman documented this potential value proposition for those organizations that successfully integrate behavioral healthcare with medical care. Specifically, they found that comparing patients with similar medical diagnoses with and without coexisting behavioral health needs, those with mental illness or substance use disorder have significantly higher healthcare costs than those without these behavioral health diagnoses. They also found that most of the additional healthcare costs for those with behavioral health needs were spent on the medical side, rather than the behavioral health side. The Milliman report estimates billions of dollars could be save in commercial, Medicare, and Medicaid spending through effective integration and management of behavioral healthcare needs. Elevance may be in a good position to succeed with health plans differentiated by such integration.

Elevance has launched several initiatives that may give it an advantage in response to the demand for greater health equity, including a new health equity index as part of the Medicare star rating measures. However, as competition to advance health equity grows, Elevance will need to clearly differentiate its health plans and benefits within the market. Competitors such as nonprofit CareSource are also innovating to address health equity. In 2023, CareSource announced a partnership with Walmart to reduce health disparities by leveraging Walmart's brand and expansion into health and wellness services. Elevance may be on the path to differentiating by addressing some root causes of health disparities that are outside of the healthcare system. For example, Elevance is working on addressing food insecurity and lack of access to the internet among disadvantaged populations. In 2024, Elevance announced a collaboration with Verizon, AT&T, T-Mobile, and Samsung to help close the digital divide by giving smart phones to eligible members of its Medicaid plans at no cost. These phones will include unlimited data, talk, and text use and virtual healthcare apps that easily connect them to their healthcare teams and access educational material. Shifting resources to partners outside of the healthcare system to address root causes of health inequities may reduce the need for healthcare and the challenges posed by powerful healthcare suppliers.

Centers for Medicare and Medicaid Services. (2023, October 13). *2024 Medicare Advantage and Part D Star Ratings.* https://www.cms.gov/newsroom/fact-sheets/2024-medicare-advantage-and-part-d-star-ratings

Melek, S. P., Norris, D. T., Paulus, J., Matthews, K., Weaver, A., & Davenport, S. (2018 January). *Potential economic impact of integrated medical-behavioral healthcare.* Milliman. https://www.milliman.com/-/media/milliman/importedfiles/uploadedfiles/insight/2018/potential-economic-impact-integrated-healthcare.ashx

Minemyer, P. (2023, October 18). Elevance Health braces for $500M hit to bonus revenue amid MA Star Ratings drop. Fierce Healthcare. https://www.fiercehealthcare.com/payers/elevance-health-boosts-guidance-it-posts-13b-q3-profit

FURTHER READINGS

Elevance Health. (2024, January 10). Elevance Health addresses healthcare's digital divide by increasing access to high-quality smartphones and health-related digital services. https://www.elevancehealth.com/newsroom/elevance-health-addresses-healthcare-digital-divide-by-increasing-access-to-high-quality-smartphones-and-health-related-digital-services

Rogers, H., Smith, M. H., & Yurkovic, M. (2023 October). *Future of Medicare Star Ratings: The reimagined CMS bonus system.* Milliman. https://us.milliman.com/-/media/milliman/pdfs/2023-articles/10-6-23_medicare-star-ratings-white-paper_20231005

Wearable Ultrasound Device by ZetrOZ Growing as a Substitute for Surgery, Pain Medication, and Physical Therapists

Abstract

While liability for the opioid epidemic has tarnished reputations among some drug companies and other healthcare organizations, the sustained acoustic medicine (sam®) device company ZetrOZ has advanced the positioning of its device as a substitute for many therapies for some injuries and pain. The sam® device can be an alternative to some surgeries, which have higher costs and risks, for pain medications, which can be addicting and have other adverse side effects, and for physical and occupational therapists, which may be less convenient and accessible than at-home treatments. However, as it grows as a substitute threat to other healthcare products and services, ZetrOZ must navigate the threat of competition from new entrants and the force of powerful buyers. In particular, health plans continue to describe the sam® device technology as investigational and, therefore, not a covered benefit under most health plans, despite ZetrOZ having received FDA clearance for the device. As new entrants receive FDA clearance for the same device classification, competition will be based on price unless ZetrOZ can differentiate. The role of regulations and health insurance practices come into play as ZetrOZ navigates growth strategies as a small business competing for buyers industry wide.

The Case

In 2013, ZetrOZ's new wearable therapeutic ultrasound system for horses was named as a finalist in the 2013 Annual Medical Design Excellence Awards. After the human version of this innovation became the first such self-treatment device to receive FDA clearance, ZetrOZ's sustained acoustic medicine (sam®) device became available by prescription in the United States for consumers to use at home or anywhere for the self-treatment of injuries and chronic pain, though generally not covered by insurance. ZetrOZ's sam® device is a classic example of a product threatening as a substitute for existing treatments—surgeries, physical and occupational therapies, and medications for some conditions such as arthritis and tendonitis.

From 2013 through 2023, ZetrOZ received competitive awards from the National Institutes of Health under the federal Small Business Innovation Research (SBIR) program. Federal law requires every federal agency with a research budget greater than $100 million to allocate a minimum set percentage of that budget (3.2% as of 2023) to SBIR awards, which are available only to small for-profit U.S. businesses. The purpose of this program is to stimulate private sector innovation, commercialize these innovations, and increase competition and economic growth. Most of the SBIR awards received by ZetrOZ have been from the National Institute on Minority Health and Health Disparities to position their technology as a way to improve affordability and access to care among rural, minority, and other underserved populations.

The prestigious NIH funding helps ZetrOZ build credibility as a product backed by science, and FDA clearance allows ZetrOZ to market its devices as available via prescription by a licensed healthcare professional for indications such as relief of pain associated with soft tissue injuries and muscle spasms. However, these accomplishments do not ensure that health insurance companies will cover the cost of the device as a benefit to health plan members. As pressure to contain healthcare costs intensifies, health plans are key gatekeepers to the adoption of new technologies. The FDA recommends that device companies communicate with health plans early in their product development to design their clinical trials to meet the data expectations of both the FDA and those making health insurance coverage determinations.

Analyzing ZetrOZ's Growth Opportunities From Porter's Framework

As ZetrOZ makes headway as a substitute threat to traditional therapies for injuries and pain, the company faces the threat of new entrants and powerful buyers. As new entrants have emerged, clearly differentiating its device from new competitors will help ZetrOZ avoid intensifying rivalry based on price, which would reduce profitability. While ZetrOZ's sam® device was the first such wearable self-treatment device to receive FDA clearance, this clearance status means that the FDA has determined the device is substantially equivalent to one or more other devices. FDA-cleared devices with the same product code as the sam® device include ManaSport by ManaMed and PainShield MD Plus by Nanovibronix, both of which received FDA clearance in 2022. Nanovibronix's PainShield device is a self-treatment version of its substantially equivalent device that received FDA clearance in 2008 for use with the assistance of physicians or therapists. Nanovibronix applied to have their PainShield device classified as Durable Medical Equipment (DME) as a pathway to reimbursement; however, in 2023, the Centers for Medicare and Medicaid Services (CMS) determined the devices do not fall within the requested DME benefit category and, thus, are not reimbursable under Medicare and Medicaid.

ZetrOZ might have success targeting health insurance companies that offer Medicare Advantage plans rather than aiming for federal Medicare and Medicaid coverage. As competition among Medicare Advantage plans intensifies, health insurance companies are seeking to differentiate. Providing coverage for alternatives to pain medications and surgery could help these insurers achieve a competitive advantage that defines healthcare more holistically and allow them to improve health equity and access to care for underserved populations. According to a 2020 ZetrOZ press release, the potential health plan benefits of covering the cost of its sam® device include that it is safer and less expensive than surgery and can be used as an adjunct to surgery to speed healing and prevent future surgeries, saving health insurance companies more than $30,000. The device may also reduce health plan expenses for physical and occupational therapists and improve satisfaction among health plan members who prefer self-treatment or who are suffering due to lack of access to these therapists in areas of short supply. ZetrOZ already has traction in coverage for worker's compensation injuries among self-insured employers, so these employers may be a good target for expanding coverage via their health plans.

Although ZetrOZ has patents to protect some aspects of its sam® device, a key challenge will be leveraging these to differentiate it from its competitors in a way that matters to buyers beyond price. ZetrOZ's history of NIH funding may be one way to build a distinct brand with a higher level of credibility and trust. The NIH National Institute on Aging showcases selected small businesses it has funded through the SBIR program, including ZetrOZ, on its website. In this NIH showcase, ZetrOZ features their scientific publications, supply contract with the Veterans Health Administration, and use by players in the National Football League, Major League Baseball, the National Basketball Association, the National Hockey League, and Major League Soccer. ZetrOZ describes its intellectual property as including patents on its treatment algorithms and technology platforms.

Perhaps the most important way for ZetrOZ to establish an enduring competitive advantage would be focusing on developing its technology platform to amplify network effects as it builds a trusted brand reputation. The company is already well positioned to leverage its popularity among professional sports teams to market the device for individual sales to the growing population of older adults. To the extent that aging adults are redefining what it means to age gracefully, ZetrOZ could use testimonials from athletes, particularly those who are retired and still using the sam® device to stay active, to appeal to aging adults who want an alternative to other therapies for a variety of muscle, tendon, bone, and joint pains. ZetrOZ could integrate the sam® device as part of a user-friendly physical fitness and wellness platform that tracks sam® device treatments along with measures of pain, mobility, exercise, sleep, mood, and other health indicators and connects the device users to a community of peers, coaches, scientists, and healthcare providers focused on alternatives to medications and surgeries. If ZetrOZ is successful in creating network effects, its sam® device, while equivalent to its competitors from the FDA perspective, would be substantially more valuable than its competitors from the perspective of potential buyers.

REFERENCES

ZetrOZ. (2020, June 23). Insurance companies benefit from reduced healthcare reimbursement, lowering costs by approving the sustained acoustic medicine (sam®) device. *PR Newswire*. https://www.prnewswire.com/news-releases/insurance-companies-benefit-from-reduced-healthcare-reimbursements-lowering-costs-by-approving-the-sustained-acoustic-medicine-sam-device-301082181.html

FURTHER READINGS

Food and Drug Administration. (2024, January). *Overview of device regulation.* https://www.fda.gov/medical-devices/device-advice-comprehensive-regulatory-assistance/overview-device-regulation

Johannes, L. (2024, March 17). New pain treatment uses ultrasound at home. *The Wall Street Journal.* https://www.wsj.com/articles/SB10001424052702303730804579439911570346896.

National Institute on Aging. (n.d.). *NIA small business showcase: ZetrOZ systems.* https://www.nia.nih.gov/research/sbir/nia-small-business-showcase/zetroz-systems.

Small Business Innovation Research. (n.d.). *About the SBIR and STTR programs.* https://www.sbir.gov/about

10

Putting Ideas Into Practice

Innovation in Care Models

The perception among those who pay for healthcare, that it has become too expensive for the level of quality provided (i.e., that it is not a good value), may be the biggest threat to investment of resources in the development of new life-saving treatments. It is expensive to bring new drugs and other technology to market, so it is risky to do so if there are uncertainties about whether the market will adopt and disseminate them in a way that produces a return on the investments. However, innovators today and into the future will still have many opportunities to bring new treatments to market and may have new opportunities as well. The key innovation challenge will be around delivering value. For decades, consumers, employers, and taxpayers have, in aggregate, been willing to spend increasing income on more and better care. Innovators during that time have not needed to worry so much about the added cost. Consumers, employers, and taxpayers, in aggregate, are no longer willing to add more cost, at least not without significantly better quality. Table 1 shows some examples of how the innovators of the future can deliver better value in contrast to the previous era of innovation that focused on quality or cost but left the question of value unanswered or unconvincingly answered.

The new era of price and quality transparency will facilitate innovation that answers the value question. Every segment of healthcare has opportunities to improve value. Many value-focused innovations have already been developed but have not yet been widely adopted as the standard of care or as a standard health plan benefit. One example is prenatal care through birth centers that offer a more holistic approach, including comprehensive patient education and psychosocial support for pregnant women with Medicaid insurance. This approach is associated with better health outcomes for babies and lower costs. Another example is the deployment of pharmacists outside of traditional medication dispensing roles, working with patients and prescribers to optimize medication regimens. These pharmacists can reduce preventable medication harm while reducing the cost of hospital care. These and many new value-based innovations will be adopted when the relevant competitive forces drive healthcare suppliers to deliver what the buyers demand. U.S. employers, as large healthcare buyers for their employees at prices that subsidize healthcare for many others, are playing a major role in driving this change. Employers like Walmart

Table 1 Quality, Cost, and Value to Consumers of Healthcare Innovations

Innovation	Quality	Cost	Value
New treatments for diseases	Increase	Unknown	Unknown
New treatments for diseases **designed and tested for value** (e.g., increased cost of treatment is more than offset by reduction in cost of hospital care and total cost of care)	Increase	Decrease	Increase
New method that improves quality (e.g., reduces errors)	Increase	Unknown	Unknown
New method that improves quality **at lower cost** (e.g., reduces errors and costs less than current technology)	Increase	Decrease	Increase
New method that improves efficiencies	Unknown	Decrease	Unknown
New method that improves efficiencies **without adverse impact on quality**	No change	Decrease	Increase
New method that improves efficiencies **and improves quality**	Increase	Decrease	Increase
New payment model that rewards better quality	Increase	Increase	Unknown
New payment model that rewards more cost savings	Unknown	Decrease	Unknown
New payment model that rewards **better quality at a lower cost**	Increase	Decrease	Increase

could play a key role in the adoption and dissemination of cost-effective birth center models for Medicaid customers while Amazon is well positioned to adopt, disseminate, and improve the deployment of pharmacists and related technology to prevent medication harm. Locally and nationally, chambers of commerce and other employer groups can advocate not only for better healthcare value for their employees but also for those whose healthcare they subsidize.

In a future where innovation is more holistically focused on value, pharmaceutical companies may be required to compare the effectiveness of their new drugs not only against other drug therapies or medical and surgical interventions but also against relatively low-cost behavioral interventions. For example, healthy food prescriptions, along with vouchers or other incentives for purchasing fruits and vegetables can improve health status among adults and children. This and other behavioral interventions could be tested head-to-head against highly effective new anti-obesity drugs to determine the cost of each treatment relative to the benefits of each.

A key barrier to implementing and disseminating value-based innovations is the reality that different stakeholders view value differently. While quality and cost both factor into decision making, there are many different views about which dimensions matter the most and how to assess or measure them. Traditionally, quality measures have focused on patient outcomes, such as morbidity and mortality. Increasingly, quality measures include population outcomes, such as disparities between groups. Similarly, assessment of cost is increasingly more complex to measure. Traditionally, cost has focused on a single unit of innovation, such as a dose of a new medication, or cumulative doses by an average patient over a period of time. Cost of a single episode of care, such as an average inpatient visit, is also a common measurement. Health insurance companies often measure cost as the total health plan expenditure per member per month. These traditional measures focus on specific costs within the traditional healthcare system. Organizations may be increasingly expected to include the cost to the primary payers (e.g., employers, employees, patients, taxpayers), the cost to the environment, the cost to health equity, and the cost in terms of economic impact in cost assessments. The economic impact of innovations that reduce business labor expenses for healthcare could be measured by how many new jobs they produce, how much they increase employee wages, how much they add to corporate profits, or how much federal tax revenue increases due to those additional profits.

Examples of Value-Based Models

Porter himself has advocated for a shift to value-based models in healthcare. He proposed a model that organizes care around medical conditions and delivers it through integrated practice units that achieve scale by growing locally in their area of expertise and through a hub-and-spoke model supported by information technology. In Porter's model, the integrated practice units measure outcomes and cost for every patient and are paid based on value. An application of this approach is Walmart's Centers of Excellence benefit model in which travel expenses are paid for employees to be treated at a center that specializes in the relevant medical condition and provides high-quality, cost-effective care.

In a new era of value, Porter's model could be criticized for not addressing quality as measured by health equity across populations or by the model's carbon footprint. Another concern is that models that focus organization of care around medical conditions may exacerbate the silos of specialty care and fail to connect with patients more holistically.

This is especially important with an aging population where multiple chronic conditions are common, and patients are at risk of adverse events because of care that is organized around medical conditions rather than around the patient with guidance from clinicians whose expertise crosses conditions.

For example, in a model organized around preventable medication harm, one of the most common preventable problems across medical conditions, pharmacists are leveraged as the healthcare industry's medication experts. According to a U.S. Department of Health and Human Services 2022 report, prescription medications account for 13% of total health expenditures in the United States. While these medications save lives, the cost of harm from less-than-optimal use of medications is estimated to be higher, 16% of total annual health expenditures, and to cause more than 275,000 deaths per year according to a 2018 report by Johnathon Watanabe and colleagues. In the new care model, pharmacists were deployed to identify inpatients at risk of medication problems and hand them off at discharge to community pharmacists who were responsible for working with the patients to identify and resolve medication problems across prescribers and across dispensing pharmacies. Compared to hospitals that did not offer this model, there was a significant reduction in medication-related hospitalizations among those age 65 and older. The cost of avoided hospitalizations produced a 264% return on investment in the cost of the pharmacists who provided this service according to a 2017 report by Karen Pellegrin and colleagues.

Health Information Technology in the Dawn of AI

The healthcare industry, particularly in the United States, has been relatively slow to adopt information technology. Much of this has been due to healthcare-specific regulations pertaining to privacy and security of health information as well as industry fragmentation and lack of resources and incentives. This changed significantly with the Health Information Technology for Economic and Clinical Health (HITECH) Act of 2009, which infused billions of federal dollars into the healthcare sector to subsidize the adoption and use of health information technology, along with payment incentives and penalties to help motivate this change. Funding focused largely on getting physician offices and hospitals to adopt an electronic health record (EHR) system that meets certain standards and initiating the establishment of local, regional, and state organizations to form health information exchanges (HIEs) that would allow connected EHRs to share information to support clinician decision making at the point of care. Prior to these advances, hospitals and clinics exchanged patient information via faxing, mailing hard copies, or not at all. According to a 2022 report by the Office of the National Coordinator for Health Information Technology, in the year before the HITECH Act, less than 20% of physician offices and less than 10% of hospitals used an EHR. As of 2021, nearly 80% of physicians and 96% of hospitals use an EHR, but these percentages are about the same as in 2014 when the adoption rate plateaued. There is evidence that the use of these technologies has improved at least somewhat since 2014. This includes an increase in the percentage of patients who were offered access to their records via a patient portal, up to 59% in 2020, with 38% of patients reporting using the portal that year.

In addition to the gaps in adoption of EHRs, there remain gaps in the electronic exchange of patient information between the EHRs in use. As shown in Figure 1, a 2023 report by the Government Accountability Office (GAO) determined that only about half of medium and large hospitals and about a third of small hospitals often send or receive health information via a local, state, or regional HIE and even fewer via a national HIE. In addition, approximately a third of medium and large hospitals and about half of small hospitals often send or receive health information via mail or fax as of 2021.

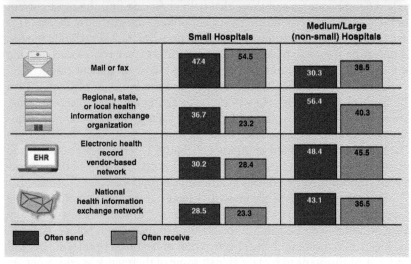

Figure 1   Exchange Methods Often Used among Acute Care Hospitals by Size, 2021

Source: GAO analysis of American Hospital Association Annual Survey Information Technology Supplement survey data (data); GAO (icons). I GAO-23-105540

The many gaps and barriers in the adoption and use of health information technology are opportunities for innovators. The value of doing so in the era of artificial intelligence (AI) may be significant enough to overcome the barriers as a fully digitized and integrated health information ecosystem would make the best use of AI. AI technology has been developed to reduce the negative impacts of pandemics through more effective infectious disease surveillance, including early warning of outbreaks through processing of news sources and social media, classification of pathogens using image processing and recognition, identification of the source of and the transmission of disease through mining electronic health data, early detection of infection hot spots through monitoring hospital waiting rooms, and improved tracking and forecasting through technology that better integrates multiple data sources.

AI is already being used to improve the efficiency of drug discovery and development. AI applications focus on screening vast numbers of potential new compounds to identify those with the most promising properties and those more likely to be effective for a specific target. While AI is not yet able to replace the expensive testing process once promising compounds are found, applications of AI in medicine have been implemented to improve the clinical trial processes used to test new treatments. This includes AI support in designing the research to ensure adequate rigor, identification, and recruitment of potential research participants, and monitoring outcomes and side effects of experimental treatments. AI is also being used to better retrieve relevant information to support clinical decision making. For example, tools that integrate information about a specific patient from multiple different sources and those that help clinicians find the most current and relevant studies to inform treatment options are currently in use. AI is also in use to improve administrative functions, such as scheduling the use of operating rooms to make efficient use of this expensive resource, billing and collections procedures, and conducting follow up patient contact.

Tiffany Kung and colleagues studied the performance of ChatGPT on the medical licensing exams without it receiving any specialized training. Collectively, the three exams cover basic science, pharmacology, pathophysiology, clinical reasoning, medical management, and bioethics. In 2023, they reported that the untrained ChatGPT performed at or near the passing rate on all three exams. The authors noted that AI will be transformative in both medical education and clinical practice.

From the perspective of competitive forces, this study demonstrates the potential of AI to dramatically weaken the power of suppliers—specifically the workforce—to ease some of the pressing industry pain points. Those in the business of training the next generation of healthcare professionals will find that AI threatens to replace at least some of their work as educators. As the cost of the technology becomes more affordable, AI might also someday reduce the cost of getting a healthcare degree, which has grown to become a key barrier to the healthcare workforce supply. If ChatGPT can pass the medical licensing exams, the nature of what is required to earn a medical degree and license may change to focus less on diagnostic skills if ChatGPT can diagnose more accurately and efficiently. Instead, physician training programs and licensure may focus more on interpersonal skills, such as those that engage patients in shared decision making and motivate them to make health-related behavior changes. However, ChatGPT might someday be more efficient and effective than humans in performing these interpersonal tasks as well. Perhaps the physician of the future will be required to take a licensing exam that focuses on competence in testing, improving, and overseeing the AI algorithms that deliver patient care.

In the nearer future, AI could ease the chronic healthcare workforce shortages and the high cost of labor by reducing burnout and improving retention among clinicians. For example, AI will likely help reduce time spent on tedious but important tasks such as documentation of care and accessing and integrating data to support clinical reasoning. Amazon's focus on user-friendly technology in primary care is aimed not only at improving the patient experience but also the clinician experience. As such, AI may dramatically improve the time clinicians can spend on quality improvements, including the rate of dissemination and implementation of new scientific findings—a longstanding challenge in medicine. AI may also reduce errors and the cost of litigation and malpractice insurance. In a 2023 report by Nikhil Sahni and colleagues analyzed the potential impact of AI on cost savings by examining use cases based on AI technology in the areas of hospital and physician office clinical operations as well as health plan operations. If these cases were to be scaled nationally, they estimated a 5–10% reduction in total U.S. healthcare expenditures. They acknowledge that these cost savings alone would not likely cover the cost of the AI investments but noted the likely quality improvements would contribute to net added value.

Where and how AI continues to develop in healthcare will be shaped by the power of buyers seeking better value, including their influence on AI-related regulations. Price sensitive buyers with bargaining power will be more likely to accept risks from AI for lower prices, creating demand for efficiency-based solutions. Other powerful buyers will drive providers to differentiate on quality. A 2023 report by Lu Tang and colleagues indicated that patients have concerns that AI will result in disengaged physicians. If so, AI could be developed to engage with patients as a substitute for physician engagement. In their review of studies on medical AI ethics, Tang and colleagues found that mistrust of AI remains a significant barrier to acceptance of AI. This includes concerns about lack of transparency regarding how AI is used and how it works. Tang and team also found that AI underperforms in populations that already experience disparities, indicating the risk of exacerbating health inequities. Gender, race, ethnicity, and insurance status biases are common in AI-based diagnoses and clinical predictions due to biases in the training data sets, including electronic health records and insurance claims. This research underscores the need to test AI-based tools across diverse patient groups to ensure performance meets appropriate standards, particularly among vulnerable patients.

In addition to concerns about bias in AI, there is evidence that AI commercialization in the healthcare industry is ahead of the science. In a 2021 report, Kicky van Leeuwen and colleagues examined 100 commercially available radiology products from 54 vendors. There were no studies of product efficacy published in peer-reviewed scientific journals for 64 of the products, and among the 36 products with such studies, the rigor of the studies varied such that only 18 products had published scientific studies supporting the validation of the product in improving diagnostic thinking, patient outcomes, or cost. Thus, radiologists who use AI products that lack adequate validation may find that perceived or actual benefits of these products are offset by risks of lawsuits or reputational damage from errors made with these products. Similarly, those vendors that can demonstrate their product benefits have been credibly tested and transparently documented in trusted scientific venues are likely to have a differentiated competitive market advantage.

Regulations regarding the use of AI in healthcare will likely be necessary to ensure patient safety and data security. While the U.S. federal government is calling for voluntary commitment to ethics in use of AI, it is also likely that many new regulatory processes will be implemented requiring AI technologies to demonstrate they are safe, effective, and fair before they can be used in healthcare. Compliance with new regulations would add costs, but value could be improved if the result is significantly better quality.

Investments in Value-Based Innovations

In addition to the federal investments in health information technology, there have been significant investments in the development of innovative care models and payment models designed to improve healthcare value, particularly for Medicare and Medicaid beneficiaries. The Affordable Care Act included establishing the Centers for Medicare & Medicaid Services (CMS) Innovation Center and funding of $10 billion per decade to support its operation and testing of new models designed to improve healthcare value without increasing costs—that is, by improving quality, reducing costs, or both. To date, the CMS Innovation Center has focused on testing new payment models that shift providers from fee-for-service payments to value-based payments. Even early supporters of the CMS Innovation Center have been critical of its performance, including failures to disseminate models that work, and have called for substantial reforms.

One key example of a value-based payment model tested with funding from the CMS Innovation Center is the Accountable Care Organization (ACO), a model in which local groups of inpatient and outpatient providers collaborate to take responsibility for providing high-value care. The collaboration of providers forms an ACO, not necessarily through launch of a new organization, but frequently through contractual arrangements. The ACO gets paid based on the number of beneficiaries it is responsible for, not based on the number of visits or services delivered to those members. If the ACO meets quality standards and provides care efficiently, it shares in the cost savings with Medicare. In a 2020 review of studies on the outcomes of ACOs, Michael Wilson and colleagues found that ACOs decrease the cost of care without reducing the quality of care; that is, ACO's improve the value of care. Specifically, they found that patient satisfaction was similar between ACOs and fee-for-service providers, that evidence on the extent to which ACOs improve quality or the provider experience was mixed, and that ACOs either reduced per capita costs or increased spending less than fee-for-service providers. The researchers found that cost savings were modest, the majority of which were a result of savings in outpatient expenses for medically complex patients and to reductions in services that do not improve quality.

If ACOs and other value-based payment models were disseminated more aggressively, providers would no longer have to operate under multiple different payment models, receiving some payments on a fee-for-service basis and some based on value. According to a 2023 Commonwealth Fund report, a survey of more than 1,000 primary care physicians in the United States found that 71% receive at least some fee-for-service payments, while only 46% receive at least some value-based payments. Larger and more urban and suburban physician practices were more likely to receive value-based payments than smaller, more rural practices. Those physicians receiving value-based payments were more likely to report involvement in quality improvement efforts and participation in an ACO.

Amazon's purchase of One Medical may accelerate the shift to value-based payments in the United States. Its growing partnerships with hospitals position Amazon to form ACOs, particularly given that Amazon is already receiving value-based payments from employer groups to provide primary care for their employees. Amazon may also facilitate the shift toward a more holistic approach to health rooted in its experience as a large employer. Amazon is one of the employers adding rather than cutting benefits. Amazon has added enhanced cancer care and mental health benefits in addition to work-life balance and flexibility programs and financial wellness benefits that include counseling, emergency savings, budgeting, goal setting, and debt consolidation.

Experts outside the United States have identified key areas where quality can be improved without adding to the total cost—in some cases reducing total costs. According to a 2018 National Academies report, low- and middle-income countries suffer the most, where up to 15% of deaths are due to poor quality care. In many socioeconomically disadvantaged regions, life-saving improvements in care can be achieved with investments in community health workers who can help address health literacy challenges along with medical mistrust. Investments in broader economic development and infrastructure in these countries might be as important as investments in the healthcare system itself to achieve health improvements in these populations. For example, better access to education, jobs, internet, and other technologies is likely synergistic with better access to healthcare.

South Korea is an instructive case, as this country has achieved dramatic improvements in life expectancy over just a few decades. According to Seungmi Yang and colleagues (2010), in 1960, South Koreans had a life expectancy of just 52.4 years, 16 years lower than the average among Organisation for Economic Co-operation and Development (OECD) countries. By 2005, life expectancy in South Korea had increased to 78.5 years, consistent with the average among OECD countries. Yang and colleagues noted that this increase was associated with an even more dramatic growth in the South Korean economy following the Korean War. They conducted an analysis of cause of death by age group and gender in South Korea to identify potential causes of the improvements in life expectancy and found mortality decreases in all age groups. Reductions in infant mortality were responsible for the largest share of life expectancy improvements based on age group, about three years. Based on cause of death, significant reductions in deaths due to cardiovascular disease accounted for the greatest improvements in life expectancy for males and females, accounting for about 30% of the improvement. The researchers point to several factors that might have contributed to the mortality reductions, including implementation of universal healthcare coverage, improvements in public health infrastructure such as water systems and housing conditions, urbanization, industrialization, access to healthcare facilities, and adherence to a traditional diet high in vegetables. Yang and colleagues cautioned that these life expectancy gains may be at risk with the cultural shift toward a Western diet among younger generations and persistently high smoking rates.

Examining the life expectancy improvements in South Korea, Stanford researcher Karen Eggleston developed a novel approach to evaluating investments in medical spending that could be used to make better decisions, including investments in high-value innovations. In 2023, Eggleston noted that current methods for measuring healthcare spending do not account for quality or outcomes of the spending. To address this limitation, Eggleston proposed a measure of the productivity of healthcare spending by examining the impact of the spending on life expectancy and quality of life—a way to measure healthcare value overall and by treatment.

At the aggregate level, Eggleston applied this approach to spending and life expectancy in South Korea from 2000 through 2019. Under a range of assumptions, Eggleston demonstrates positive return on medical spending investment. During this period, there was a three-fold increase in inflation-adjusted per capita medical spending in South Korea that was more than offset by a 7.3-year increase in life expectancy.

Innovations designed to improve health and healthcare value globally and locally will continue to attract investors. Today, it is not uncommon for healthcare providers, including nonprofit organizations, to establish investment arms to attract venture capital and other financing to support commercialization of innovations. While private equity firms may help innovation, they may also invest in healthcare to gain short-term profits that jeopardize achieving longer-term value. Conversely, while price controls in the United States may mean lower drug costs for consumers, these controls may threaten innovation. A movement toward value-based care is likely to continue growing and attracting investors as the demand for cost-effective care with better outcomes increases.

Healthcare and the U.S. Economy

Warren Buffett warned that the healthcare industry is consuming too much of the U.S. economy, depleting investment opportunities across all sectors as healthcare costs have escalated. Through his healthcare venture, Haven, Buffett tried to counteract these detrimental effects. Ultimately, he conceded that the organization failed to transform healthcare. As one of the most successful investors of all time, Buffett has not invested much in the healthcare industry. Perhaps this is because he is a value investor, and healthcare has yet to reflect the fundamentals of Buffett's value investment strategy, or this may be because he recommends investors invest in businesses they understand and is following his own advice. The complexities and opacity of the healthcare industry remain frustrating and confusing. Buffett has acknowledged avoiding investing in technology companies because he did not understand them or have confidence in them as long-term investments. Before the Haven venture and before Amazon's entry into healthcare, Buffett acknowledged missing out on investing in Amazon as he did not understand the transformative value of the internet for new business models.

Buffett remains a long-term investor, even at age 93, but he has changed his spending. In 2006, Buffett announced that he would start giving away his wealth, with the majority going to the Bill and Melinda Gates Foundation, which has a core focus on world health. As of 2023, he has donated more than $50 billion to this foundation and inspired others to donate their wealth to philanthropic endeavors. As an employer and major taxpayer, Buffett remains a large buyer of healthcare. In Buffett's 2022 letter to Berkshire Hathaway shareholders, while he does not mention healthcare, he shares his insights that inspire hope that businesses will continue to be the force that delivers healthcare value and funds so much of the nation's safety net. In the letter, he noted that "during the decade ending in 2021, the United States Treasury received about $32.3 trillion in taxes while it spent $43.9 trillion," a deficit so large it would surely have consequences. He also emphasized that, via corporate income tax payments, Berkshire Hathaway contributed "$32 billion during the decade, almost exactly a tenth of 1% of all money that the Treasury collected." Buffett accentuated this fact by pointing out that had there been just 1,000 U.S. businesses performing as well as Berkshire, "no other businesses nor any of the country's 131 million households would have needed to pay *any* taxes to the federal government." He stated that at Berkshire Hathaway, they "hope *and expect* to pay much more in taxes during the next decade" because "America's dynamism has made a huge contribution to whatever success Berkshire has achieved." Indeed, Buffett insisted this was the business's most important contribution, that "America would have done fine without Berkshire. The reverse is *not* true." These statements are likely apropos for every organization that does business successfully in the United States, including in its healthcare industry.

While Buffett remains optimistic about the United States in terms of its climate for business, Michael Porter's assessment is more cautious. He and others at Harvard Business School started the U.S. Competitiveness Project in 2011 due to concerns about structural weaknesses in the U.S. economy and society. As of 2019, they indicated that dysfunction in the U.S. political system remains a primary weakness that undermines America's global competitive advantage across industries. Because the healthcare industry is so heavily regulated, it is particularly susceptible to impairment in the government's ability to pass effective laws.

As unique, complex, and regulated as it is, the healthcare industry is more clearly understood when viewed through Porter's evidence-based analysis because competitive forces are the same across industries. The threats of new entrants and substitutes motivate change among incumbents, suppliers and buyers vie for greater power, and existing competitors position themselves to compete on price or differentiation. Application of this rigorous approach in the healthcare industry allows organizations to see new opportunities, be better prepared for challenges, and sustain performance over the long term. Porter's framework and the values of nations that shape the competitive forces have collectively produced the global health and healthcare industry of today, and they will continue to provide the windows of opportunity within which organizations can innovate to make it better tomorrow.

REFERENCES

Assistant Secretary for Planning and Evaluation. (2022). *Trends in prescription drug spending, 2016–2021.* Office of Science and Data Policy, U.S. Department of Health and Human Services. https://aspe.hhs.gov/sites/default/files/documents/88c547c976e915fc31fe2c6903ac0bc9/sdp-trends-prescription-drug-spending.pdf

Buffett, W. (2022). *Letter to shareholders.* Berkshire Hathaway. https://www.berkshirehathaway.com/letters/2022ltr.pdf

Eggleston, K. (2023). Valuing longer, healthier lives: Assessing the productivity of health spending in South Korea. *Asia-Pacific Issues,* (158), 1-8. https://www.eastwestcenter.org/sites/default/files/2023-03/EWC%20API-N158.pdf

Horstman, C., & Lewis, C. (2023, April 13). Engaging primary care in value-based payment: New findings from the 2022 Commonwealth Fund Survey of primary care physicians. *To the Point.* Commonwealth Fund. https://doi.org/10.26099/k3v8-0k69

Kung, T. H., Cheatham, M., Medenilla, A., Sillos, C., De Leon, L., Elepaño, C., Madriaga, M., Aggabao, R., Diaz-Candido, G., Maningo, J., & Tseng, V. (2023). Performance of ChatGPT on USMLE: Potential for AI-assisted medical education using large language models. *PLOS Digital Health,* 2(2), e0000198. https://doi.org/10.1371/journal.pdig.0000198

Office of the National Coordinator for Health Information Technology. (2022). *2022 report to Congress: Update on access, exchange, and use of electronic health information.* https://www.healthit.gov/sites/default/files/page/2023-02/2022_ONC_Report_to_Congress.pdf

Pellegrin, K. L., Krenk, L., Oakes, S. J., Ciarleglio, A., Lynn, J., McInnis, T., Bairos, A. W., Gomez, L., McCrary, M. B., Hanlon, A. L., & Miyamura, J. (2017). Reductions in medication-related hospitalizations in older adults with medication management by hospital and community pharmacists: A quasi-experimental study. *Journal of the American Geriatrics Society,* 65(1), 212–219. https://doi.org/10.1111/jgs.14518

Sahni, N., Stein, G., Zemmel, R., & Cutler, D. M. (2023). The potential impact of artificial intelligence on healthcare spending (No. w30857). In Agrawal, A., Gans, J., Goldfarb, A., & Tucker, C. (Eds.), *The economics of artificial intelligence: Health care challenges.* University of Chicago Press. https://www.nber.org/system/files/chapters/c14760/c14760.pdf

Tang, L., Li, J., & Fantus, S. (2023). Medical artificial intelligence ethics: A systematic review of empirical studies. *Digital Health,* 9, 20552076231186064. https://doi.org/10.1177/20552076231186064

U.S. Government Accountability Office. (2023, April). *Electronic health information exchange*. https://www.gao.gov/assets/gao-23-105540.pdf

van Leeuwen, K. G., Schalekamp, S., Rutten, M. J. C. M., van Ginneken, B., & de Rooij, M. (2021, April 15). Artificial intelligence in radiology: 100 commercially available products and their scientific evidence. *European Radiology, 31*(6), 3797–3804. https://doi.org/10.1007/s00330-021-07892-z

Watanabe, J. H., McInnis, T., & Hirsch, J. D. (2018). Cost of prescription drug-related morbidity and mortality. *The Annals of Pharmacotherapy, 52*(9), 829–837. https://doi.org/10.1177/1060028018765159

Wilson, M., Guta, A., Waddell, K., Lavis, J., Reid, R., & Evans, C. (2020). The impacts of accountable care organizations on patient experience, health outcomes and costs: a rapid review. *Journal of Health Services Research & Policy, 25*(2), 130–138. https://doi.org/10.1177/1355819620913141

Yang, S., Khang, Y. H., Harper, S., Davey Smith, G., Leon, D. A., & Lynch, J. (2010). Understanding the rapid increase in life expectancy in South Korea. *American Journal of Public Health, 100*(5), 896–903. https://doi.org/10.2105/AJPH.2009.160341

FURTHER READINGS

Berwick, D. M., & Gilfillan, R. (2021). Reinventing the Center for Medicare and Medicaid Innovation. *JAMA, 325*(13), 1247–1248. https://doi.org/10.1001/jama.2021.3203

Brownstein, J. S., Rader, B., Astley, C. M., & Tian, H. (2023). Advances in artificial intelligence for infectious-disease surveillance. *The New England Journal of Medicine, 388*(17), 1597–1607. https://doi.org/10.1056/NEJMra2119215

Dubay, L., Hill, I., Garrett, B., Blavin, F., Johnston, E., Howell, E., Morgan, J., Courtot, B., Benatar, S., & Cross-Barnet, C. (2020). Improving birth outcomes and lowering costs for women on Medicaid: Impacts of "strong start for mothers and newborns." *Health Affairs (Project Hope), 39*(6), 1042–1050. https://doi.org/10.1377/hlthaff.2019.01042

Haug, C. J., & Drazen, J. M. (2023). Artificial intelligence and machine learning in clinical medicine, 2023. *The New England Journal of Medicine, 388*(13), 1201–1208. https://doi.org/10.1056/NEJMra2302038

Mayer, K. (2023, July 31). *Amazon latest employer to bulk up benefits to address employee challenges*. Society for Human Resource Management. https://www.shrm.org/topics-tools/news/benefits-compensation/amazon-latest-employer-to-bulk-benefits-to-address-employee-challenges

National Academies of Sciences, Engineering, and Medicine, Health and Medicine Division, Board on Health Care Services, Board on Global Health, & Committee on Improving the Quality of Health Care Globally. (2018). *Crossing the global quality chasm: Improving health care worldwide*. National Academies Press (US). https://doi.org/10.17226/25152

Zhu, H. (2020). Big data and artificial intelligence modeling for drug discovery. *Annual Review of Pharmacology and Toxicology, 60,* 573–589. https://doi.org/10.1146/annurev-pharmtox-010919-023324

Bibliography

Academy of Managed Care Pharmacy. (2019). *Formulary management.* https://www.amcp
.org/about/managed-care-pharmacy-101/concepts-managed-care-pharmacy/
formulary-management

Agocs, S. (2011). Chiropractic's fight for survival. *AMA Journal of Ethics, 13*(6), 384–
388. https://doi.org/10.1001/virtualmentor.2011.13.6.mhst1-1106

Allen, L. N., Wigley, S., & Holmer, H. (2021). Implementation of non-communicable
disease policies from 2015 to 2020: A geopolitical analysis of 194 countries.
The Lancet Global Health, 9(11), e1528–e1538. https://doi.org/10.1016/
S2214-109X(21)00359-4

Alliance for Safe Online Pharmacies. (2021). *American perceptions and use of online
pharmacies.* https://buysaferx.pharmacy//wp-content/uploads/2021/07/ASOP-
Global-Foundation-2021-Consumer-Behavior-Survey-Key-Findings_Final-
7.9.2021.pdf

Amazon. (n.d.). Prime now offers medical care. https://health.amazon.com/prime

Amazon. (2022). Annual report. https://www.annualreports.com/HostedData/Annual-
Reports/PDF/NASDAQ_AMZN_2022.pdf

America's Health Rankings. (2022). Annual report. *United Health Foundation.* https://
assets.americashealthrankings.org/app/uploads/ahr_2022annualreport.pdf

American Association of Colleges of Nursing. (2023, July). *Nursing workforce fact sheet.*
https://www.aacnnursing.org/news-data/fact-sheets/nursing-workforce-
fact-sheet

American Hospital Association. (2017, September). *Fact sheet: Hospital billing explained.*
https://www.aha.org/system/files/2018-01/factsheet-hospital-billing-
explained-9-2017.pdf

American Hospital Association. (2023). *5 things to know about Amazon's recent One
Medical acquisition.* https://www.aha.org/aha-center-health-innovation-
market-scan/2023-03-07-5-things-know-about-amazons-recent-one-
medical-acquisition

American Hospital Association. (2023). *Fast facts on U.S. hospitals.* https://www.aha
.org/statistics/fast-facts-us-hospitals

American Hospital Association. (2023, March 28). *Civica Rx gets more backing in effort
to reduce drug prices and shortages.* https://www.aha.org/aha-center-health-
innovation-market-scan/2023-03-28-civica-rx-gets-more-backing-effort-
reduce-drug-prices-and-shortages

American Hospital Association. (2023, April). *The financial stability of America's hospitals
and health systems is at risk as the costs of caring continue to rise.* https://www
.aha.org/system/files/media/file/2023/04/Cost-of-Caring-2023-The-
Financial-Stability-of-Americas-Hospitals-and-Health-Systems-Is-at-Risk.pdf

American Medical Association. (2023). *Bipartisan graduate medical education and physician workforce legislation.* https://www.ama-assn.org/system/files/2023-nac-
action-kit-gme-physician-workforce.pdf

American Medical Association. (2023, May 15). *AMA successfully fights scope of practice expansions that threaten patient safety.* https://www.ama-assn.org/practice-
management/scope-practice/ama-successfully-fights-scope-practice-expansions-
threaten

American Psychological Association. (2022, November). *Psychologists struggle to meet demand amid mental health crisis.* https://www.apa.org/pubs/reports/practitioner/2022-covid-psychologist-workload

Anell, A., Dietrichson, J., Ellegård, L. M., & Kjellsson, G. (2021). Information, switching costs, and consumer choice: Evidence from two randomised field experiments in Swedish primary health care. *Journal of Public Economics, 196.* 104390. https://doi.org/10.1016/j.jpubeco.2021.104390

Arias, E., Heron, M., & Hakes, J. K. (2016). The validity of race and Hispanic-origin reporting on death certificates in the United States: An update. National Center for Health Statistics. *Vital Health Stat, 2*(172). https://www.cdc.gov/nchs/data/series/sr_02/sr02_172.pdf

Assistant Secretary for Planning and Evaluation. (2022). *Trends in prescription drug spending, 2016–2021.* Office of Science and Data Policy, U.S. Department of Health and Human Services. https://aspe.hhs.gov/sites/default/files/docum ents/88c547c976e915fc31fe2c6903ac0bc9/sdp-trends-prescription-drug-spending.pdf

Assistant Secretary for Planning and Evaluation, Office of Health Policy. (2022, April 20). *Changes of ownership of hospital and skilled nursing facilities.* U.S. Department of Health and Human Services. https://aspe.hhs.gov/sites/default/files/documents/be6f3366294bd30a08a8ae90c84f3894/aspe-datapoint-change-ownership-pecos.pdf

Assistant Secretary for Planning and Evaluation, Office of Health Policy. (2022, May 3). *Impact of the COVID-19 pandemic on the hospital and outpatient clinician workforce.* U.S. Department of Health and Human Services. https://aspe.hhs.gov/sites/default/files/documents/9cc72124abd9ea25d58a22c7692dccb6/aspe-covid-workforce-report.pdf

Atherly, A., Feldman, R. D., Dowd, B., & van den Broek-Altenburg, E. (2020). Switching costs in Medicare Advantage. *Forum for Health Economics & Policy, 23*(1), 20190023. https://doi.org/10.1515/fhep-2019-0023

Atwoli, L., Baqui, A. H., Benfield, T., Bosurgi, R., Godlee, F., Hancocks, S., Horton, R., Laybourn-Langton, L., Monteiro, C. A., Norman, I., Patrick, K., Praities, N., Rikkert, M., Rubin, E. J., Sahni, P., Smith, R., Talley, N., Turale, S., & Vázquez, D. (2021). Call for emergency action to limit global temperature increases, restore biodiversity, and protect health. *PLoS Med 18*(9), e1003755. https://doi.org/10.1371/journal.pmed.1003755

Bays, C. W. (1983). Why most private hospitals are nonprofit. *Journal of Policy Analysis and Management, 2*(3), 366–385. https://doi.org/10.2307/3324447

Beakes-Read, G., Neisser, M., Frey, P., & Guarducci, M. (2022). Analysis of FDA's accelerated approval program performance December 1992–December 2021. *Therapeutic Innovation & Regulatory Science, 56*(5), 698–703. https://doi.org/10.1007/s43441-022-00430-z

Berkshire Hathaway. (2018, January 30). *Amazon, Berkshire Hathaway and JPMorgan Chase & Co. to partner on U.S. employee healthcare.* https://berkshirehathaway.com/news/jan3018.pdf

Berwick, D. M., & Gilfillan, R. (2021). Reinventing the Center for Medicare and Medicaid Innovation. *JAMA, 325*(13), 1247–1248. https://doi.org/10.1001/jama.2021.3203

Beyene, K. A., Sheridan, J., & Aspden, T. (2014). Prescription medication sharing: a systematic review of the literature. *American Journal of Public Health, 104*(4), e15–e26. https://doi.org/10.2105/AJPH.2013.301823

Bhargava, S., Loewenstein, G., & Sydnor, J. (2017). Choose to lose: Health plan choices from a menu with dominated option. *The Quarterly Journal of Economics, 132*(3), 1319–1372. http://doi.org/10.1093/qje/qjx011

Boyle, P. (2023, January 12). What's your specialty? New data show the choices of America's doctors by gender, race, and age. *Association of American Medical Colleges. AAMCNews.* https://www.aamc.org/news/what-s-your-specialty-new-data-show-choices-america-s-doctors-gender-race-and-age

Bradburd, R. M., & Ross, D. R. (1989). Can small firms find and defend strategic niches? A test of the Porter hypothesis. *The Review of Economics and Statistics,* 258–262. https://doi.org/10.2307/1926971

Brady, D., Kohler, U., & Zheng, H. (2023). Novel estimates of mortality associated with poverty in the US. *JAMA Internal Medicine, 183*(6), 618–619. https://doi.org/10.1001/jamainternmed.2023.0276

Braveman, P. (2023). *Social determinants of health and health disparities.* Oxford University Press, Incorporated.

Braveman, P., Egerter, S., & Williams, D. R. (2011). The social determinants of health: coming of age. *Annual Review of Public Health, 32,* 381–398. https://doi.org/10.1146/annurev-publhealth-031210-101218

Brownstein, J. S., Rader, B., Astley, C. M., & Tian, H. (2023). Advances in artificial intelligence for infectious-disease surveillance. *The New England Journal of Medicine, 388*(17), 1597–1607. https://doi.org/10.1056/NEJMra2119215

Buffett, W. (2022). *Letter to shareholders.* Berkshire Hathaway. https://www.berkshirehathaway.com/letters/2022ltr.pdf

Button, B. L., Taylor, K., McArthur, M., Newbery, S., & Cameron, E. (2022). The economic impact of rural healthcare on rural economies: A rapid review. *Canadian Journal of Rural Medicine, 27*(4), 158–168. https://doi.org/10.4103/cjrm.cjrm_70_21

Carlton, S., Lee, M., & Prakash, A. (2022, August 3). *Insights into the 2022 individual health insurance market.* McKinsey & Company. https://www.mckinsey.com/industries/healthcare/our-insights/insights-into-the-2022-individual-health-insurance-market

Casadevall, A., & Fang, F. C. (2014). Specialized science. *Infection and Immunity, 82*(4), 1355–1360.

Centers for Disease Control and Prevention. (n.d.). *CDC WONDER.* Centers for Disease Control and Prevention. https://wonder.cdc.gov/

Centers for Disease Control and Prevention. (2017). *Table 89. Hospitals, beds, and occupancy rates, by type of ownership and size of hospital: United States, selected years 1975–2015.* https://www.cdc.gov/nchs/data/hus/2017/089.pdf

Centers for Disease Control and Prevention. (2023, May). *COVID data tracker.* https://covid.cdc.gov/covid-data-tracker/#vaccination-states-jurisdictions

Centers for Disease Control and Prevention. (2023, August). *Federal retail pharmacy program: A collaboration between the federal government, states and territories, and 21 national pharmacy partners and independent pharmacy networks nationwide.*

Centers for Disease Control and Prevention Archive. https://archive.cdc
.gov/#/details?url=https://www.cdc.gov/vaccines/covid-19/retail-pharmacy-
program/index.html

Centers for Medicare and Medicaid Services. (2023, March 15). *Medicare drug price
negotiation program: Initial guidance.* https://www.cms.gov/files/document/
medicare-drug-price-negotiation-program-initial-guidance.pdf

Centers for Medicare & Medicaid Services. (2023, September 6). *National health expenditure data.* U.S. Department of Health and Human Services. https://www
.cms.gov/research-statistics-data-and-systems/statistics-trends-and-reports/
nationalhealthexpenddata

Centers for Medicare and Medicaid Services. (2023, October 13). *2024 Medicare Advantage and Part D Star Ratings.* https://www.cms.gov/newsroom/
fact-sheets/2024-medicare-advantage-and-part-d-star-ratings

Chung, A. P., Gaynor, M., & Richards-Shubik, S. (2017). Subsidies and structure:
The lasting impact of the Hill-Burton program on the hospital industry. *The
Review of Economics and Statistics, 99*(5), 926–943. https://www.jstor.org/
stable/26616170

Clark, B., & Puthiyath, M. S. (2022). *The federal 340b drug pricing program: What it
is, and why it's facing legal challenges.* Commonwealth Fund. https://doi
.org/10.26099/c4z8-pf65

Cochran, S. D., Björkenstam, C., & Mays, V. M. (2016). Sexual orientation and all-cause
mortality among US adults aged 18 to 59 years, 2001–2011. *American Journal
of Public Health, 106*(5), 918–920. https://doi.org/10.2105/ajph.2016.303052

Cohen, E. (n.d.). *PharmacyOS.* PillPack by Amazon Pharmacy. https://www.pharmacyos
.com/

Cohen, R. A., Bernstein, A. B., Bilheimer, L. T., Makuc, D. M., & Powell-Griner, E.
(2009). Health insurance coverage trends, 1959–2007: Estimates from the
National Health Interview Survey. *National Health Statistics Reports,* (17),
1–25. https://www.cdc.gov/nchs/data/nhsr/nhsr017.pdf

CommonSpirit. (2022). *Unaudited annual report: For the years ended June 30, 2023 and
2022.* https://www.commonspirit.org/investor-resources

Congressional Budget Office. (2021, April). *Research and development in the pharmaceutical industry.* https://www.cbo.gov/publication/57126

Congressional Budget Office. (2022, January). *The prices that commercial health insurers
and Medicare pay for hospitals' and physicians' services.* https://www.cbo.gov/
system/files/2022-01/57422-medical-prices.pdf

Congressional Budget Office. (2022, September). *Policy approaches to reduce what commercial insurers pay for hospitals' and physicians' services.* https://www.cbo.gov/
publication/58541

Cooper, R. L., Ramesh, A., Radix, A. E., Reuben, J. S., Juarez, P. D., Holder, C. L., Belton,
A. S., Brown, K. Y., Mena, L. A., & Matthews-Juarez, P. (2023). Affirming and
inclusive care training for medical students and residents to reduce health
disparities experienced by sexual and gender minorities: A systematic review.
Transgender Health, 8(4), 307–327. https://doi.org/10.1089/trgh.2021.0148

Cooper, Z., Craig, S. V., Gaynor, M., & Van Reenen, J. (2019). The price ain't right?
Hospital prices and health spending on the privately insured. *The Quarterly
Journal of Economics, 134*(1), 51–107. https://doi.org/10.1093/qje/qjy020

Cordina, J., Fowkes, J., Malani, R., & Medford-Davis, L. (2022, February 22). *Patients love telehealth—physicians are not so sure*. McKinsey & Company. https://www.mckinsey.com/industries/healthcare/our-insights/patients-love-telehealth-physicians-are-not-so-sure

Costa, F., Lago, A., Rocha, V., Barros, Ó., Costa, L., Vipotnik, Z., Silva, B., & Tavares, T. (2019). A review on biological processes for pharmaceuticals wastes abatement—a growing threat to modern society. *Environmental Science & Technology, 53*(13), 7185–7202. https://doi.org/10.1021/acs.est.8b06977

Crimmins, E. M., Shim, H., Zhang, Y. S., & Kim, J. K. (2019). Differences between men and women in mortality and the health dimensions of the morbidity process. *Clinical Chemistry, 65*(1), 135–145. https://doi.org/10.1373/clinchem.2018.288332

Cubanski, J., & Neuman, T. (2023, January 19). *What to know about Medicare spending and financing*. Kaiser Family Foundation. https://www.kff.org/medicare/issue-brief/what-to-know-about-medicare-spending-and-financing/

Cubanski, J., Neuman, T., & Freed, M. (2023, January 24). *Explaining the prescription drug provisions in the Inflation Reduction Act*. Kaiser Family Foundation. https://www.kff.org/medicare/issue-brief/explaining-the-prescription-drug-provisions-in-the-inflation-reduction-act/#bullet02

Definitive Healthcare. (2022). *Top 10 largest independent hospitals*. https://www.definitivehc.com/blog/top-10-largest-independent-hospitals

Deloitte. (2019). *The role of distributors in the US health care industry*. https://www2.deloitte.com/us/en/pages/life-sciences-and-health-care/articles/the-role-of-distributors-in-the-us-health-care-industry.html

Dess, G. G., & Davis, P. S. (1984). Porter's (1980) generic strategies as determinants of strategic group membership and organizational performance. *Academy of Management Journal, 27*(3), 467–488. https://doi.org/10.2307/256040

Doty, M. M., Tikkanen, R., Shah, A., & Schneider, E. C. (2020). Primary care physicians' role in coordinating medical and health-related social needs in eleven countries. *Health Affairs (Project Hope), 39*(1), 115–123. https://doi.org/10.1377/hlthaff.2019.01088

Dredge, C., & Scholtes, S. (2023). Vaccinating health care supply chains against market failure: The case of civica rx. *NEJM Catalyst Innovations in Care Delivery, 4*(10), CAT-23. https://doi.org/10.1056/CAT.23.0167

Drexel University Online. (2021, August 26). *Authentic or virtue signaling? Marketing professor breaks down corporate social responsibility* [Video]. https://www.youtube.com/watch?v=FvJXD5BHaIQ

Drug Channels Institute. (2023, March 8). The top 15 U.S. pharmacies of 2022: Market shares and revenues at the biggest companies. https://www.drugchannels.net/2023/03/the-top-15-us-pharmacies-of-2022-market.html

Dubay, L., Hill, I., Garrett, B., Blavin, F., Johnston, E., Howell, E., Morgan, J., Courtot, B., Benatar, S., & Cross-Barnet, C. (2020). Improving birth outcomes and lowering costs for women on Medicaid: Impacts of "strong start for mothers and newborns." *Health Affairs (Project Hope), 39*(6), 1042–1050. https://doi.org/10.1377/hlthaff.2019.01042

Dunleavy, K. (2023, April 18). *The top 20 pharma companies by 2022 revenue*. Fierce Pharma. https://www.fiercepharma.com/pharma/top-20-pharma-companies-2022-revenue

Dunleavy, K. (2023, May 12). *Medicare IRA measure as 'negotiation with a gun to your head.'* Fierce Pharma. https://www.fiercepharma.com/pharma/pfizer-ceo-bourla-calls-medicare-ira-measure-negotiation-gun-your-head

Edelman Trust Institute. (2023). *Edelman Trust Barometer global report.* https://www.edelman.com/sites/g/files/aatuss191/files/2023-01/2023%20Edelman%20Trust%20Barometer%20Global%20Report.pdf

Eggleston, K. (2023). Valuing longer, healthier lives: Assessing the productivity of health spending in South Korea. *Asia-Pacific Issues,* (158), 1–8. https://www.eastwestcenter.org/sites/default/files/2023-03/EWC%20API-N158.pdf

Elevance Health. (2024, January 10). Elevance Health addresses healthcare's digital divide by increasing access to high-quality smartphones and health-related digital services. https://www.elevancehealth.com/newsroom/elevance-health-addresses-healthcare-digital-divide-by-increasing-access-to-high-quality-smartphones-and-health-related-digital-services

Emerson, J. (2023, February 16). *Meet America's largest employer of physicians: United Health Group.* Becker's Healthcare. https://www.beckerspayer.com/payer/meet-americas-largest-employer-of-physicians-unitedhealth-group.html

Employee Benefit Research Institute and Greenwald Research. (2022). *Consumer engagement in health care survey.* https://www.ebri.org/docs/default-source/cehcs/2022-cehcs-report.pdf?sfvrsn=da56392f_2

Employee Benefit Research Institute and Greenwald Research. (2023, April 6). *What leads to greater satisfaction with health plan coverage?* https://www.ebri.org/docs/default-source/fast-facts/ff-463-cehcs7-6apr23.pdf?sfvrsn=c599392f_2

Evans, B. R., & Leighton, F. A. (2014). A history of One Health. *Revue Scientifique et Technique (International Office of Epizootics),* 33(2), 413–420. https://doi.org/10.20506/rst.33.2.2298

Executive Office of the President, Office of Management and Budget. (1997, October 30). *Revisions to the standards for the classification of federal data on race and ethnicity.* Federal Register Notice. https://obamawhitehouse.archives.gov/omb/fedreg_1997standards

Federal Trade Commission. (2021). *Notice of penalty offenses concerning deceptive or unfair conduct around endorsements and testimonials.* https://www.ftc.gov/system/files/attachments/penalty-offenses-concerning-endorsements/notice-penalty_offenses-endorsements.pdf

Federal Trade Commission. (2022, December) *Mobile health app interactive tool.* https://www.ftc.gov/business-guidance/resources/mobile-health-apps-interactive-tool

Federal Trade Commission. (2023, April 13). *FTC warns almost 700 marketing companies that they could face civil penalties if they can't back up their product claims.* https://www.ftc.gov/news-events/news/press-releases/2023/04/ftc-warns-almost-700-marketing-companies-they-could-face-civil-penalties-if-they-cant-back-their

Fein, A. J. (2022, March). *The 2022 economic report on U.S. pharmacies and pharmacy benefit managers.* Drug Channels Institute. https://drugchannelsinstitute.com/files/2022-PharmacyPBM-DCI-Overview.pdf

Fein, A. J. (2022, August 2). *The shady business of specialty carve-outs, a.k.a., alternative funding programs.* Drug Channels. https://www.drugchannels.net/2022/08/the-shady-business-of-specialty-carve.html

Fidler, D. P. (2022, July 28). *Geopolitics, global health, and the group of seven*. Council on Foreign Relations. https://www.cfr.org/article/geopolitics-global-health-and-group-seven

Flaherty, M., & Lou, R. (2020, October 1). *Direct-to-patient (DTP) sales channels might be the next frontier for pharmaceutical companies*. Deloitte Consulting LLP. https://www2.deloitte.com/us/en/blog/health-care-blog/2020/direct-to-patient-sales-channels-might-be-the-next-frontier-for-pharmaceutical-companies.html

Food and Drug Administration. (2023). *New drug therapy approvals 2022*. Food and Drug Administration. https://www.fda.gov/drugs/new-drugs-fda-cders-new-molecular-entities-and-new-therapeutic-biological-products/new-drug-therapy-approvals-2022

Food and Drug Administration. (2024, January). *Overview of device regulation*. https://www.fda.gov/medical-devices/device-advice-comprehensive-regulatory-assistance/overview-device-regulation

Fortune PINC AI. (2023). *100 Top Hospitals*. https://cdn.sanity.io/files/dcd4gsuh/production/7db7428df32516f4d30368ebb6c4cb17d884c0b3.pdf

Fry, S., Kapur, V., Jain, N., Klingan, F., Podpolny, D., & Murphy, K. (2022, March 15). *Healthcare private equity deal returns: Look to revenues and multiples*. Bain & Company. https://www.bain.com/insights/deal-returns-global-healthcare-private-equity-and-ma-report-2022/

Fuller, R., Landrigan, P. J., Balakrishnan, K., Bathan, G., Bose-O'Reilly, S., Brauer, M., Caravanos, J., Chiles, T., Cohen, A., Corra, L., Cropper, M., Ferraro, G., Hanna, J., Hanrahan, D., Hu, H., Hunter, D., Janata, G., Kupka, R., Lanphear, B., Lichtveld, M., … & Yan, C. (2022). Pollution and health: a progress update. *The Lancet. Planetary health*, 6(6), e535–e547. https://doi.org/10.1016/S2542-5196(22)00090-0

Gao, W., Sanna, M., Hefler, M., & Wen, C. P. (2020). Air pollution is not "the new smoking": comparing the disease burden of air pollution and smoking across the globe, 1990–2017. *Tobacco Control*, 29(6), 715–718. https://doi.org/10.1136%2Ftobaccocontrol-2019-055181

Godwin, J., Levinson, Z., & Hulver, S. (2023, March 14). *The estimated value of tax exemption for nonprofit hospitals was about $28 billion in 2020*. Kaiser Family Foundation https://www.kff.org/health-costs/issue-brief/the-estimated-value-of-tax-exemption-for-nonprofit-hospitals-was-about-28-billion-in-2020/

Goldsworthy, R. C., & Mayhorn, C. B. (2009). Prescription medication sharing among adolescents: prevalence, risks, and outcomes. *The Journal of Adolescent Health: Official Publication of the Society for Adolescent Medicine*, 45(6), 634–637. https://doi.org/10.1016/j.jadohealth.2009.06.002

Grant, M. (2021). Walmart: Healthcare for all? In *Sage Business Cases*. SAGE. https://doi.org/10.4135/9781529762884

Gunja, M. Z., Gumas, E. D., & Williams II, R. D. (2023, January 31). *U.S. health care from a global perspective, 2022: Accelerating spending, worsening outcomes*. The Commonwealth Fund. https://www.commonwealthfund.org/publications/issue-briefs/2023/jan/us-health-care-global-perspective-2022#:~:text=The%20U.S.%20has%20the%20lowest,nearly%20twice%20the%20OECD%20average.

Guth, M., Ammula, M., & Hinton, E. (2021, September 9). *Understanding the impact of Medicaid premiums and cost sharing: Updated evidence from the literature and section 1115 waivers.* Kaiser Family Foundation. https://www.kff.org/medicaid/issue-brief/understanding-the-impact-of-medicaid-premiums-cost-sharing-updated-evidence-from-the-literature-and-section-1115-waivers/

Hall, K. L., Vogel, A. L., Huang, G. C., Serrano, K. J., Rice, E. L., Tsakraklides, S. P., & Fiore, S. M. (2018). The science of team science: A review of the empirical evidence and research gaps on collaboration in science. *American Psychologist, 73*(4), 532. https://doi.org/10.1037/amp0000319

Hamed, S., Bradby, H., Ahlberg, B. M., & Thapar-Björkert, S. (2022). Racism in healthcare: A scoping review. *BMC Public Health, 22*(1), 988. https://doi.org/10.1186/s12889-022-13122-y

Haque, W., Ahmadzada, M., Janumpally, S., Haque, E., Allahrakha, H., Desai, S., & Hsiehchen, D. (2022). Adherence to a federal hospital price transparency rule and associated financial and marketplace factors. *JAMA, 327*(21), 2143–2145. https://doi.org/10.1001/jama.2022.5363

Harris, J. K., Beatty, K., Leider, J. P., Knudson, A., Anderson, B. L., & Meit, M. (2016). The double disparity facing rural local health departments. *Annual Review of Public Health, 37*, 167–184. https://doi.org/10.1146/annurev-publhealth-031914-122755

Haug, C. J., & Drazen, J. M. (2023). Artificial intelligence and machine learning in clinical medicine, 2023. *The New England Journal of Medicine, 388*(13), 1201–1208. https://doi.org/10.1056/NEJMra2302038

Hayes, D., Killian, R., & Kolli, S. (2020, February). *Capital requirements for health insurers.* Milliman. https://www.milliman.com/-/media/milliman/pdfs/articles/capital_requirements_for_health_insurers.ashx

HCA Healthcare. (2022). *Annual report to shareholders.* https://s23.q4cdn.com/949900249/files/doc_financials/2022/ar/274375-HCA-Healthcare-Annual-Report.pdf

Health Resources and Services Administration. (2022). *National Health Center Program Uniform Data System (UDS) awardee data, Table 9D.* https://data.hrsa.gov/tools/data-reporting/program-data/national

Healthcare Distribution Alliance. (2022). *HDA Factbook.* https://www.hda.org/publications/93rd-edition-hda-factbook-the-facts,-figures-and-trends-in-healthcare/

Hernando-Amado, S., Coque, T. M., Baquero, F., & Martínez, J. L. (2019). Defining and combating antibiotic resistance from One Health and Global Health perspectives. *Nature Microbiology, 4*(9), 1432–1442. https://doi.org/10.1038/s41564-019-0503-9

Hero, J. O., Sinaiko, A. D., Kingsdale, J., Gruver, R. S., & Galbraith, A. A. (2019). Decision-making experiences of consumers choosing individual-market health insurance plans. *Health Affairs (Project Hope), 38*(3), 464–472. https://doi.org/10.1377/hlthaff.2018.05036

Hickey, K. J., Kirchhoff, S. M., & Rogers H. A. (2023, December 8). *Medicare Drug price negotiation under the Inflation Reduction Act: Industry responses and potential effects.* Congressional Research Service. https://crsreports.congress.gov/product/pdf/R/R47872

Hickman, C., Marks, E., Pihkala, P., Clayton, S., Lewandowski, R. E., Mayall, E. E., Wray, B., Mellor, C., & Van Susteren, L. (2021). Climate anxiety in children and young people and their beliefs about government responses to climate change: a global survey. *The Lancet Planetary Health, 5*(12), e863–e873. https://doi.org/10.1016/s2542-5196(21)00278-3

Hill, E., Goodwill, A. M., Gorelik, A., & Szoeke, C. (2019). Diet and biomarkers of Alzheimer's disease: a systematic review and meta-analysis. *Neurobiology of Aging, 76*, 45–52. https://doi.org/10.1016/j.neurobiolaging.2018.12.008

Holgash, K., & Heberlein, M. (2019). *Physician acceptance of new Medicaid patients: what matters and what doesn't.* Medicaid and CHIP Payment and Access Commission. https://www.macpac.gov/wp-content/uploads/2019/01/Physician-Acceptance-of-New-Medicaid-Patients.pdf

Hopkins, J. S. (2023, February 2). Drug prices increase 5.6% as government ramps up pressure to lower costs. *Wall Street Journal.* https://www.wsj.com/articles/drugmakers-raise-prices-on-nearly-1-000-medicines-but-show-restraint-11675313960

Horstman, C., & Lewis, C. (2023, April 13). Engaging primary care in value-based payment: New findings from the 2022 Commonwealth Fund Survey of primary care physicians. *To the Point.* Commonwealth Fund. https://doi.org/10.26099/k3v8-0k69

IHS Markit Ltd. (2021, June). *The complexities of physician supply and demand: Projections from 2019 to 2034.* Association of American Medical Colleges. https://www.aamc.org/media/54681/download

Illinois Department of Public Health (2008, December 31). *Final report of the Task Force on Health Planning Reform.* http://www.idph.state.il.us/tfhpr/reports/TFHPR%20Final%20Report.pdf

J.D. Power. (2022, July 28). *Innovations at retail pharmacies accelerate as digital competition, health and wellness offerings grow, J.D. Power Finds.* https://www.jdpower.com/business/press-releases/2022-us-pharmacy-study

Jackson, S. S., Brown, J., Pfeiffer, R. M., Shrewsbury, D., O'Callaghan, S., Berner, A. M., Gadalla, S. M., & Shiels, M. S. (2023). Analysis of mortality among transgender and gender diverse adults in England. *JAMA Network Open, 6*(1), e2253687–e2253687. https://doi.org/10.1001/jamanetworkopen.2022.53687

Janin, A. (2023, July 10). The longevity clinic will see you now—for $100,000: The clinics cater to a growing number of people obsessed with fighting aging. *Wall Street Journal.* https://www.wsj.com/articles/longevity-clinics-aging-living-longer-2b98e773

Japsen, B. (2023, October 9). Amazon's One Medical to add more health services in existing markets. *Forbes.* https://www.forbes.com/sites/brucejapsen/2023/10/09/amazon-clinics-and-pharmacy-are-opportunities-to-make-things-easier-for-people/?sh=46ef7a0e5c62

Jennings, K. (2023, November 8). Amazon Prime's new $9 primary care subscription undercuts Amazon's other health services. *Forbes.* https://www.forbes.com/sites/katiejennings/2023/11/08/amazon-primes-new-one-medical-discount-undercuts-amazon-clinic-prices/?sh=494be18230d6

Johannes, L. (2000, August 29). M.D. Anderson works to build ties with the HMOs it once combated. *Wall Street Journal.* https://www.wsj.com/articles/SB967500656782012753

Johannes, L. (2024, March 17). New pain treatment uses ultrasound at home. *The Wall Street Journal*. https://www.wsj.com/articles/SB10001424052702303730804 579439911570346896.

Kaiser Family Foundation. (2019). *Medicaid-to-Medicare fee index*. https://www.kff.org/medicaid/state-indicator/medicaid-to-medicare-fee-index/

Kaiser Family Foundation. (2013, April 25). *Summary of the Affordable Care Act*. https://www.kff.org/health-reform/fact-sheet/summary-of-the-affordable-care-act/

Kaiser Family Foundation. (2021). *Health insurance coverage of the total population*. https://www.kff.org/other/state-indicator/total-population/

Kane, C. K. (2021). *Recent changes in physician practice arrangements: Private practice dropped to less than 50 percent of physicians in 2020*. American Medical Association. https://www.ama-assn.org/system/files/2021-05/2020-prp-physician-practice-arrangements.pdf

Kaplan, R. S., & Norton, D. P. (1992). The balanced scorecard—measures that drive performance. *Harvard Business Review, 70*(1), 71–79. https://hbr.org/1992/01/the-balanced-scorecard-measures-that-drive-performance-2

Kaplan, R. S., & Norton, D. P. (2015). *Balanced scorecard success: The Kaplan-Norton collection* (4 ebooks). Harvard Business Review.

Karam, G., Agarwal, A., Sadeghirad, B., Jalink, M., Hitchcock, C. L., Ge, L., Kiflen, R., Ahmed, W., Zea, A. M., Milenkovic, J., Chedrawe, M. A., Rabassa, M., El Dib, R., Goldenberg, J. Z., Guyatt, G. H., Boyce, E., & Johnston, B. C. (2023). Comparison of seven popular structured dietary programmes and risk of mortality and major cardiovascular events in patients at increased cardiovascular risk: systematic review and network meta-analysis. *BMJ, 380*, e072003. https://doi.org/10.1136/bmj-2022-072003

KaufmanHall. (2022, May 11). *A special workforce edition of the national hospital flash report*. https://www.kaufmanhall.com/insights/research-report/special-workforce-edition-national-hospital-flash-report

Keeling, A. W. (2016, May 31). Historical perspectives on an expanded role for nursing. *OJIN The Online Journal of Issues in Nursing, 20*(2). https://doi.org/10.3912/OJIN.Vol20No02Man02

Klein, S., & Hostetter, M. (2022, April 1). *Tackling high health care prices: A look at four purchaser-led efforts. Do employers have any leverage to bring down prices?* The Commonwealth Fund. https://www.commonwealthfund.org/publications/2022/apr/tackling-high-health-care-prices-look-four-purchaser-led-efforts

Kling, J. A., & Smith, K. A. (1995). Identifying strategic groups in the US airline industry: An application of the Porter model. *Transportation Journal*, 26–34.

Kominski, G. F., Nonzee, N. J., & Sorensen, A. (2017). The Affordable Care Act's impacts on access to insurance and health care for low-income populations. *Annual Review of Public Health, 38*, 489–505. https://doi.org/10.1146/annurev-publhealth-031816-044555

Kona, M., & Corlette, S. (2022). *Hospital and insurer price transparency rules now in effect but compliance is still far away*. Georgetown University Center on Health Insurance Reforms. https://chirblog.org/hospital-and-insurer-price-transparency-rules-in-effect/

Kung, T. H., Cheatham, M., Medenilla, A., Sillos, C., De Leon, L., Elepaño, C., Madriaga, M., Aggabao, R., Diaz-Candido, G., Maningo, J., & Tseng, V. (2023). Performance of ChatGPT on USMLE: Potential for AI-assisted medical education using large language models. *PLOS Digital Health, 2*(2), e0000198. https://doi.org/10.1371/journal.pdig.0000198

Kurani, N., Rae, M., Pollitz, K., Amin, K., & Cox, C. (2021, January 13). *Price transparency and variation in U.S. health services.* Peterson-KFF Health System Tracker. https://www.healthsystemtracker.org/brief/price-transparency-and-variation-in-u-s-health-services/

Lamiraud, K., & Stadelmann, P. (2020). Switching costs in competitive health insurance markets: The role of insurers' pricing strategies. *Health Economics, 29*(9), 992–1012. https://doi.org/10.1002%2Fhec.4111

Landi, H. (2022, July 25). *What Amazon's $4B One Medical play reveals about its healthcare ambitions.* Fierce Healthcare. https://www.fiercehealthcare.com/health-tech/how-amazons-one-medical-deal-could-boost-its-healthcare-ambitions-and-heat-competition

Landi, H. (2023, February 22). *Amazon closes $3.9B One Medical deal as it builds out healthcare strategy.* https://www.fiercehealthcare.com/providers/amazon-closes-39b-one-medical-deal-build-its-ambitions-healthcare-player

LaVeist, T. A., Pérez-Stable, E. J., Richard, P., Anderson, A., Isaac, L. A., Santiago, R., Okoh, C., Breen, N., Farhat, T., Assenov, A., & Gaskin, D. J. (2023). The economic burden of racial, ethnic, and educational health inequities in the US. *JAMA, 329*(19), 1682–1692. https://doi.org/10.1001/jama.2023.5965

Lazaro, E., Ullrich, F., & Mueller, K. J. (August 2022). *Update on rural independently owned pharmacy closures in the United States, 2003–2021* (Brief No. 2022-3). Rural Policy Research Institute Center for Rural Health Policy Analysis. https://rupri.public-health.uiowa.edu/publications/policybriefs/2022/Independent%20Pharmacy%20Closures.pdf

Lee, E. L., Richards, N., Harrison, J., & Barnes, J. (2022). Prevalence of use of traditional, complementary and alternative medicine by the general population: A systematic review of national studies published from 2010 to 2019. *Drug Safety, 45*(7), 713–735. https://doi.org/10.1007/s40264-022-01189-w

Leigh, S., Ouyang, J., & Mimnagh, C. (2017). Effective? Engaging? Secure? Applying the ORCHA-24 framework to evaluate apps for chronic insomnia disorder. *Evidence-Based Mental Health, 20*(4), e20. https://doi.org/10.1136/eb-2017-102751

Leste, T., Siegal, Y., Shukla, M. (2019, April 30). *Return on capital performance in life sciences and health care.* Deloitte. https://www.deloitte.com/global/en/our-thinking/insights/industry/health-care/return-on-capital-health-care.html

Lite, S., Gordon, W. J., & Stern, A. D. (2020). Association of the meaningful use electronic health record incentive program with health information technology venture capital funding. *JAMA Network Open, 3*(3), e201402. https://doi.org/10.1001/jamanetworkopen.2020.1402

Long, A. S., Hanlon, A. L., & Pellegrin, K. L. (2018). Socioeconomic variables explain rural disparities in US mortality rates: Implications for rural health research and policy. *SSM - Population Health, 6,* 72–74. https://doi.org/10.1016/j.ssmph.2018.08.009

Madureira Lima, J., & Galea, S. (2019). The Corporate Permeation Index - A tool to study the macrosocial determinants of non-communicable disease. *SSM - Population Health, 7,* 100361. https://doi.org/10.1016/j.ssmph.2019.100361

Mahase, E. (2023). Private providers see surge in demand as PM blames long NHS waiting lists on strikes. *BMJ (Clinical research ed.), 382*, 2126. https://doi.org/10.1136/bmj.p2126

Mathews, A. W. (2023, September 28). These employers took on healthcare costs, and the fight got nasty. *The Wall Street Journal*. https://www.wsj.com/health/healthcare/these-employers-took-on-healthcare-costs-and-the-fight-got-nasty-54674114

Mathews, A. W., McGinty, T., & Evans, M. (2022, July 25). Big hospitals provide skimpy charity care—Despite billions in tax breaks. *The Wall Street Journal*. https://www.wsj.com/articles/nonprofit-hospitals-vs-for-profit-charity-care-spending-11657936777

Mayer, K. (2023, July 31). *Amazon latest employer to bulk up benefits to address employee challenges.* Society for Human Resource Management. https://www.shrm.org/topics-tools/news/benefits-compensation/amazon-latest-employer-to-bulk-benefits-to-address-employee-challenges

Mazurenko, O., Buntin, M. J. B., & Menachemi, N. (2019). High-deductible health plans and prevention. *Annual Review of Public Health, 40*, 411–421. https://doi.org/10.1146/annurev-publhealth-040218-044225

Mazzarol, T. W., & Soutar, G. N. (2008). Strategy matters: Strategic positioning and performance in the education services sector. *International Journal of Nonprofit and Voluntary Sector Marketing 13*(2), 141–151. https://doi.org/10.1002/nvsm.313

McKinsey & Company. (2022, September 19). *Still feeling good: The US wellness market continues to boom.* https://www.mckinsey.com/industries/consumer-packaged-goods/our-insights/still-feeling-good-the-us-wellness-market-continues-to-boom

Medicare Payment Advisory Commission. (2023). Chapter 11, The Medicare Advantage program: Status report. In *Report to the Congress: Medicare Payment Policy.* Medicare Payment Advisory Commission. https://www.medpac.gov/wp-content/uploads/2023/03/Ch11_Mar23_MedPAC_Report_To_Congress_SEC.pdf

Megibow, E., Orgera, K., & Piepenbrink, S. (2023, May 1). *Generation Z takes the reins.* Association of American Medical Colleges, Center for Health Justice. https://www.aamchealthjustice.org/news/polling/generation-z-takes-reins

Melek, S. P., Norris, D. T., Paulus, J., Matthews, K., Weaver, A., & Davenport, S. (2018 January). *Potential economic impact of integrated medical-behavioral healthcare.* Milliman. https://www.milliman.com/-/media/milliman/importedfiles/uploadedfiles/insight/2018/potential-economic-impact-integrated-healthcare.ashx

Micha, R., Peñalvo, J. L., Cudhea, F., Imamura, F., Rehm, C. D., & Mozaffarian, D. (2017). Association between dietary factors and mortality from heart disease, stroke, and type 2 diabetes in the United States. *JAMA, 317*(9), 912–924. https://doi.org/10.1001/jama.2017.0947

Miller, K. E. M., Chatterjee, P., & Werner, R. M. (2023). Trends in supply of nursing home beds, 2011–2019. *JAMA Network Open, 6*(3), e230640. https://doi.org/10.1001/jamanetworkopen.2023.0640

Minemyer, P. (2023, October 18). Elevance Health braces for $500M hit to bonus revenue amid MA Star Ratings drop. *Fierce Healthcare*. https://www.fiercehealthcare.com/payers/elevance-health-boosts-guidance-it-posts-13b-q3-profit

Moher, D., Shamseer, L., Cobey, K. D., Lalu, M. M., Galipeau, J., Avey, M. T., Ahmadzai, N., Alabousi, M., Barbeau, P., Beck, A., Daniel, R., Frank, R., Ghannad, M., Hamel, C., Hersi, M., Hutton, B., Isupov, I., McGrath, T. A., McInnes, M. D. F., Page, M. J., ... & Ziai, H. (2017). Stop this waste of people, animals and money. *Nature, 549*(7670), 23–25. https://doi.org/10.1038/549023a

Mulcahy, A. W., & Kareddy, V. (2021). *Prescription drug supply chains: An overview of stakeholders and relationships.* RAND Corporation. https://www.rand.org/pubs/research_reports/RRA328-1.html

Mulcahy, A. W., Whaley, C., & Tebeka, M. G. (2021). *International prescription drug price comparisons.* RAND Corporation. https://www.rand.org/pubs/research_reports/RR2956.html

Nahin, R. L., Barnes, P. M., & Stussman, B. J. (2016). *Expenditures on complementary health approaches: United States, 2012.* National Health Statistics Reports, National Center for Health Statistics. https://www.cdc.gov/nchs/data/nhsr/nhsr095.pdf

National Academies of Sciences, Engineering, and Medicine, Health and Medicine Division, Board on Health Care Services, Board on Global Health, & Committee on Improving the Quality of Health Care Globally. (2018). *Crossing the global quality chasm: Improving health care worldwide.* National Academies Press (US). https://doi.org/10.17226/25152

National Association of Boards of Pharmacy. (2022). *Rogue Rx activity report.* https://nabp.pharmacy/wp-content/uploads/2022/10/Rogue-Rx-Activity-Report-Disrupting-Illegal-Online-Pharmacies-2022.pdf

National Conference of State Legislatures. (2021, December 20). *Certificate of need state laws.* https://www.ncsl.org/health/certificate-of-need-state-laws

National Health Care Anti-Fraud Association. (n.d.). *The challenge of health care fraud.* https://www.nhcaa.org/tools-insights/about-health-care-fraud/the-challenge-of-health-care-fraud/

National Institute on Aging. (n.d.). *NIA small business showcase: ZetrOZ systems.* https://www.nia.nih.gov/research/sbir/nia-small-business-showcase/zetroz-systems.

Newman, D. J., & Cragg, G. M. (2020). Natural products as sources of new drugs over the nearly four decades from 01/1981 to 09/2019. *Journal of Natural Products, 83*(3), 770–803. https://doi.org/10.1021/acs.jnatprod.9b01285

Newsweek. (2022). *America's most trusted brands 2022.* https://www.newsweek.com/americas-most-trusted-brands-2022

Nunn, R., Parsons, J., Shambaugh, J., & Contreras, A. (2020, March 10). *A dozen facts about the economics of the US healthcare system.* Brookings. https://www.brookings.edu/research/a-dozen-facts-about-the-economics-of-the-u-s-health-care-system/

Occupational Safety and Health Administration. (2015, December). *Workplace violence in healthcare.* https://www.osha.gov/sites/default/files/OSHA3826.pdf

Ochieng, N., Biniek, J. F., Freed, M., Damico, A., & Neuman, T. (2023, August 9). *Medicare Advantage in 2023: Enrollment update and key trends.* Kaiser Family Foundation. https://www.kff.org/medicare/issue-brief/medicare-advantage-in-2023-enrollment-update-and-key-trends/

Office of Inspector General. (2023, January 25). *The National Institutes of Health and EcoHealth Alliance did not effectively monitor awards and subawards, resulting in missed opportunities to oversee research and other deficiencies.* U.S. Department of Health and Human Services Office of Inspector General. https://oig.hhs.gov/oas/reports/region5/52100025.pdf

Office of the National Coordinator for Health Information Technology. (2022). *2022 report to Congress: Update on access, exchange, and use of electronic health information.* https://www.healthit.gov/sites/default/files/page/2023-02/2022_ONC_Report_to_Congress.pdf

Office of the National Coordinator for Health Information Technology. (2023 March). *Use of telemedicine among office-based physicians, 2021* [Data Brief No. 65]. https://www.healthit.gov/data/data-briefs/use-telemedicine-among-office-based-physicians-2021

Oliffe, J. L., Rossnagel, E., Kelly, M. T., Bottorff, J. L., Seaton, C., & Darroch, F. (2020). Men's health literacy: A review and recommendations. *Health Promotion International, 35*(5), 1037–1051. https://doi.org/10.1093/heapro/daz077

Organisation for Economic Co-operation and Development. (2020). *Trade in counterfeit pharmaceutical products.* OECD Publishing. https://www.oecd-ilibrary.org/sites/a7c7e054-en/index.html?itemId=/content/publication/a7c7e054-en

Organisation for Economic Co-operation and Development. (2022, September). *Understanding differences in health expenditure between the United States and OECD countries.* https://www.oecd.org/health/Health-expenditure-differences-USA-OECD-countries-Brief-July-2022.pdf

Ostler, C. (2022). Intermountain healthcare: Utilizing technology to bring value to patients. In *Sage Business Cases.* SAGE. https://doi.org/10.4135/9781529780604

Ozawa, S., Evans, D. R., Bessias, S., Haynie, D. G., Yemeke, T. T., Laing, S. K., & Herrington, J. E. (2018). Prevalence and estimated economic burden of substandard and falsified medicines in low- and middle-income countries: A systematic review and meta-analysis. *JAMA network open, 1*(4), e181662. https://doi.org/10.1001/jamanetworkopen.2018.1662

Patel, N., & Singhal, S. (2023, January 9). *What to expect in US healthcare in 2023 and beyond.* McKinsey & Company. https://www.mckinsey.com/industries/healthcare/our-insights/what-to-expect-in-us-healthcare-in-2023-and-beyond#_

Pellegrin, K. L., & Pezzuto, J. M. (2011). Strategic direction for high demand degrees: an analysis of the US pharmacy degree competitive market. *International Journal of Management in Education, 5*(2–3), 285–300. https://doi.org/10.1504/IJMIE.2011.039490

Pellegrin, K. (2017). CVS health: Checking the vital signs of the largest pharmacy company in the US. In *Sage Business Cases.* SAGE. https://doi.org/10.4135/9781526408006

Pellegrin, K., & Duerler, T. (2017). Mango medical: Growing a fresh healthcare model. In *Sage Business Cases.* SAGE. https://doi.org/10.4135/9781526410900

Pellegrin, K. L., Krenk, L., Oakes, S. J., Ciarleglio, A., Lynn, J., McInnis, T., Bairos, A. W., Gomez, L., McCrary, M. B., Hanlon, A. L., & Miyamura, J. (2017). Reductions in medication-related hospitalizations in older adults with medication management by hospital and community pharmacists: A quasi-experimental study. *Journal of the American Geriatrics Society, 65*(1), 212–219. https://doi.org/10.1111/jgs.14518

Pellegrin, K., & Corbin, K. (2018). A public "safety net" hospital aims for excellence: Mission-driven transformation to improve health in east Hawaii. In *Sage Business Cases.* SAGE. https://doi.org/10.4135/9781526444301

Pellegrin, K., & Krenk, L. (2018). Maui clinic pharmacy: An independent community pharmacy considers strategic options. In *Sage Business Cases*. SAGE. https://doi.org/10.4135/9781526444981

Pellegrin, K. L. (2021). Haven: Amazon, Berkshire Hathaway, and JP Morgan chase launch nonprofit to improve healthcare for U.S. employees. In *Sage Business Cases*. SAGE. https://doi.org/10.4135/9781529767766

Pellegrin, K. L. (2021). Kodak's faded picture of health: A COVID-19 moment to exit photos and enter pharmaceuticals? In *Sage Business Cases*. SAGE. https://doi.org/10.4135/9781529767773

Pellegrin, K. L. (2023). Cerebral: Response to service failures in a booming digital mental health market. In *Sage Business Cases*. SAGE. https://doi.org/10.4135/9781071920305

Pendzialek, J. B., Simic, D., & Stock, S. (2016). Differences in price elasticities of demand for health insurance: A systematic review. *The European Journal of Health Economics, 17*, 5–21. Patient Protection and Affordable Care Act of 2010. https://www.govinfo.gov/content/pkg/PLAW-111publ148/pdf/PLAW-111publ148.pdf

Perez, J. C. (2004, January 8). Amazon records first profitable year in its history. *Computerworld*. https://www.computerworld.com/article/2575106/amazon-records-first-profitable-year-in-its-history.html.

Pew Research Center. (2017, February 2). 2. *Americans' health care behaviors and use of conventional and alternative medicine.* Pew Research Center. https://www.pewresearch.org/science/2017/02/02/americans-health-care-behaviors-and-use-of-conventional-and-alternative-medicine/

Pichler, P. P., Jaccard, I. S., Weisz, U., & Weisz, H. (2019). International comparison of health care carbon footprints. *Environmental research letters, 14*(6), 064004. https://doi.org/10.1088/1748-9326/ab19e1

Pierson, L. (2022, March 15). *The AMA can help fix the health care shortages it helped create.* Bill of Health. https://blog.petrieflom.law.harvard.edu/2022/03/15/ama-scope-of-practice-lobbying/

Porter, M. E. (1976). Please note location of nearest exit: Exit barriers and planning. *California Management Review, 19*(2), 21–33. https://doi.org/10.2307/41164693

Porter, M. E. (1980). *Competitive strategy: Techniques for analyzing industries and competitors.* New York: Free Press.

Porter, M. E. (2008). The five competitive forces that shape strategy. *Harvard Business Review, 86*(1), 78.

Porter, M. E., & Kramer, M. R. (2006, December). Strategy and society: The link between competitive advantage and corporate social responsibility. *Harvard Business Review, 84*(12), 78–92. https://hbr.org/2006/12/strategy-and-society-the-link-between-competitive-advantage-and-corporate-social-responsibility

Posadzki, P., Pieper, D., Bajpai, R., Makaruk, H., Könsgen, N., Neuhaus, A. L., & Semwal, M. (2020). Exercise/physical activity and health outcomes: An overview of Cochrane systematic reviews. *BMC Public Health, 20*, 1–12. https://doi.org/10.1186/s12889-020-09855-3

Public Health Emergency. *National strategy for a resilient public health supply chain.* (2021, July). U.S. Department of Health & Human Services. https://www.phe.gov/Preparedness/legal/Documents/National-Strategy-for-Resilient-Public-Health-Supply-Chain.pdf

Rakshit, S., Wager, E., Hughes-Cromwick, P., Cox, C., & Amin, K. (2023, July 26). *How does medical inflation compare to inflation in the rest of the economy?* Peterson-KFF

Health System Tracker. https://www.healthsystemtracker.org/brief/how-does-medical-inflation-compare-to-inflation-in-the-rest-of-the-economy/

Rhoades, C. A., Whitacre, B. E., & Davis, A. F. (2023 January). *Community sociode-mographics and rural hospital survival analysis* [Policy brief]. Center for Economic Analysis of Rural Health, University of Kentucky. https://cearh.ca.uky.edu/sites/cearh.ca.uky.edu/files/Community_Sociodemographics_Rural_Hospital_Survival_CEARH_policy_brief_JAN_23.pdf

Rhodes, J., Abdolrasouli, A., Dunne, K., Sewell, T. R., Zhang, Y., Ballard, E., Brackin, A. P., van Rhijn, N., Chown, H., Tsitsopoulou, A., Posso, R. B., Chotirmall, S. H., McElvaney, N. G., Murphy, P. G., Talento, A. F., Renwick, J., Dyer, P. S., Szekely, A., Bowyer, P., Bromley, M. J., ... & Fisher, M. C. (2022). Population genomics confirms acquisition of drug-resistant Aspergillus fumigatus infection by humans from the environment. *Nature Microbiology, 7*(5), 663–674. https://doi.org/10.1038/s41564-022-01091-2

Rogers, H., Smith, M. H., & Yurkovic, M. (2023 October). *Future of Medicare Star Ratings: The reimagined CMS bonus system.* Milliman. https://us.milliman.com/-/media/milliman/pdfs/2023-articles/10-6-23_medicare-star-ratings-white-paper_20231005

Rudowitz, R., Drake, P., & Tolbert, J. (2023, March 31). *How many uninsured are in the coverage gap and how many could be eligible if all states adopted the Medicaid expansion?* Kaiser Family Foundation. https://www.kff.org/medicaid/issue-brief/how-many-uninsured-are-in-the-coverage-gap-and-how-many-could-be-eligible-if-all-states-adopted-the-medicaid-expansion/

Russell, D., Mathew, S., Fitts, M., Liddle, Z., Murakami-Gold, L., Campbell, N., Ramjan, M., Zhao, Y., Hines, S., Humphreys, J. S., & Wakerman, J. (2021). Interventions for health workforce retention in rural and remote areas: a systematic review. *Human Resources for Health, 19*(1), 103. https://doi.org/10.1186/s12960-021-00643-7

Saad, L. (2023, January 19). Americans sour on U.S. healthcare quality. *Gallup News.* https://news.gallup.com/poll/468176/americans-sour-healthcare-quality.aspx

Sahni, N., Stein, G., Zemmel, R., & Cutler, D. M. (2023). The potential impact of artificial intelligence on healthcare spending (No. w30857). In Agrawal, A., Gans, J., Goldfarb, A., & Tucker, C. (Eds.), *The economics of artificial intelligence: Health care challenges.* University of Chicago Press. https://www.nber.org/system/files/chapters/c14760/c14760.pdf

Saiki, S. (2020). Amazon Rx: Growing from books to pharmacy. In *Sage Business Cases.* SAGE. https://doi.org/10.4135/9781529720259

Scheil-Adlung, X. (2015). *Global evidence on inequities in rural health protection: new data on rural deficits in health coverage for 174 countries.* International Labour Organization. https://www.ilo.org/secsoc/information-resources/publications-and-tools/Workingpapers/WCMS_383890/lang--en/index.htm

Schultz, M. (2008). Rudolf Virchow. *Emerging Infectious Diseases, 14*(9), 1480–1481. https://doi.org/10.3201/eid1409.086672

Seeley, E. (2022, July 20). *The impact of pharmaceutical wholesalers on U.S. drug spending.* The Commonwealth Fund. https://www.commonwealthfund.org/publications/issue-briefs/2022/jul/impact-pharmaceutical-wholesalers-drug-spending

Shafer, P. R., Dusetzina, S. B., Sabik, L. M., Platts-Mills, T. F., Stearns, S. C., & Trogdon, J. G. (2023). High deductible health plans and use of free preventive services under the Affordable Care Act. *Inquiry: A Journal of Medical Care Organization, Provision and Financing, 60.* https://doi.org/10.1177/00469580231182512

Shimizu, S. (2022). As CVS pharmacists vaccinate millions, the new CEO of CVS health navigates the transition. In *Sage Business Cases.* SAGE. https://doi .org/10.4135/9781529793956

Siconolfi, M. (2023, May 26). Elizabeth Holmes to report to prison: A history of the WSJ Theranos investigation. *The Wall Street Journal.* https://www.wsj.com/articles/elizabeth-holmes-sentencing-a-history-of-the-wsj-theranos-investigation-11668741222

Small Business Innovation Research (n.d.). *About the SBIR and STTR programs.* https://www.sbir.gov/about

Smith, S. D., Newhouse, J. P., & Cuckler, G. A. (2022). *Health care spending growth has slowed: Will the bend in the curve continue?* (No. w30782). National Bureau of Economic Research. http://dx.doi.org/10.2139/ssrn.4336976

Sood, N. (2023, March 23). *Should the government restrict direct-to-consumer prescription drug advertising? Six takeaways on their effects.* University of Southern California. https://healthpolicy.usc.edu/article/should-the-government-restrict-direct-to-consumer-prescription-drug-advertising-six-takeaways-from-research-on-the-effects-of-prescription-drug-advertising/.

Stobierski, T. (2020, November 12). *What are network effects?* Business Insights Blog. Harvard Business School Online. https://online.hbs.edu/blog/post/what-are-network-effects

Tang, L., Li, J., & Fantus, S. (2023). Medical artificial intelligence ethics: A systematic review of empirical studies. *Digital Health, 9,* 20552076231186064. https://doi.org/10.1177/20552076231186064

Tang, M., Chernew, M. E., & Mehrotra, A. (2022). How emerging telehealth models challenge policymaking. *The Milbank Quarterly, 100*(3), 650–672. https://doi .org/10.1111/1468-0009.12584

Taparra, K., & Pellegrin, K. (2022). Data aggregation hides Pacific Islander health disparities. *Lancet (London, England), 400*(10345), 2–3. https://doi.org/10.1016/S0140-6736(22)01100-X

Terp, S., Seabury, S. A., Arora, S., Eads, A., Lam, C. N., & Menchine, M. (2017). Enforcement of the Emergency Medical Treatment and Labor Act, 2005 to 2014. *Annals of Emergency Medicine, 69*(2), 155–162.e1. https://doi.org/10.1016/j .annemergmed.2016.05.021

Tikkanen, R., Osborn, R., Mossialos, E., Djordjevic, A., Wharton, G. (2020 December). *2020 international profiles of health care systems.* The Commonwealth Fund. https://www.commonwealthfund.org/sites/default/files/2020-12/International_Profiles_of_Health_Care_Systems_Dec2020.pdf

Travis, D. A., Sriramarao, P., Cardona, C., Steer, C. J., Kennedy, S., Sreevatsan, S., & Murtaugh, M. P. (2014). One medicine one science: A framework for exploring challenges at the intersection of animals, humans, and the environment. *Annals of the New York Academy of Sciences, 1334*(1), 26–44. https://doi .org/10.1111/nyas.12601

Trinh, A. (2022). Moderna Inc. and the future of vaccine technologies: Management and protection of intellectual property. In *Sage Business Cases.* SAGE. https://doi.org/10.4135/9781529793208

Tulloch, A. I., Borthwick, F., Bogueva, D., Eltholth, M., Grech, A., Edgar, D., . . . & McNeill, G. (2023). How the EAT–Lancet Commission on food in the

Anthropocene influenced discourse and research on food systems: A systematic review covering the first 2 years post-publication. *The Lancet Global Health,* *11*(7), e1125-e1136. https://doi.org/10.1016/s2214-109x(23)00212-7

Turrini, G., Branham, D. K., Chen, L., Conmy, A. B., Chappel, A. R., & De Lew, N. (2021, July). *Access to affordable care in rural America: Current trends and key* *challenges* [Research Report No. HP-2021-16]. Office of the Assistant Secretary for Planning and Evaluation, U.S. Department of Health and Human Services. https://aspe.hhs.gov/sites/default/files/2021-07/rural-health-rr.pdf

U.S. Bureau of Labor Statistics. (2020, April). *Workplace violence in healthcare, 2018.* https://www.bls.gov/iif/factsheets/workplace-violence-healthcare-2018.htm

U.S. Bureau of Labor Statistics. (2020, November). *How have healthcare expenditures* *changed? Evidence from the Consumer Expenditure Surveys.* https://www.bls.gov/opub/btn/volume-9/how-have-healthcare-expenditures-changed-evidence-from-the-consumer-expenditure-surveys.htm

U.S. Bureau of Labor Statistics. (2023, September 21). *Employee benefits in the United* *States.* https://www.bls.gov/news.release/ebs2.toc.htm

U.S. Census Bureau. (n.d.). *Measuring race and ethnicity across the decades: 1790–2010.* https://www.census.gov/data-tools/demo/race/MREAD_1790_2010.html

U.S. Department of Agriculture. (n.d.). *Honey bees.* https://www.usda.gov/peoples-garden/pollinators/honey-bees#:~:text=Beehives%20are%20often%20important%20elements,fruits%2C%20nuts%2C%20and%20vegetables.

U.S. Department of Agriculture and U.S. Department of Health and Human Services. (2020, December) *Dietary guidelines for Americans, 2020–2025, 9th Edition.* https://www.dietaryguidelines.gov/sites/default/files/2020-12/Dietary_Guidelines_for_Americans_2020-2025.pdf

U.S. Department of Justice. (2008, September 15). *Competition in health care and* *certificates of need.* https://www.justice.gov/archive/atr/public/press_releases/2008/237153a.htm

U.S. Food and Drug Administration. (2019). *Drug shortages: Root causes and potential* *solutions.* https://www.fda.gov/media/131130/download?attachment

U.S. Food and Drug Administration. (2020 September 21). *BeSafeRx: Frequently asked* *questions.* https://www.fda.gov/drugs/besaferx-your-source-online-pharmacy-information/besaferx-frequently-asked-questions-faqs

U.S. Food and Drug Administration. (2023, December 22). *Counterfeit medicine.* https://www.fda.gov/drugs/buying-using-medicine-safely/counterfeit-medicine

U.S. Government Accountability Office. (2021, May). *Caps on Medicare-funded gradu-* *ate medical education at teaching hospitals.* https://www.gao.gov/assets/gao-21-391.pdf

U.S. Government Accountability Office. (2022, June). *Report to congressional addressees:* *COVID-19 Pandemic lessons highlight need for public health situational awareness* *network.* https://www.gao.gov/assets/gao-22-104600.pdf

U.S. Government Accountability Office. (2023, April). *Electronic health information* *exchange.* https://www.gao.gov/assets/gao-23-105540.pdf

U.S. Government Accountability Office. (2023, April 26). *Tax administration: IRS oversight* *of hospitals' tax-exempt status.* https://www.gao.gov/products/gao-23-106777#:

U.S. Justice Department. (2000, December 14). *HCA—the health care company and* subsidiaries to pay $840 million in criminal fines and civil damages and penalties—largest government fraud settlement in U.S. history [Press release]. https://www.justice.gov/archive/opa/pr/2000/December/696civcrm.htm#

U.S. Preventive Services Task Force. (2018, October). *Grade definitions.* https://www.uspreventiveservicestaskforce.org/uspstf/about-uspstf/methods-and-processes/grade-definitions

U.S. Senate Finance Committee. (2023, December 5). *Testimony of Allan Coukell.* https://www.finance.senate.gov/imo/media/doc/1205_coukell_testimony.pdf

Uygur, B., Ferguson, S., & Pollack, M. (2022). Hiding in plain sight: surprising pharma and biotech connections to NIH's national cancer institute. *Journal of Commercial Biotechnology, 27*(2), 5. https://doi.org/10.5912/jcb1020

van Leeuwen, K. G., Schalekamp, S., Rutten, M. J. C. M., van Ginneken, B., & de Rooij, M. (2021, April 15). Artificial intelligence in radiology: 100 commercially available products and their scientific evidence. *European Radiology, 31*(6), 3797–3804. https://doi.org/10.1007/s00330-021-07892-z

Venable, H. P. (1961). The history of Homer G. Phillips Hospital. *Journal of the National Medical Association, 53*(6), 541–551. http://www.ncbi.nlm.nih.gov/pmc/articles/pmc2642069/

Verweij, P. E., Lucas, J. A., Arendrup, M. C., Bowyer, P., Brinkmann, A. J., Denning, D. W., Dyer, P. S., Fisher, M. C., Geenen, P. L., Gisis, U., Hermann, D., Hoogendijk, A., Kiers, E., Lagrou, K., Melchers, W. J. G., Rhodes, J., Rietveld, A. G., Schoustra, S. E., Stenzel, K., & Fraaije, B. A. (2020). The one health problem of azole resistance in Aspergillus fumigatus: Current insights and future research agenda. *Fungal Biology Reviews, 34*(4), 202–214.

Wall Street Journal. (2022). *Nonprofit hospitals are big business.* https://www.wsj.com/news/collection/nonprofit-hospitals-679fab59

Walters, R., Leslie, S. J., Polson, R., Cusack, T., & Gorely, T. (2020). Establishing the efficacy of interventions to improve health literacy and health behaviours: a systematic review. *BMC Public Health, 20*(1), 1040. https://doi.org/10.1186/s12889-020-08991-0

Wang, P. (2022, November 3). The pros and cons of Medicare advantage. *Consumer Reports.* https://www.consumerreports.org/money/health-insurance/pros-and-cons-of-medicare-advantage-a6834167849/

Watanabe, J. H., McInnis, T., & Hirsch, J. D. (2018). Cost of prescription drug-related morbidity and mortality. *The Annals of Pharmacotherapy, 52*(9), 829–837. https://doi.org/10.1177/1060028018765159

Whaley, C. M., Briscombe, B., Kerber, R., O'Neill, B., & Kofner, A. (2022). *Prices paid to hospitals by private health plans: Findings from round 4 of an employer-led transparency initiative.* RAND Corporation. https://www.rand.org/pubs/research_reports/RRA1144-1.html

White, C. (2017). *Hospital prices in Indiana: Findings from an employer-led transparency initiative.* RAND Corporation. https://www.rand.org/pubs/research_reports/RR2106.html

White, R. E. (1986). Generic business strategies, organizational context and performance: An empirical investigation. *Strategic Management Journal, 7*(3), 217–231. https://doi.org/10.1002/smj.4250070304

Wicklum, S. C., Nuique, K., Kelly, M. A., Nesbitt, C. C., Zhang, J. J., & Svrcek, C. P. (2023). Greening Family Medicine clinic operations and clinical care, where do we start? A scoping review of toolkits and aids. *Family Practice, 40*(3), 473–485. https://doi.org/10.1093/fampra/cmad006

Willett, W., Rockström, J., Loken, B., Springmann, M., Lang, T., Vermeulen, S., Garnett, T., Tilman, D., DeClerck, F., Wood, A., Jonell, M., Clark, M., Gordon, L. J., Fanzo, J., Hawkes, C., Zurayk, R., Rivera, J. A., De Vries, W., Majele Sibanda, L., Afshin, A., ... & Murray, C. J. L. (2019). Food in the Anthropocene: the EAT-Lancet Commission on healthy diets from sustainable food systems. *Lancet (London, England), 393*(10170), 447–492. https://doi.org/10.1016/S0140-6736(18)31788-4

Williams, E., Rudowitz, R., & Burns, A. (2023, April 13). *Medicaid financing: The basics.* Kaiser Family Foundation. https://www.kff.org/medicaid/issue-brief/medicaid-financing-the-basics/

Wilson, M., Guta, A., Waddell, K., Lavis, J., Reid, R., & Evans, C. (2020). The impacts of accountable care organizations on patient experience, health outcomes and costs: a rapid review. *Journal of Health Services Research & Policy, 25*(2), 130–138. https://doi.org/10.1177/1355819620913141

Wilson, R. (2023, June 1). 50 things to know about UnitedHealth Group. *Becker's Payer Issues.* https://www.beckerspayer.com/payer/50-things-to-know-about-unitedhealth-group.html

World Health Organization. (n.d). *Global health expenditure database.* https://apps.who.int/nha/database/Select/Indicators/en

World Health Organization. (n.d). *Indicators.* https://www.who.int/data/gho/data/indicators/indicators-index

World Health Organization. (2022). *Global expenditure on health.* https://apps.who.int/iris/bitstream/handle/10665/365133/9789240064911-eng.pdf

World Health Organization. (2023, August 10). *Traditional medicine has a long history of contributing to conventional medicine and continues to hold promise.* https://www.who.int/news-room/feature-stories/detail/traditional-medicine-has-a-long-history-of-contributing-to-conventional-medicine-and-continues-to-hold-promise

World Health Organization. (2023, September 16). *Noncommunicable diseases.* https://www.who.int/news-room/fact-sheets/detail/noncommunicable-diseases

Wouters, O. J., McKee, M., & Luyten, J. (2020). Estimated research and development investment needed to bring a new medicine to market, 2009–2018. *JAMA, 323*(9), 844–853. https://doi.org/10.1001/jama.2020.1166

Xu, J. Q., Murphy, S. L., Kochanek, K. D., & Arias, E. *Mortality in the United States, 2021.* NCHS Data Brief, no 456. Hyattsville, MD: National Center for Health Statistics. 2022. https://doi.org/10.15620/cdc:122516

Yang, S., Khang, Y. H., Harper, S., Davey Smith, G., Leon, D. A., & Lynch, J. (2010). Understanding the rapid increase in life expectancy in South Korea. *American Journal of Public Health, 100*(5), 896–903. https://doi.org/10.2105/AJPH.2009.160341

Zelman, W. N., Pink, G. H., & Matthias, C. B. (2003). Use of the balanced scorecard in health care. *Journal of Health Care Finance, 29*(4), 1–16. Ascension 2022 annual report. https://about.ascension.org/-/media/project/ascension/about/section-about/financials/2023/consolidated-ascension-financial-statements-q4-fy23.pdf

ZetrOZ. (2020, June 23). Insurance companies benefit from reduced healthcare reimbursement, lowering costs by approving the sustained acoustic medicine (*sam®*) device. *PR Newswire.* https://www.prnewswire.com/news-releases/insurance-companies-benefit-from-reduced-healthcare-reimbursements-lowering-costs-by-approving-the-sustained-acoustic-medicine-sam-device-301082181.html

Zhu, H. (2020). Big data and artificial intelligence modeling for drug discovery. *Annual Review of Pharmacology and Toxicology, 60,* 573–589. https://doi.org/10.1146/annurev-pharmtox-010919-023324

Index

Hall, K., 149–150
Hamed, S., 132
HCA Healthcare Inc.
  composite score, 178
  outpatient and inpatient care, 177
  payor mix chains, 179, 179 (figure)
  Porter's framework, 178–182
  quality and cost issues, 176–177
  resilience, 177
Healthcare innovations
  exchange methods, 203 (figure)
  healthy food prescriptions, 200–201
  information technology, 202–206
  investments, 206–209
  patient and population outcomes, 201
  prenatal care, 199
  price and quality transparency, 199
  quality, cost, and consumers value, 199,
    200 (table)
  U.S. economy, 209–210
  value-based models, 201–202
Healthcare professionals, 93, 96
Healthcare Transformation Alliance
    (HTA), 171
Health disparities
  CDC system, 127
  defined, 123
  funding research, 124
  gender. See Gender-based disparities
  life expectancy, 123
  political identity, 124
  poverty, 125
  quality of life, 126
  rurality. See Urban-rural disparities
  See also Geopolitical disparities; Racial
    and ethnic disparities
Health information exchanges (HIEs), 202
Health Information Technology for
    Economic and Clinical Health
    (HITECH) Act of 2009, 53, 202–203
Health insurance exchange system, 22
Health insurance payers
  consumers, 72–75
  Departments of Defense and Veterans
    Affairs, 71–72
  Medicaid and CHIP, 69–71
  Medicare, 68–69
  private health insurance, 66–68

third-party payers and programs, 72
total annual cost households/
    consumers, 74 (table)
Health savings account (HSA), 77
Health threats, 147
Healthy lifestyles, 90–95
Hero, J. O., 76
HHS vs. CPI method, 73, 73 (table)
Hickman, C., 152
Hill, E., 92
Holmes, E., 119
Home health care, 52
Hospitalists, 27, 46
Hospital Survey and Construction Act of
    1946, 53
HSA-eligible plans, 77

Inflation Reduction Act of 2022,
    187–189
Information technology, 202–206
Intensity of competition
  exit barriers, 107
  industry growth, 104–107,
    106 (figure)
  Medicare Advantage plans, 116
  motivation, 107
  number and sizing, 103–104
  signals, 107
International Labour Organization
    (ILO), 133
Interpersonal skills, 205

Jackson, S., 139
Joint Commission reports, 150–151

Kaiser Family Foundation (KFF), 66–67,
    76, 116
Kaplan, R. S., 180
Karam, G., 92
Kelleher, D., 114
Kung, T., 204
Kurani, N., 67

LaVeist, T., 125
Lee, E. L., 89
Leigh, S., 98
Lite, S., 53
Long, A., 125, 135